KU-069-990

Contents

THE INTERNATIONAL LAW OF OCCUPATION

THE INTERNATIONAL LAW
OF OCCUPATION

With a new preface by the author

Eyal Benvenisti

PRINCETON UNIVERSITY PRESS   PRINCETON AND OXFORD

Second printing, and first paperback printing, with a new preface, 2004
Paperback ISBN 0-691-12130-3

The Library of Congress has cataloged the cloth edition of this book as follows

Benvenisti, Eyal.
The international law of occupation / Eyal Benvenisti.
p. cm.
Includes bibliographical references (p.   ) and index.
ISBN 0-691-05666-8 (acid-free paper)
1. Military occupation. I. Title.
JX4093.B46   1992
341.6'6—dc20   92-15185

British Library Cataloging-in-Publication Data is available

This book has been composed in Linotron Galliard

Printed on acid-free paper. ∞

pup.princeton.edu

Printed in the United States of America

10   9   8   7   6   5   4   3   2

Preface to the Paperback Edition _____

THE DOZEN or so years that have elapsed since this book went to press in 1992 have seen several new instances of occupations. A number of them, where neighbors clashed, became the sites of horrific crimes. Forces controlled by Croatia and Serbia committed mass atrocities in occupied parts of Bosnia and Herzegovina between 1992 and 1995. Both Ethiopian and Eritrean occupation forces were responsible for numerous war crimes committed in areas held under the control of both armies during the 1998–2000 Eritrean-Ethiopian war. In Congo, parts of which have been occupied since 1998 by the armed forces of Uganda, Rwanda, Burundi, or their proxies, it is estimated that up to three million people have been killed, millions more have become internally displaced or have sought asylum in neighboring countries, and the country's natural resources have been pillaged by the occupants.

The law of occupation, which requires the occupant to care for individuals—"protected persons"—in the areas under its control, was, of course, not recognized by any of those occupants as applicable to those cases. This in itself was not a new phenomenon. The great majority of post–World War II occupations have honored the law of occupation by virtue of its breach. The declaration by the International Military Tribunal in Nuremberg that the Hague Regulations on the law on occupation reflected customary international law did not hinder most occupants from disregarding this law using a variety of disingenuous claims. Occupants either asserted their own sovereign title to the occupied land, disputed the sovereign title of the ousted government to the land, denied having control over the occupied area, or assigned responsibility to ostensibly independent proxies. But for the first time since the military tribunals at the end of World War II, international tribunals dealing with the consequences of the violations of the law of occupation have had the opportunity to react to such claims in a clear and resolute fashion. Cutting through the traditional pretexts of occupants for disregarding the laws of war in general and the law of occupation in particular, the International Criminal Tribunal for the Former Republic of Yugoslavia (ICTY) opted for an approach that centered on the individuals who find themselves as "protected persons" in the hands of powers to whom they owe no allegiance. The Appeals Chamber of the ICTY declared in the Tadic case (1999) the necessary implications of the evolution of the law from a tool that defined armies' obligations toward each other into "international humanitarian law" that aimed at securing the well-being of individual civilians:

> Article 4 of Geneva Convention IV, if interpreted in the light of its object and purpose, is directed to the protection of civilians to the maximum extent possible. It therefore does not make its applicability dependent on formal bonds and purely legal relations. Its primary purpose is to ensure the safeguards afforded by the Convention to those civilians who do not enjoy the diplomatic protection, and correlatively are not subject to the allegiance and control, of the State in whose hands they may find themselves. In granting its protection, Article 4 intends to look to the substance of relations, not to their legal characterisation as such.[1]

Similarly, the Eritrea-Ethiopia Claims Commission rejected the link between the disputed status of certain territories and the protection of individuals present in those territories. "The alternative," the Commission opined, "could deny vulnerable persons in disputed areas the important protections provided by international humanitarian law. These protections should not be cast into doubt because the belligerents dispute the status of territory."[2] The international law of occupation, according to the Commission, does not suggest that "only territory the title to which is clear and uncontested can be occupied territory."[3]

The atrocities committed against civilian populations by occupying armies raised questions relating to the enforcement of international humanitarian law in general and the law of occupation in particular. The collective response—criminal prosecution—was ultimately institutionalized as the International Criminal Court, whose Statute includes grave breaches of the law of occupation as initially defined in the Fourth Geneva Convention of 1949. In addition, several European countries have recognized their universal jurisdiction to prosecute such crimes, and have exercised this jurisdiction with respect to war crimes committed in the former Yugoslavia. Both the focus on civilians rather than on governments' disingenuous claims, and the earnest collective effort to impose criminal sanctions for grave breaches are welcome responses to unwelcome crimes.

Besides the acute question of enforcement, the more theoretically challenging task for international lawyers in the context of the law of occupation has been that of adapting the law to the challenges of modern governance. This is why the 2003 occupation of Iraq by the United States and the United Kingdom has been the most significant development in the

---

[1] *Prosecutor v. Tadic* (Case IT-94-1-A) (1999) paragraph 168 (http://www.un.org/icty/tadic/appeal/judgement/tad-aj990715e.pdf).
[2] Partial Award, Central Front, Ethiopia's Claim No. 2, April 28, 2004, paragraph 28 (http://www.pca-cpa.org/ENGLISH/RPC/EECC/ET%20Partial%20Award.pdf).
[3] *Id.* at paragraph 29.

law of occupation in recent years. The occupants did not explicitly acknowledge their status as occupying powers, nor did they invoke the Hague Regulations of 1907 or the Fourth Geneva Convention as applicable to their actions in Iraq. In fact, they were initially reluctant to use the term *occupation*.[4] But they did declare their mission in Iraq using concepts and even language reminiscent of the Hague and Geneva instruments. The letter of May 8, 2003,[5] from the permanent representatives of the United Kingdom and the United States to the president of the UN Security Council communicates the two states' pledge to "strictly abide by their obligations under international law, including those relating to the essential humanitarian needs of the people of Iraq." It also outlines specific goals and mechanisms to attain these goals. The Security Council, in its Resolution 1483 "noted" this letter but moved on to explicitly "recogniz[e] the specific authorities, responsibilities, and obligations under applicable international law of these states as occupying powers under unified command." The two occupants set up the "Coalition Provisional Authority" (CPA) which replaced the domestic system of governance with a temporary command structure that ruled the country based on the authority of the "relevant U.N. Security Council resolutions, and the laws and usages of war."[6] The setting up of an occupation administration based on the law of occupation provided a mechanism to legitimate the temporary control of Iraq, granting considerable powers to the occupying authorities but for a limited period of time. The establishment of the CPA also ensured that

---

[4] During the fighting, the U.S. military was of the opinion that the areas that were occupied were still not occupied in the legal sense, perhaps implying that the determination of an area as occupied requires something more than a factual test. *See* Briefing on Geneva Convention, EPW's and War Crimes (April 7, 2003) (Q&A with W. Hays Parks, Special Assistant to the Army Judge Advocate General), Defense*LINK* (http://www.defenselink.mil/news/Apr2003/t04072003_t407genv.html). ("The term 'military occupation' is one of those that's very, very misunderstood. When you are an infantry company commander, and you're told to take the hill, you physically occupy it. That's military occupation with a smaller—lower-case 'm' and lower-case 'o.' It certainly does not mean that you have taken over it with the intent to run the government in that area. That's the very clear-cut distinction, that until the—usually, until the fighting has concluded and is very conclusive, do you reach the point where technically there might be Military Occupation—capital 'M,' capital 'O'—and a declaration of occupation is issued. That's a factual determination; it's a determination by the combatant commander in coordination with others, as well. Obviously, we occupy a great deal of Iraq at this time. But we are not, in the technical sense of the law of war, a military occupier or occupation force.")

[5] Letter dated May 8, 2003, from the Permanent Representatives of the United Kingdom of Great Britain and Northern Ireland and the United States of America to the United Nations, addressed to the President of the Security Council, UN *Doc.* S/2003/538.

[6] *See, e.g.,* the preamble to the Coalition Provisional Authority Order Number 1 (De-Baathification of Iraqi Society), May 16, 2003 (http://www.cpa-iraq.org/regulations/CPAORD1.pdf). The CPA was formally recognized by the UN Security Council in Resolution 1511 of October 16, 2003.

it would have a monopoly on the exercise of governmental powers in Iraq,[7] thereby excluding other "coalition members," the United Nations, and other states and organizations from claims to authority.[8]

This recourse to the law of occupation was a complicated undertaking, because it was not simply a task of looking up the relevant articles in the Hague Regulations or the Fourth Geneva Convention. International law has evolved significantly since the time these two instruments were drafted. The fundamental concepts of human rights and self-determination of peoples, which had transformed international law in the latter half of the twentieth century, have not been duly reflected in the constituting documents of the law of occupation. Issues concerning the management of public resources, including scarce natural resources, and even transboundary natural resources, had to be governed by rules that reflected the late nineteenth-century conception of public property as one that belongs to the sovereign ruler but not to his people. The law of occupation had to adapt itself to offer responses to enormous challenges such as the effort at transforming a previous dictatorship into a complex constitutional democracy, the rebuilding of its economy, and the management of its natural resources, primarily its abundant oil reserves and its share of the Tigris and the Euphrates rivers.

Security Council Resolution 1483 of May 22, 2003, which recognized the presence of U.S. and U.K. forces in Iraq as occupying powers subject to the law of the Hague Regulations and the Fourth Geneva Convention, is therefore a significant event in the history of the troubled law of occupation. A rich body of laws developed during the late nineteenth century and early twentieth century, and honored more by its breach since then, was set in motion to face contemporary challenges. When the Security Council announced the applicability of the law of occupation to 2003 Iraq, it had to adapt a law that initially reflected the premise that kings were the sovereigns and that international law should protect their possessions during wartime, to a new philosophy—the philosophy of international *humanitarian* law—which posited that peoples were the true sovereigns and that human rights had to be respected. These fundamental changes in international law required the law of occupation to revise its

[7] CPA Regulation Number 1, Section 1(1): "The CPA shall exercise powers of government temporarily . . . "; Section 1(2): "The CPA is vested with all executive, legislative and judicial authority to achieve its objectives . . . " (May 16, 2003) (http://www.cpa-iraq.org/regulations/REG1.pdf).

[8] CPA Regulation Number 5 from June 17, 2003, established the Council for International Coordination whose task is to "work, on behalf of the CPA, to support, encourage and facilitate participation of the international community in relief, recovery and development efforts with respect to Iraq" (Section 1). This Council was to be composed of representatives from Coalition member states and other countries whose participation would be approved by the Council (Section 2).

approach toward the consequences of the downfall of the domestic regime and take into due account the relevancy of human rights law.

Resolution 1483 can be seen as the latest and most authoritative restatement of several basic principles of the contemporary law of occupation. It endorses several theses developed in this book. First, it revives the neutral connotation of the doctrine. Occupation is a temporary measure for reestablishing order and civil life after the end of active hostilities, benefiting also, if not primarily, the civilian population. As such, occupation does not amount to unlawful alien domination that entitles the local population to struggle against it. Second, sovereignty inheres in the people, and consequently regime collapse does not extinguish sovereignty. Thus, the Resolution implicitly confirms the demise of the doctrine of *debellatio*, which would have passed sovereign title to the occupant in case of total defeat and disintegration of the governing regime. Instead, and notwithstanding the requirement of Article 43 of the Hague Regulations to "respect . . . , unless absolutely prevented, the laws in force in the country,"[9] Resolution 1483 grants a mandate to the occupants to transform the previous legal system to enable the Iraqi people "freely to determine their own political future and control their own natural resources . . . to form a representative government based on the rule of law that affords equal rights and justice to all Iraqi citizens without regard to ethnicity, religion, or gender." Hence, the law of occupation, according to Resolution 1483, connotes respect to popular sovereignty, not to the demised regime. Third, the Resolution recognizes in principle the continued applicability of international human rights law in occupied territories in tandem with the law of occupation. Human rights law may thus complement the law of occupation on specific matters. Fourth, Resolution 1483 envisions the role of the modern occupant as the role of the heavily involved regulator, when it calls upon the occupants to pursue an "effective administration" of Iraq. This call stands in contrast to the initial orientation of the Hague Regulations, which envisioned a disinterested occupant who does not intervene in the lives of the occupied population. In the years since, such an "inactive custodian" approach has been rejected as unacceptable. The call to administer the occupied area "effectively" acknowledges the several duties that the occupants must perform to protect the occupied population. It precludes the occupant from hiding behind the limits imposed on its powers as a pretext for inaction.

In the context of managing Iraq's natural resources, the Resolution offered further two important contributions. It acknowledged that the

---

[9] Regulations Respecting the Laws and Customs of War on Land, annexed to Convention Respecting the Laws and Customs of War on Land, October 18, 1907.

occupant was fully entitled to utilize public resources provided such use benefits the lawful owner, namely, the people of Iraq. This reading was consonant with the traditional reading of Article 55 of the Hague Regulations, and ended a debate over whether oil could be exploited by the occupant and, if so, for what purposes. Even more important was the institutional innovation of the Resolution, the establishment of monitoring processes to oversee the occupant's measures. This was a necessary addition to a law that virtually lacked effective international mechanisms to monitor occupants' decision making as being compatible with the law.[10]

Resolution 1483 did not address a number of key questions concerning the further adaptation of the law of occupation to contemporary governance. One gray area concerns the question of whether an occupant can undertake international obligations as part of its temporary administration of the occupied territory. Contemporary management is no longer an exercise in domestic policing. Rather, it requires cooperation with neighboring countries, for example in the area of transboundary resources management, and with the international community at large, for example in the context of international trade. But does the occupant have the authority to negotiate agreements with other states? And will such negotiations yield agreements that would be binding after the expiration of the occupant's control? Given the contemporary philosophy underlying this law, which emphasizes humanitarian concerns, an initial response would not restrict the occupant's choice of legal means in realizing its duties. The occupant may implement existing legislation or amend those if necessary to promote the legitimate goals of the administration. The same logic would apply with equal force to the occupant's authority to coordinate its activities with neighboring states. This perspective would suggest that there should be no *a priori* restriction on the occupant's authority to negotiate or renegotiate agreements with other neighboring states. But the occupant's authority is essentially limited in time—it lasts only as long as the occupant exercises effective control. Therefore the occupant cannot create rights and obligations that will bind the sovereign power of the post-occupation government once it regains authority and until that government manages to renegotiate the treaty or to show that a "fundamental change of circumstances"[11] has occurred which entitles it to terminate the treaty. Hence it is suggested that agreements between

---

[10] The International Advisory and Monitoring Board (IAMB). The IAMB's members include representatives of the Secretary-General of the UN, the Managing Director of the International Monetary Fund, the Director-General of the Arab Fund for Economic and Social Development, and the President of the International Bank for Reconstruction and Development. For the terms of reference of IAMB, *see* http://www.iamb.info/tor.htm.

[11] Article 62 of the 1969 Vienna Convention on the Law of Treaties.

the occupant as the administrator of the occupied country and other states, whether or not formally qualified as "treaties" under the Vienna Convention on the Law of Treaties, would be valid for the duration of the occupation and subject to the sovereign's authority to renegotiate such agreements when occupation ends. But this response is not free from complications. A question of conflict of interests may arise when the occupant is itself an interested party. May the occupant negotiate an agreement with its own government as the second party to an international agreement? And in cases of partial occupation of a territory, when the sovereign government continues to act in the international plane, who has the authority to represent the occupied area vis-à-vis other states?[12]

Another possible area of contention concerns the international responsibility of the occupant itself, or the independent responsibility of the administration that the occupant has established in the occupied area (whose authority is independent of the occupant state), for acts committed in the occupied territory by the occupant (or the occupation administration) acting on behalf of the civilian population, or for its omission to control activities of the local population that adversely affect the interests of third parties in or outside the occupied territory.

The year that elapsed since the beginning of the occupation in Iraq does not offer sufficient perspective to assess the performance of the Coalition Provisional Authority. Thus far the record seems mixed. On the one hand, the orders the CPA has issued reflect an earnest effort to transform Iraq into a market-oriented democracy.[13] The CPA committed itself to conform with international human rights standards. It established a Ministry of Human rights[14] and prohibited "torture and cruel, degrading or inhuman treatment or punishment" by Iraqi judges and police.[15] While these policies depart from a strict reading of Article 43 of the Hague

---

[12] For more on these questions, see Eyal Benvenisti, *Water Conflicts During the Occupation of Iraq*, 97 AJIL 860 (2003).

[13] See, e.g., Order no. 1 (De-Baathification of Iraqi Society) (May 16, 2003); Order no. 39 (Foreign Investment) (September 19, 2003); Order no. 40 (Bank Law) (September 19, 2003); Order no. 64 (Amendment to the Company Law No. 21 of 1997) (March 3, 2004); Order no. 74 (Interim Law on Securities Markets) (April 19, 2004); Order no. 87 (Patent, Industrial Design, Undisclosed Information, Integrated Circuits and Plant Variety Law) (April 26, 2004). Full text for all CPA orders and regulations can be found at http://www.cpa-iraq.org/regulations/.

[14] On September 3, 2003, the CPA appointed an Interim Minister of Human Rights and on February 22, 2004, established the Ministry of Human Rights (Order no. 60). The Ministry's tasks were to promote human rights and fundamental freedoms in Iraq and to "assist all the people of Iraq . . . in healing from the atrocities committed by the Ba'athist regime" (Section 2).

[15] Order no. 7 (Penal Code) (June 10, 2003), Section 3(2).

Regulations,[16] they would seem to conform to a contemporary reading of the law.[17] On the other hand, several months into the occupation it became apparent that Iraqis detained by U.S. forces in Iraq had been subjected to coercive interrogation practices. These practices, approved by a U.S. Army field manual, included the forcing of prisoners to crouch for up to forty-five minutes; sleep deprivation; the use of blindfolds, earmuffs, and other materials, all for up to seventy-two hours; the use of loud music and bright lights; isolation for more than thirty days; and interrogations in the presence of "trained" dogs.[18] Moreover, U.S. Army personnel have been recorded subjecting Iraqi detainees under their control to perverse acts of torture, including sexual abuse of male and female prisoners. It remains to be seen how the U.S. Army and the CPA will react to these clear violations of the Fourth Geneva Convention, of basic standards of international human rights law,[19] and of the pledges of the CPA to the Iraqi people and to the international community.

Security Council Resolution 1546 of June 8, 2004, endorsed the transferal by June 30, 2004, of authority in Iraq from the CPA to the interim Iraqi government, which had been set up on June 1, 2004. Resolution 1546 deemed that with this transfer of authority, the occupation of Iraq would come to an end. Noting that the presence of the multinational force in Iraq was at the request of the Iraqi interim government, the Council granted that force "the authority to take all necessary measures to contribute to the maintenance of security and stability in Iraq" in accordance with the letters exchanged between the Prime Minister of the Iraqi interim government and the U.S. Secretary of State.[20] The Council viewed these two letters as establishing a "security partnership"—indeed a "full partnership"—between the interim Iraqi government and the multinational force (Article 11).

Resolution 1546 does not elaborate on the international legal obligations to which the multinational force is subject when exercising its authorities. The only reference to this issue appears in the letter of Secretary of State Colin Powell, who asserts that "the forces that make up the [multinational force] are and will remain committed at all times to act consistently with their obligations under the law of armed conflict, including the Geneva Conventions." The law of occupation, part of

---

[16] *See supra* note 9 and accompanying text.

[17] *See infra* Chapter 2.

[18] *Precise Rules for Handling Iraq Detainees*, N.Y. Times, May 14, 2004.

[19] Leila Nadya Sadat, *International Legal Issues Surrounding the Mistreatment of Iraqi Detainees by American Forces*, ASIL Insights (May 2004) (http://www.asil.org/insights/insigh134.htm).

[20] Article 10, Resolution 1546. The two letters, dated June 5, 2004, are annexed to the Resolution.

which is set out in the Fourth Geneva Convention, requires such a commitment. Although the formal occupation of Iraq ended on June 28, 2004, to the extent that the United States and other foreign troops operating in Iraq continue to wield effective control over Iraqis and Iraqi property, they are bound by this body of laws.[21] As the ICTY noted in the Tadic case mentioned above,[22] the Fourth Geneva Convention "does not make its applicability dependent on formal bonds and purely legal relations. . . . Article 4 [of that Convention] intends to look to the substance of relations, not to their legal characterisation as such."

Aside from the various challenges posed by the occupation of Iraq and other contemporary occupations, another set of questions arises related to the applicability of the law of occupation to UN peacekeeping operations that derive their authority from Chapter VII of the UN Charter. In its various interventions under Chapter VII during the 1990s to end conflicts, the UN preferred not to assume direct governmental functions in the territories that came under its control, but instead relied upon domestic institutions. But when such institutions were not available, responsibility had to be assigned to the forces in charge. In the case of Somalia, the Security Council essentially left the question of authority open. Instead, its Resolution 794 of December 3, 1992, authorized the Secretary General and "Member States cooperating" to "use all necessary means to establish as soon as possible a secure environment for humanitarian relief operations in Somalia" (Article 10). Only the Australian contingency responsible for parts of Somalia chose to apply the law of occupation to the areas under its authority.[23] In 1999 the UN had to address this question again in the context of its governance of both Kosovo and East Timor. Security Council Resolution 1244 of June 19, 1999, established "international civil and security presences" (Article 5). This resolution granted the UN Interim Administration Mission in Kosovo (UNMIK) wide-ranging powers, without any restrictions. The Special Representative who was appointed to direct UNMIK issued a regulation, by which he declared that "[a]ll legislative and executive authority with respect to Kosovo, including the administration of the judiciary, is vested in UNMIK and is exercised by the Special Representative."[24] This asser-

[21] *See also* Adam Roberts, *Iraq's Day of Reckoning*, The Guardian, May 25, 2004. ("If coalition forces are used against insurgents, if they take prisoners, or if they find themselves exercising authority in an operational area, then they will continue to be bound by the Geneva conventions.")

[22] *Supra* note 1.

[23] For an in-depth analysis of the applicability of the law of occupation to UN-supported peace-enforcement operations in general and the operation in Somalia in particular, *see* Michael J. Kelly, *Peace Operations* (1997).

[24] Article 1(1) of Regulation No. 1999/1 on The Authority of the Interim Administration in Kosovo, July 25, 1999 (http://www.unmikonline.org/regulations/1999/reg01-99.htm).

tion of wide-ranging authority was subject only to "internationally recognized human rights standards" and "the mandate given to UNMIK under United Nations Security Council resolution 1244."[25] In Resolution 1272 of October 25, 1999, the Security Council, acting under Chapter VII, established the United Nations Transitional Administration in East Timor (UNTAET) and endowed it with "overall responsibility for the administration of East Timor" and the power to "exercise all legislative and executive authority, including the administration of justice" (Article 1). Regulation Number 1 of UNTAET declared that

> All legislative and executive authority with respect to East Timor, including the administration of the judiciary, is vested in UNTAET and is exercised by the Transitional Administrator. In exercising these functions the Transitional Administrator shall consult and cooperate closely with representatives of the East Timorese people.[26]

Similarly to UNMIK, UNTAET was to be subjected only to international human rights standards and the UN Security Council.[27]

The UN peacekeeping forces came to control these areas not through international armed conflicts. Formally, in the absence of such conflict the laws of war are inapplicable. But as suggested in Chapter 1 of this book, the law of occupation should apply to any case of "effective control of a power (be it one or more states or an international organization, such as the United Nations) over a territory to which that power has no sovereign title, without the volition of the sovereign of that territory." The resolutions in both cases created trusteeships toward the indigenous communities and the ousted governments, trusteeships of the kind the law of occupation is designed to address.[28] The application of this law seems pertinent in these two cases. Particularly in Kosovo, the lack of any clear guidelines on the exercise of those wide-ranging governmental powers led to confusion as well as to pressures by domestic interests to amend the

---

[25] *Id.* Articles 2 and 3.

[26] Article 1.1 of Regulation No. 1999/1 on The Authority of the Transitional Administration in East Timor, November 27, 1999 (http://www.un.org/peace/etimor/untaetR/etreg1.htm).

[27] *Id.* Articles 2 and 3.

[28] *See also* Tobias H. Irmscher, *The Legal Framework for the Activities of the United Nations Interim Administration Mission in Kosovo: The Charter, Human Rights, and the Law of Occupation,* 44 German Yb. of Int'l L. 353, 383–87 (2001); but *see* David J. Scheffer, *Beyond Occupation Law,* 97 AJIL 842, 851 (2003). ("[L]iberating armies that operate with international authority, advance democracy, and save civilian populations from atrocities should be regulated by a modern occupation regime that can be created under the UN Charter.")

existing laws to suit their political demands.[29] Recourse to the framework of the law of occupation may have enabled both the government and the governed to draw upon the rich experience that has accumulated over the years and to inform their policies and expectations.

In its advisory opinion of July 9, 2004, on the *Legal Consequences of the Construction of a Wall in the Occupied Palestinian Territory*,[30] the International Court of Justice found Israel in breach of several international law obligations by its construction of a separation wall on West Bank territory. The opinion addresses several significant questions that arise in relation to the Israeli occupation in particular and to the law of occupation in general. The Court flatly rejects the Israeli claims concerning the inapplicability of the Fourth Geneva Convention to the West Bank and concerning the inapplicability of Article 49 to the Jewish settlements in the areas occupied by Israel. Neither have these claims gained serious support from the international community.[31] The Court views the wall as obstructing the Palestinians' right to self-determination on West Bank territory and as a violation of several rights that individual Palestinians are entitled to under both international humanitarian law and human rights law.

The opinion confirms the applicability of human rights law to occupied territories. The Court enumerates several rights arising from the Covenant on Civil and Political Rights; the Covenant on Economic, Social, and Cultural Rights; and the Convention on the Rights of the Child that are applicable also in occupied territories. The Court further finds the occupant's obligations under international humanitarian law to be *erga omnes* obligations, whose violation raises the obligation of other states to ensure compliance by the occupant with its obligations. In particular, the Court declares that states party to the Fourth Geneva Convention have an obligation, "while respecting the United Nations Charter and international law, to ensure compliance by Israel [as an occupant] with international humanitarian law as embodied in that Convention."[32] This assertion remains "without any argument in its reasoning" and without elaboration of the scope of that obligation.[33]

---

[29] *See* Hansjoerg Strohmeyer, *Collapse and Reconstruction of a Judicial System: The United Nations Mission in Kosovo and East Timor*, 95 AJIL 46, 58–59 (2001); Irmscher, note 28, at 392.

[30] Advisory Opinion, July 9, 2004 (http://www.icj-cij.org/icjwww/idocket/imwp/imwpframe.htm).

[31] On these questions *see* pp. 109–14, 140–41.

[32] Advisory Opinion, *supra* note 30, paragraph 159. *But see* the dissent of Judge Kooijmans on this question: separate opinion of Judge Kooijmans, paragraphs 40–50.

[33] *See* the separate opinion of Judge Kooijmans, paragraph 50.

In 1993, when this book was first published, there was a fresh promise of global cooperation in a post–Cold War world. Attention was given to conflict prevention rather than to conflict management, let alone to conflict regulation. A truly active Security Council was poised to reduce and even eliminate regional violence. Europe was collectively devising means to ensure stabilization and justice in Central and Eastern Europe. Following the 1993 Oslo Accords, hopes were even high for the cessation of conflict in the Middle East and the end of occupation of Palestinian territories. This promise was only partially fulfilled. In the following years, new occupations presented new challenges. Some of these challenges called for more effective enforcement measures, such as the establishment of an international criminal court and other tribunals. Other challenges call for adaptation of the law to contemporary perceptions and needs. Such adaptation requires an understanding of the basic premises of the law of occupation and its links to other spheres of international law. Such an understanding is what this book tries to offer.

Tel Aviv
July 2004

Acknowledgments _____

THIS BOOK is based on a doctoral dissertation presented to the Yale Law School in 1990. The dissertation benefited immeasurably from the guidance of Professor W. Michael Reisman, whose advice and suggestions were invaluable. Professors Lea Brilmayer and Mirjan Damaska read the dissertation and offered many insightful comments.

I am very grateful to the Yale Law School for the considerable support it gave me during my stay there in the LL.M. and J.S.D. programs. Special thanks go to Associate Dean Barbara J. Safriet for her constant support in academic and administrative matters, and to Mr. Daniel Wade, the Foreign and International Law Librarian, who was always very helpful in locating various sources. I am also indebted to the Nathan Feinberg Foundation for the support it extended for the preparation of the manuscript, and to Mr. Doron Narkiss for his careful editing.

Lastly, I would like to express my deepest thanks to my wife, Rivka, for her support and encouragement during our stay at Yale. This work is dedicated to her and to our sons, Haggai and Amir.

Abbreviations

AD   Annual Digest of Public International Law Cases
AJIL   American Journal of International Law
BYIL   British Yearbook of International Law
EPIL   R. Bernhardt, ed., Encyclopedia of Public International Law
FJG   Fontes Juris Gentium
ICJ Rep. International Court of Justice Reports
ICLQ   International and Comparative Law Quarterly
ILM   International Legal Materials
ILN   International Law Notes
ILQ   International Law Quarterly
ILR   International Law Reports
ISLR   Israeli Law Review
IYHR   Israeli Yearbook of Human Rights
JCLIL   Journal of Comparative Legislation in International Law
PD   Piskei Din (Judgments of the Israeli Supreme Court)
PSM   Psakim Mekhoziim (Judgments of the Israeli District Courts)
RIAA   Reports of International Arbitral Awards
TGS   Transactions of the Grotius Society

THE INTERNATIONAL LAW OF OCCUPATION

1

Overview: The Phenomenon of Occupation

INTERNATIONAL LAW has sought since the nineteenth century to regulate
the conduct of occupying forces. Rules were prescribed through military
manuals, multilateral instruments, and state practice. These rules stemmed
from the universally accepted principle that sovereignty may not be alienated through the use of force. The occupying power is thus precluded from
annexing the occupied territory or otherwise changing its political status
and is bound to respect and maintain the political and other institutions
that exist in that territory. During the period of occupation, the occupant
is responsible for the management of public order and civil life in the territory under its control.

The law of occupation developed as part of the law of war. Initially,
occupation was viewed as a possible by-product of military actions during
war,[1] and therefore it was referred to in legal literature as "belligerent occupation." But the history of the twentieth century has shown that occupation is not necessarily the outcome of actual fighting: it could be the
result of a threat to use force that prompted the threatened government to
concede effective control over its territory to a foreign power;[2] occupation
could be established through an armistice agreement between the enemies;[3] and it also could be the product of a peace agreement.[4] Moreover,

---

[1] One necessary element of belligerent occupation is the establishment of "authority," of
effective control, by the invading army over the relevant territory. Article 42 of the Regulations Respecting the Laws and Customs of War on Land, annex to the Convention (IV)
Respecting the Laws and Customs of War on Land, signed at The Hague, October 18, 1907
[hereinafter Hague Regulations], defines the situation: "Territory is considered occupied
when it is actually placed under the authority of the hostile army. The occupation extends
only to the territory where such authority has been established and can be exercised."

Mere invasion does not amount to occupation. *See, e.g.*, 2 L. Oppenheim, *International
Law* 434–35 (7th ed., by H. Lauterpacht, 1948); E. Feilchenfeld, *The International Economic
Law of Belligerent Occupation* 6 (1942); M. Greenspan, *The Modern Law of Land Warfare* 213–
14 (1959).

[2] Examples of this type of occupation are the German occupation of Bohemia and Moravia
in March 1939, *see, e.g.*, *Anglo-Czechoslovak and Prague Credit Bank v. Janssen*, [1943–1945]
AD Case no. 11, at 47 (Australia, Supreme Court of Victoria); and the German occupation
during World War II of Denmark, *see, e.g.*, Ross, *Denmark's Legal Status during the Occupation*, 1 Jus Gentium 1 (1949).

[3] For example, the "Armistice Agreement" that established Allied control over the Rhineland in Germany in 1918. On this occupation, *see infra* Chapter 2.

[4] The Israeli occupation of the Gaza Strip did not change its status despite the 1979 Peace

because of many occupants' reluctance to admit the existence of a state of "war" or of an international armed conflict, or their failure to acknowledge the true nature of their activities on foreign soil, the utility of retaining the adjectives "belligerent" or "wartime" has become rather limited. Today the more inclusive term, "occupations," is generally used.[5] The emphasis is thus put not on the course through which the territory came under the foreign state's control, whether through actual fighting or otherwise, but rather on the phenomenon of occupation. This phenomenon can be defined as the effective control of a power (be it one or more states or an international organization, such as the United Nations) over a territory to which that power has no sovereign title, without the volition of the sovereign of that territory.

This movement toward a more encompassing definition of occupation is also reflected in the most important international instruments that prescribed the law of warfare, namely, the Hague Regulations and the 1949 Fourth Geneva Convention.[6] Article 42 of the Hague Regulations linked occupation to war: "[t]erritory is considered occupied when it is actually placed under the authority of the *hostile army*" (my emphasis). In the Fourth Geneva Convention this link is attenuated: Article 2 provides that the convention shall apply even to an occupation that "meets with no armed resistance." The rationale for the inclusive definition of occupation is that at the heart of all occupations exists a potential—if not an inherent— conflict of interest between occupant and occupied. This special situation is the result of the administration of the affairs of a country by an entity that is not its sovereign government. The issues that this type of administration raise are characterized by this possible conflict of interest, and are largely independent of the process through which the occupant established its control.

The Hague Regulations assumed that upon gaining control, the occupant would establish its authority over the occupied area, introducing a system of direct administration.[7] But this is more then a descriptive assumption: it is the law. There is a duty to establish such system of a government.[8] In 1907 there was no need to emphasize this point: the estab-

---

Treaty with Egypt. Egypt controlled Gaza prior to the Israeli occupation of 1967. On the status of this occupation, *see infra* Chapter 5.

[5] Adam Roberts gives a very thorough account of the variety of types of occupations. Roberts, *What Is Military Occupation?* 55 BYIL 249 (1985).

[6] The Convention Relative to the Protection of Civilian Persons in Time of War of August 12, 1949.

[7] This assumption is implicit, *inter alia*, in Article 43, which refers to the situation in which "[t]he authority of the legitimate power ha[s] in fact passed *into the hands of the occupant*" (my emphasis). On this assumption, *see also* Roberts, *supra* note 5, at 252.

[8] *See, e.g., The Law of Land Warfare* at paragraph 362 (U.S. Army Field Manual, FM 27-

lishment of a system of administration by the occupant was widely accepted in practice and in the literature as mandatory. Today, however, such practice is the rare exception rather than the rule.[9] Modern occupants came to prefer, from a variety of reasons, not to establish such a direct administration. Instead, they would purport to annex or establish puppet states or governments, make use of existing structures of government, or simply refrain from establishing any form of administration. In these cases, the occupants would tend not to acknowledge the applicability of the law of occupation to their own or their surrogates' activities, and when using surrogate institutions, would deny any international responsibility for the latter's actions. Acknowledgment of the status of occupant is the first and the most important initial indication that the occupant will respect the law of occupation. Such an acknowledgment is also likely to restrict the occupant's future actions and limit its claims regarding the ultimate status of that territory. This is a compelling reason for international law to stress what was self-evident not too long ago: the existence of the duty to establish a direct system of administration.[10] In any case, the failure to do so does not relieve the occupant of its other duties under the law of occupation: after all, the definition of occupation is not dependent on the establishment of an occupation administration. This principle is asserted in Article 47 of the Fourth Geneva Convention, which provides that "the benefits under the Convention shall not be affected by any change introduced, as a result of the occupation of a territory, into the institutions or government of the said territory, nor by any agreement concluded between the authorities of the occupied territories and the Occupying Power, nor by any annexation by the latter of the whole or part of the occupied territory."[11]

The foundation upon which the entire law of occupation is based is the principle of inalienability of sovereignty through the actual or threatened use of force. Effective control by foreign military force can never bring about by itself a valid transfer of sovereignty. From the principle of inalien-

---

10, 1956) ("Military government is the form of administration by which an occupying power exercises governmental authority over occupied territory.").

[9] This issue and the consequences of failure to abide by the requirement to establish a direct administration are treated in Chapter 6.

[10] In this respect, it is of little significance whether the occupant chooses to establish a system of military administration or a civil one, or a mixture of both. What is important is the establishment of a separate system by the occupant to execute the powers and duties allotted to it by the law of occupation. *See* (British) War Office, *The Law of War on Land, Being Part III of the Manual of Military Law* at 145, paragraph 518 (1958).

[11] Or as the British military manual, *id*. at paragraph 518(2), states: "The duties and constraints laid upon an Occupant cannot be circumvented by carrying out illegal acts through the instrumentality of a 'puppet government' set up in the occupied territory, or by a system of orders through local government officials operating in occupied territory."

able sovereignty over a territory spring the constraints that international law imposes upon the occupant. The power exercising effective control within another sovereign's territory has only temporary managerial powers, for the period until a peaceful solution is reached. During that limited period, the occupant administers the territory on behalf of the sovereign. Thus the occupant's status is conceived to be that of a trustee.[12] Changes over time have affected both the identity of the beneficiaries of this trust and the powers of the trustee, namely, the occupant. The occupant's powers have expanded through time to cover almost all the areas in which modern governments assert legitimacy to police, a far cry from the turn of the century laissez-faire conception of minimal governmental intervention. Other developments in the areas of political thought, namely, the emerging principles of self-determination and self-rule, were responsible for the shift in focus regarding the beneficiary of the trust: contemporary attention is paid more to the interests of the indigenous community under occupation rather than to the wishes of the ousted government. These two trends together form a striking departure from the Hague law, in which the emphasis was on the state elites as the primary beneficiaries and on minimal involvement of the occupant in the management of the affairs of the population under its temporary rule. These conceptual changes are reflected in the law of occupation, which came to recognize certain important modifications to the occupant's powers and duties.

In exploring the phenomenon of occupation, I was struck by the fact that most contemporary occupants ignored their status and their duties under the law of occupation. The examination of these cases and the motives for the occupants' positions (see Chapter 5) has led me to conclude that the tendency to avoid the recognition of the applicability of the law of occupation is not likely to disappear. This practice of occupants poses another decisive challenge that the law of occupation has to face in order to maintain its relevance.

This book sets out to explore the phenomenon of occupation. It examines the law of occupation as it was codified around the turn of this century in the Hague conferences, contrasting that law with the practice of occupants throughout the twentieth century and with more recent efforts to prescribe optimal standards of conduct. The object of this examination is to understand the arrangement that the international community has devised for settling the possible conflicts of interest between occupant and occupied and to assess the shortcomings and challenges of such a system.

[12] *See* Wilson, *The Laws of War in Occupied Territory*, 18 TGS 17, at 38 (1933) ("enemy territories in the occupation of the armed forces of another country constitute . . . a sacred trust"); Roberts, *supra* note 5, at 295 ("the idea of trusteeship is implicit in all occupation law"); G. von Glahn, *Law among Nations* 686 (5th ed. 1986) (the "occupant . . . exercises a temporary right of administration on a sort of trusteeship basis").

2

The Framework of the Law of Occupation

Article 43 of the Hague Regulations: A Profile of the Occupant's Role

Article 43 of the 1907 Hague Regulations states:

> The authority of the legitimate power having in fact passed into the hands of the occupant, the latter shall take all the measures in his power to restore and ensure, as far as possible, public order and [civil life], while respecting, unless absolutely prevented, the laws in force in the country.[1]

This concise statement is the gist of the law of occupation. Very few words are used to describe both the nature of the occupation regime and the scope of the occupant's legitimate powers. These words represent the culmination of prescriptive efforts made throughout the nineteenth century by national courts,[2] military manuals,[3] nonbinding international in-

---

[1] The official French version reads: "L'autorité du pouvoir légal ayant passé de fait entre les mains de l'occupant, celui-ci prendra toutes les measures qui dépendent de lui en vue de rétablir et d'assurer, autant qu'il est possible, l'ordre et la vie publics en respectant, sauf empêchement absolu, les lois en vigueur dans le pays." An identical version appeared in Article 43 of the Hague Regulations of 1899. As noted by Schwenk, *Legislative Power of the Military Occupant under Article 43, Hague Regulations*, 54 Yale L.J. 393 (1945), the first English translation of Article 43, which used the phrase "public order and *safety*" in lieu of "l'ordre et la *vie publics*," was incorrect. Schwenk suggested the use of the more comprehensive phrase used here, namely "public order and *civil life*." *See also infra* text accompanying notes 11–16.

[2] *See, e.g., Thirty Hogsheads of Sugar v. Boyle*, 13 U.S. (9 Cranch) 191 (1815); *United States v. Rice*, 17 U.S. (4 Wheat.) 246 (1819); *Fleming and Marshall v. Page*, 50 U.S. (9 How.) 603 (1850).

[3] The most famous is the Lieber Code, the first attempt to codify the laws of war, which was prepared in 1863 by Francis Lieber to be used as the U.S. war manual during the Civil War. The text is reproduced in D. Schindler and J. Toman, eds., *The Laws of Armed Conflicts* 3 (2d ed. 1981). Other military codes following the basic principles are the Bluntschli Code, prepared in 1866 for the German army, and the French manual for officers prepared in 1893, as well as the manuals of the British, Italian, and Russian armies. *See* D. Graber, *The Development of the Law of Belligerent Occupation 1863–1914*, at 26–27, 114–15, 132–33 (1949). The Lieber Code provides that an occupied area is put under martial law of the invading army, which "consists in the suspension . . . of the criminal and civil law, and of the domestic administration and government . . . and in the substitution of military rule and force for the same, as well as in the dictation of general laws, as far as military necessity requires this suspension, substitution, or dictation." Articles 1 and 3; *see also* Article 6.

struments,[4] and many legal scholars.[5] Article 43 was, in fact, a combination of Articles 2 and 3 of the Brussels Declaration.[6] Accordingly, the text of Article 43 was accepted by scholars as mere reiteration of the older law,[7] and subsequently the article was generally recognized as expressing customary international law.[8]

Among the two issues dealt with in Article 43 there is one which was not contested during the efforts to formulate the law of occupation. This is the notion that the occupation does not confer upon the occupant sovereignty over the occupied territory. In Article 43 this idea is expressed, quite vaguely, in the opening phrase: "The authority of the legitimate power having *in fact* passed into the hands of the occupant" (my emphasis).[9]

During the discussions at the second Hague Peace Conference in 1907, this basic premise served as the starting point for the more controversial

[4] The Brussels Declaration of 1874 provides as follows: Article 2: "The authority of the legitimate power being suspended and having in fact passed into the hands of the occupant, the latter shall take all the measures in his power to restore and ensure, as far as possible, public order and safety." Article 3: "With this object he shall maintain the laws which were in force in the country in time of peace and shall not modify, suspend or replace them unless necessary." The Oxford Manual on the Laws of War on Land of 1880, Article 6, provides: "No invaded territory is regarded as conquered until the end of the war; until that time the occupant exercises, in such territory, only a de facto power, essentially provisional in character." The texts of both codes appear in D. Schindler and J. Toman, *supra* note 3, at 26 and 35, respectively. On the background of these two codes *see* Graber, *supra* note 3, at 20–30.

[5] See Graber, *supra* note 3, at 110–48.

[6] On this issue, *see infra* notes 22–24 and accompanying text.

[7] *See* Graber, *supra* note 3, at 143 ("Nothing distinguishes the writing of the period following the 1899 Hague code from the writing prior to that code.").

[8] This view was expressed by the International Military Tribunal in Nuremberg. *See The Trial of the Major War Criminals* 253–54 (1947), *also published in* 41 AJIL 172, 248–49 (1947). *See also, e.g.,* G. von Glahn, *The Occupation of Enemy Territory* 10–12 (1957). Municipal courts have also regarded the Hague Regulations as codified customary international law. Morgenstern, *Validity of Acts of the Belligerent Occupant,* 28 BYIL 291, 292 (1951).

[9] This expression led von Glahn to say that "[t]he Hague Regulations give no clear-cut answer to the problem of sovereignty in occupied territory, inasmuch as there is only reference to a passage of de facto authority into the hands of the occupant." von Glahn, *supra* note 8, at 31. It is, however, quite clear that the framers of the Hague Regulations unanimously took the view that an occupant could not claim sovereign rights only because of its effective control over the occupied territory. Moreover, many authorities even went further, denying the occupant any *legal right* to control such territory. According to this latter view, Article 43 did not grant the occupant an entitlement to administer the territory; rather, it merely recognized *the fact* of its effective control, and set out to delimit it. For more modern reiterations of this view, *see, e.g.,* Bothe, *Belligerent Occupation, in* 4 EPIL 65 (1982) ("International law does not grant rights to the occupying powers, but limits the occupier's exercise of its *de facto* powers."); Baxter, *The Duty of Obedience to the Belligerent Occupant,* 27 BYIL 235, 243 (1950). Compare this view with that of other commentators who *do* find international law as granting certain legal powers to the occupant. *See, e.g.,* Morgenstern, *supra* note 8, at 296; J. Stone, *Legal Controls of International Conflicts* 724 (1954).

debate regarding the scope of the occupant's authority. In fact, this second issue was the subject of intense controversy even before the first Hague Conference of 1899. This debate, which was not resolved in the conferences, is reflected in the compromise formula of Article 43, which is sufficiently vague to carry various meanings. Indeed, the debate regarding the issue of the occupant's powers is still alive today, and the differences between the opposing views have grown. Since Article 43 is the cornerstone of the law of occupation in the twentieth century, it is pertinent to discuss this issue here.

Delimitation of the Occupant's Powers

Article 43, dealing with the general powers of the occupant, mentions both the obligations of the occupying power and its rights in the course of fulfilling these obligations. In this sense, Article 43 is a sort of miniconstitution for the occupation administration; its general guidelines permeate any prescriptive measure or other acts taken by the occupant.[10]

The obligations of the occupant are to "take all the measures in his power to restore and ensure, as far as possible, public order and [civil life]." It is required to do so "while respecting, unless absolutely prevented, the laws in force in the country." From the latter duty emerges the implicit recognition of the right of the occupant *not* to respect some of the local laws.

The Subjects of The Occupant's Legitimate Concerns: Public Order and Civil Life

The phrases in Article 43, "public order" and what should be translated as "civil life," delimit the scope of the occupant's powers and duties. They prescribe, however, only a vague and intuitive course. Moreover, these phrases are susceptible to changing conceptions regarding the role of the central government in society. Between 1874, when these terms were first coined, and the late twentieth century, the conceptions regarding the issues involved have changed dramatically. Indeed, they have become the focal point of deep ideological differences between nations.

[10] Other articles deal with specific issues, such as collection of taxes (Article 48), requisitions (Article 52), and taking possession of various assets (Articles 46, 52–56). These specific grants of authority are in turn subject to the overriding delimiting principle of Article 43. *See, e.g., Abu-Aita et al. v. Commander of Judea and Samaria et al.,* 37 PD (2) 197, 260 (1983), *translated in 7 Selected Judgments of the Supreme Court of Israel* 1, 54 (1983–1987) (the powers and delimitations regarding taxation, as set by Article 48, are subject to those of Article 43).

To nineteenth-century politicians and legal scholars, there was nothing problematic about recognizing the occupant's power to prescribe measures for the purpose of restoring and ensuring public order and civil life. Based on the then-prevailing notions of the proper role of central governments and assumptions as to the short duration and nature of war, giving this power to the occupant did not seem to raise any grave concerns on the part of societies susceptible to occupations. In fact, these terms, which would later be used by occupants as justification for increased intervention in local affairs, were originally elaborated by the delegates of the weaker countries, those most susceptible to being occupied. They wanted to impress this duty upon occupants, who otherwise, they thought, might choose not to get involved in matters concerning the civilian population of an occupied territory.

In the debate over the Brussels Declaration of 1874, it was the Belgian delegate who suggested that "l'ordre publique" meant "la securité ou la sureté generale," while "la vie publique" stood for "des fonctions sociales, des transactions ordinaires, qui constituent la vie de tous les jours."[11] It seems safe to assume that the weaker parties to the convention, more than the major powers, wanted to enlarge the scope of the occupant's duty toward the local inhabitants, thus ensuring their ability to return as quickly and as much as possible to their regular daily life. It was not expected at that time that the occupant would have any self-interest in regulating those social functions. Consequently, no one raised the possibility of the occupant's intervention in these areas to further its own policies. International scholars still viewed the likely motives of the occupant to be short-term military concerns, not impinging upon the local civil and criminal orders.[12]

With the advent of the twentieth century and the ever-increasing regulation of the markets and other social activities by central governments, especially during and after hostilities, the duty imposed on the occupant turned into a grant of authority to prescribe and create changes in a wide spectrum of affairs. With the modern conceptions of the state, both in the Western world and in the socialist countries, it became "difficult to point with much confidence to any of the usual subjects of governmental action as being *a priori* excluded from the sphere of administrative authority conferred upon the occupant."[13] Indeed, the term "l'ordre et la vie publics," in an interesting historical twist, was soon invoked by the occupants to justify

---

[11] *See* Ministère des Affaires Étrangeres, Actes de la Conference de Bruxelles de 1874 23 (1874), *reproduced in* Schwenk, *supra* note 1, at 398.

[12] The occupant was not expected to introduce legal changes in the civil and criminal laws. Military necessity, a recognized justification for legislation by the occupant, did not seem to be linked with those areas. *See* the description of the opinion of the numerous commentators of that period in Graber, *supra* note 3, at 123–25, 132–34, 143–45.

[13] M. McDougal and F. Feliciano, *Law and Minimum World Public Order* 746 (1961).

their extensive use of prescriptive powers.[14] The duty was transformed into a legal tool extensively invoked by occupants in those areas in which they wished to intervene. Article 43 proved an extremely convenient tool for the occupant: if it wished, it could intervene in practically all aspects of life;[15] if it was in its interest to refrain from action, it could invoke the "limits" imposed on its powers.[16]

The Objects of the Occupant's Action: "Restore and Ensure"

The need to "restore" public order and civil life arises in the wake of hostilities that disrupt them. The restoration process includes immediate acts needed to bring daily life as far as possible back to the previous state of affairs. The occupant's discretion in this process is limited. It is the other term, the command "to ensure," that poses some difficulties. At issue is the extent to which the occupant must adhere to the *status quo ante bellum*. This question becomes more pressing as the occupation is protracted. A strict reading of "ensure," as the preservation of the status quo,[17] could well mean the freezing of the economic infrastructure and stagnation in the occupied territory. Starting with the cessation of actual hostilities, a new era begins, which could continue for many years before the occupation is ended. During this period, "human existence requires organic growth, and it is impossible for a state to mark time indefinitely. Political decisions must be taken, policies have to be formulated and carried out."[18] Could all these decisions be regarded as "ensuring" public order and civil life?

Many occupants during this century answered this question affirmatively. In implementing the duty "to ensure," they often created a whole

[14] *See, e.g., Grahame v. Director of Prosecution,* [1947] AD Case no. 103, at 228, 232 (Germany, British Zone of Control, Control Commission Court of Criminal Appeal) (" '[L]'ordre et la vie publics'[is] a phrase which refers to the whole social, commercial and economic life of the community."). The Israeli High Court of Justice has also subscribed to this view. *See, e.g., Abu-Aita, supra* note 10 (concerning the introduction of a new value-added tax). For other decisions of Israeli courts in this direction, *see infra* Chapter 5.

[15] McDougal and Feliciano, *supra* note 13, at 747 ("Occupants did in fact intervene in and subject to regulation practically every aspect of life in a modern state which legitimate sovereigns themselves are generally wont to regulate."); O. Debbasch, *L'occupation militaire* 172 (1962) ("L'occupant . . . a souvent tenté d'accroître exagérément sa compétence réglementaire et de predre des mesures que seul le souverain aurait du normalement décider.").

[16] This has been the position of the British occupation government in post–World War II Tripolitania, where the former denied desperate requests of the local inhabitants to ameliorate their conditions. For a discussion of that occupation, *see infra* Chapter 4.

[17] This interpretation was suggested in the early period of the Israeli occupation by Justice H. Cohn, in a minority opinion in *The Christian Society for the Sacred Places v. Minister of Defence et al.,* 26(1) PD 574 (1972).

[18] M. Greenspan, *The Modern Law of Land Warfare* 225 (1959).

cycle of events: new policies brought about new outcomes, which in their turn necessitated multiple other social decisions, and so forth. Since "ensuring" is linked to the wide spectrum of social activity—the "public order and civil life"—it does not take too long after the occupation administration is established for the command "to ensure" to connote not much less than full discretionary powers, amounting to those of a sovereign government.[19] This latitude that Article 43 entrusts to occupants is not a simple matter. My analysis of occupations shows—and this should not be surprising—that social decisions taken and implemented in occupied territories were never incompatible with outcomes sought by occupants. Often these outcomes proved detrimental to the occupied country. This brings us to the second part of Article 43, which tries to strike a balance between stability and change, between the interests of the occupant and those of the occupied population.

Stability versus Change: "While Respecting, Unless Absolutely Prevented, the Laws in Force in the Country"

The second part of Article 43 was a separate article in the 1874 Brussels Declaration, linked to the duty of the occupant to restore and ensure public order and safety.[20] Implicit in this duty is the recognition of the occupant's power to prescribe laws or otherwise act in ways not in conformity with the legal system that was laid down by the sovereign government. This implicit recognition was the only issue regarding Article 43 that was contested during the 1899 Hague Peace Conference.[21] Beernaert, the delegate of Belgium, and den Beer Portugael, of the Netherlands, opposed the inclusion of Article 3 of the Brussels Declaration in the proposed Hague Regulations. Beernaert explained that he did not want officially to sanction such a power: "The country invaded submits to the law of the invader; that is a fact; that is might; but we should not legalize the exercise of this power

---

[19] Mossner, *Military Government, in* 3 EPIL 269, 273 (1982) (after more than a decade of Israeli occupation, "it is questionable as to whether [the Hague Regulations] prohibit any changes in economic, legal, and cultural affairs whatsoever"); Liszt, *Das Völkerrecht* 491 (12th ed. 1925) ("The longer the occupation lasts, the more comprehensive will be the interference with the administration and legislation of the occupied country for its own sake" (*translated in* Schwenk, *supra* note 1, at 399 n.25).). On long-term occupations and international law, *see infra* Chapter 5.

[20] Article 3 of the Brussels Declaration: "With this object [expressed in Article 2, the occupant] shall maintain the laws which were in force in the country in time of peace, and shall not modify, suspend or replace them unless necessary."

[21] *See, e.g.,* W. Hull, *The Two Hague Conferences and Their Contributions to International Law* 243–45 (1908).

in advance, and admit that might makes right."[22] Several formulations were put forward, trying to satisfy the strong and the weak countries alike.[23] The compromise that was finally agreed upon, suggested by Bilhourd, the French delegate, probably seemed more acceptable to the representatives of the weaker states, because "respecting" and "unless absolutely prevented" seemed more restrictive than the phrases "maintaining" and "unless necessary" in the Brussels Declaration.[24] In retrospect, this change of tone proved of little value. From the point of view of the occupants, the meaning of "unless absolutely prevented" remained conveniently vague. The Belgians, on the other hand, did not consider themselves hindered by this article from claiming that the German occupant of their land during World War I (or any other occupant, for that matter) had no power to enact legally binding laws.[25]

The requirement to "respect" the existing laws "unless absolutely prevented" has no meaning of its own, since the occupant is almost never absolutely prevented, in the technical sense, from respecting them.[26] This phrase becomes meaningful only when it is linked to the considerations that the occupants are entitled or required to weigh while contemplating the desirability of change vis-à-vis the interest in stability and respect for the status quo. But delineating the legitimate concerns of the occupant is not enough. One must also determine the proper balances: the desired balance between stability and change in general, and the balance between the conflicting considerations that the occupant faces in a particular matter. Thus, if general emphasis should be laid on maintaining the status quo, then no conflicting acts would be permitted unless (for example) the public order had deteriorated significantly. More particularly, if the occupant's security interests merit no more deference than does the welfare of the population, then not all changes that may promote its army's needs would be deemed lawful. The interpretation of the vague phrase "unless absolutely prevented" is therefore critical: if the general emphasis is on change

[22] *Reprinted in id.* at 244.

[23] A succinct description of the suggestions exists in Graber, *supra* note 3, at 141–43, and Schwenk, *supra* note 1, at 396–97.

[24] The linkage between the duty concerning legislation (to respect local laws unless absolutely prevented) and the duty to restore and ensure public order and civil life, which existed in the Brussels Declaration is retained in Article 43. It is, nevertheless, widely accepted that the duty to respect local laws is a general principle, which is not limited to issues related to public order and civil life. There is no freedom to disregard local law in other matters, Schwenk, *supra* note 1, at 397.

[25] This was essentially a reiteration of the argument of their delegate to the 1899 Hague Peace Conference. On the later Belgian claims with respect to the 1914–1918 occupation, *see infra* notes 58 and 60, and Chapter 7, text accompanying notes 13–21.

[26] E. Feilchenfeld, *The International Economic Law of Belligerent Occupation* 89 (1942); Schwenk, *supra* note 1, at 400.

and not on stability, then this phrase would merely create a rebuttable presumption in favor of the preoccupation law. If this is the case, the question of whether or not to enact new laws will not be very different from the same question posed to any sovereign government contemplating new policies.

It seems that the drafters of this phrase viewed military necessity as the sole relevant consideration that could "absolutely prevent" an occupant from maintaining the old order.[27] As was mentioned earlier, under the prevailing laissez-faire view, the occupant was not expected, during the anticipated short period of occupation, to have pressing interests in changing the law to regulate the activities of the population, except for what was necessary to the safety of its forces. The only relevant question under this restrictive view would therefore be whether or not the occupant could—in the technical sense—accommodate its security interests with the existing laws. However, as early as World War I, this test proved to be insufficient as it could not properly conform with the occupant's duty to protect the interests of the local population, interests that at times could be best met by amending the local laws.

Scholars in the post–World War II period already conceded other legitimate subjects for the occupant's lawmaking. Von Glahn contended that the occupant might lawfully enact laws for nonmilitary goals. In his view, "the secondary aim of any lawful military occupation is the safeguarding of the welfare of the native population, and this secondary and lawful aim would seem to supply the necessary basis for such new laws that are passed by the occupant for the benefit of the population and are not dictated by his own military necessity and requirements."[28] McNair and Watts drew three grounds for legitimate lawmaking: "the maintenance of order, the safety of [the occupant's] forces and the realization of the legitimate purpose of his occupation."[29] Debbasch mentioned "la sécurité de l'armée et l'ordre public local" as the two lawful grounds for changing the law.[30] In

---

[27] See the many citations in Schwenk, supra note 1. See also Greenspan, supra note 18, at 224 ("if demanded by the exigencies of war"), but Greenspan adds that "[t]hose exigencies may, in fact demand a great deal," and gives as an example the elimination of undemocratic and inhumane institutions. Bothe, supra note 9, at 66, is a modern voice advocating this strict interpretation.

[28] According to von Glahn, the view confining lawmaking to military necessity "fails to take cognizance of the fact that there are certain categories of laws which may be necessary during the course of belligerent occupation but which nevertheless have nothing to do with military necessity in the strict sense of the term." von Glahn, supra note 8, at 97. But still, in von Glahn's view, military necessity remains the primary grant of prescription, well before the "public order": the welfare of the native population is "a secondary aim" of the lawful occupation. Id.

[29] Lord A. McNair and A. Watts, The Legal Effects of War 369 (4th ed. 1966).

[30] Debbasch, supra note 15, at 172.

addition, especially in light of the oppressive laws that the occupants found in Nazi Germany, some scholars have argued that at times moral arguments, and not only technical difficulties, could be considered as preventing an occupant from respecting local laws and, in fact, requiring change.[31] With the enlargement of the legitimate subjects for changes came a more positive view regarding change in principle. Scholars in that postwar period, all writing from a Western perspective, were less averse to changes to be introduced by the occupant. Thus, some interpreted "absolutely prevented" as meaning "absolute necessity,"[32] or just "necessity."[33] Ernst Feilchenfeld suggested the test of "sufficient justification" to change the law.[34] Still another approach was to use the "reasonableness" test.[35]

This recognition of broader powers for changing the legal landscape of the occupied territory implied more discretion for the occupant, and less formal constraints on its measures. Realizing that occupants could invoke the needs of the civilian population as grounds for legislation under Article 43, while "there [was] no objective criterion in practice for drawing a distinction between sincere and insincere concern for the civilian population," Yoram Dinstein suggested a simple rule for such "sincerity": the test for the legality of such legislative changes would generally be "whether or not the occupant is equally concerned about his own population."[36] Thus the existence of a law in the occupant's own country will generally serve as evidence of the occupant's lawfulness in introducing a similar law in the occupied territory. This is a practical test, and as such could serve as a useful compass in evaluating occupation measures. However, this cannot be viewed as the ultimate test for lawfulness. First, the social and economic conditions in the two areas could be different, and therefore communal needs may vary. Second, if the sincerity of the occupant is at issue, the use of similar laws cannot allay the concerns involved, since different implementations of the same texts can yield disparate outcomes. Finally, the test

---

[31] *See, e.g.,* McDougal and Feliciano, *supra* note 13, at 770 (The Allied occupants of Germany "may fairly be said to have been 'absolutely prevented' by their own security interests from respecting, for instance, the German laws with respect to the Nazi Party and other Nazi organizations and the 'Nuremberg' racial laws."); similarly, Greenspan, *supra* note 18, at 225 ("If, in those circumstances [of complete German surrender], the victors are not 'absolutely prevented' . . . from respecting those institutions, then those words have no sensible meaning."). *See also* the British Military Manual, *supra* Chapter 1, note 10, at paragraph 510 n.1.

[32] *See, e.g.,* Schwenk, *supra* note 1, at 401 ("It is therefore submitted that the term 'empêchement absolu' means nothing but 'absolute necessity'.").

[33] Dinstein, *The International Law of Belligerent Occupation and Human Rights*, 8 IYHR 104, 112 (1978) ("absolute prevention means necessity").

[34] Feilchenfeld, *supra* note 26, at 89.

[35] McDougal and Feliciano, *supra* note 13, at 767; Debbasch, *supra* note 15, at 317; Greenspan, *supra* note 18, at 224 ("International law allows a reasonable latitude in such circumstances.").

[36] Dinstein, *supra* note 33, at 113.

seem to open the door wide enough to allow almost any law to be duplicated in the occupied territory; consequently, it might be abused as an excuse for the assimilation of the legal landscape of the two regions, which could well be a de facto annexation of the occupied territory.[37]

The various scholarly efforts to explore the limits of the occupant's power and duty to modify the legal landscape of the occupied territory can provide no more than general guidelines. No a priori formulation can furnish concrete rules for the specific circumstances of every occupation. Ultimately there is no general formula that could substitute for the process of analyzing each and every act, taking note of all the relevant interests at stake and the available alternatives.

Having said that, it should be added that certain specific issues have been addressed in greater detail by scholars, and some specific rules have gained wide acceptance. One of these is the rule that occupants may suspend the operation of laws concerning conscription to military service and granting licenses to carry weapons, as well as laws relating to political activity in the territory, such as laws concerning elections to national institutions. Another generally expected act, often required by military necessity, is the suspension of certain civil liberties, such as freedom of speech and freedom of movement.[38] Considerable agreement exists among scholars with respect to the occupant's power to regulate the local currency and determine exchange rates.[39] Scholars also generally agree that the indigenous court system should be left intact if it is operative.[40] Other specific issues have received special attention, but no consensus has been formed, for example, regarding the occupant's powers to introduce changes in fiscal laws (including custom duties).[41] Besides the discussion concerning the scope of

[37] For a similar critique of this test, *see* Meron, *Applicability of Multilateral Conventions to Occupied Territories*, 72 AJIL 542, 550 (1978); Roberts, *Prolonged Military Occupation: The Israeli-Occupied Territories since 1967*, 84 AJIL 44, 94 (1990).

[38] *See, e.g.*, von Glahn, *supra* note 8, at 98–99; Schwenk, *supra* note 1, at 403–4.

[39] *See* Feilchenfeld, *supra* note 26, at 70–83; K. Skubiszewski, *Pieniadz na Terytorium Okupowanym* [Money in Occupied Territories] (1960) (in Polish, summary in English at 360–83); A. Nussbaum, *Money in the Law* 495 (1950); F. Mann, *The Legal Aspect of Money* 485–91 (4th ed. 1982); Stone, *supra* note 9, at 718.

[40] E. Wolff, *Municipal Courts in Enemy-Occupied Territory*, 29 TGS 99 (1944); Stone, *supra* note 9, at 701; von Glahn, *supra* note 8, at 106.

[41] The specific article dealing with such laws is Article 48 of the Hague Convention. On taxation, *see, e.g.*, Feilchenfeld, *supra* note 26, at 49; Stone, *supra* note 9, at 712–13; Greenspan, *supra* note 18, at 229; McNair and Watts, *supra* note 29, at 386. On custom duties *see, e.g.*, Feilchenfeld, *supra* note 26, at 83; Stone *supra* note 9, at 712 n.118; Greenspan, *supra* note 18, at 228; Schwenk, *supra* note 1, at 404; E. Castrén, *The Present Law of War and Neutrality* 224 (1954). Of special interest would be the decision of the Israeli Supreme Court in the case of *Abu-Aita*, which sanctioned the introduction of the Value Added Tax into the Israeli-occupied territories, and also approved the free passage of goods across the borders

the authorized legislation by the occupant, two issues exist with respect to the relevant portions of the local legal system that the occupant should respect: Does the duty to respect "*the laws* in force" extend not only to primary legislation but also to secondary legislation and maybe even court precedents? And what weight should be given to the term "the laws *in force in the country*"? Do these laws include new laws introduced by the sovereign government subsequent to the commencement of the occupation, and enforced in the unoccupied part of the country?

Only a very narrow and technical reading of Article 43 can support a claim that the occupant has no duty to respect prescriptions that are not embedded in primary legislation. Public order and civil life are maintained through laws, regulations, court decisions, administrative guidelines, and even customs, all of which form an intricate and balanced system. Even in democratic societies, which differentiate between the legislative powers of the elected parliament and the delegation of authority to other lawmaking bodies, it is accepted that all the prescriptive functions are equally important.[42] Schwenk argued that the legislature, by delegating its legislative authority to other branches, has a priori implicitly consented to any changes made by the occupant and therefore such changes do not have to pass the muster of international law.[43] But this opinion overlooks the fact that by delegating its authority, the legislature did not waive its power to intervene and correct abuses made by the delegated power. That opportunity to react to abuses or misuses of authority is, of course, lacking under occupation. Hence, the occupant's duty to respect the laws under Article 43 should be construed as including the duty to respect nonstatutory prescriptions,[44] and even the local administration's interpretation of the local statutes and other instruments. Any deviation from such an interpretation should not be justified as a "fresh reading" of the interpreted instrument, but rather by the necessity to deviate from the former operative interpretation, necessity that must be justified under Article 43.

More complicated is the second question, regarding subsequent legislation by the ousted government. Occupants,[45] some national courts,[46] and

---

between Israel and the territories. *Abu-Aita, supra* note 10; *see also infra* Chapter 5, text accompanying notes 179–80.

[42] *But cf.* von Glahn, *supra* note 8, at 99, arguing that "administrative regulations and executive orders are quite sharply distinct from the constitutional and statute law of a country and . . . they do not constitute as important or as vital a part of the latter's legal structure."

[43] Schwenk, *supra* note 1, at 408.

[44] *See, e.g.*, De Visscher, *L'occupation de guerre d'après la jurisprudence de la Cour de cassation de Belgique*, 34 LQR 72, 80 (1918); K. Strupp, *Das Internationale Landkriegsrecht* 99 n.2 (1914).

[45] The German occupation government in Belgium during World War I, the Allied forces in World War II, and the Israeli administration in 1967 did not recognize these laws as applicable. *See* Stein, *Application of the Law of the Absent Sovereign in Territories under Belligerent*

some scholars[47] have rejected any duty to respect legislation made outside the occupied area. The majority of post–World War II scholars, relying also on the practice of various national courts, have, however, agreed that with respect to those issues in which the occupant has no power to amend the local law, the absent sovereign government is entitled to legislate and expect the occupant to respect its dictates.[48] Even if the occupant does not respect such new legislation, it is nevertheless valid, and could be invoked retroactively upon the conclusion of the occupation.[49]

Occupation: The Schio Massacre, 46 Mich. L. Rev. 341, 352–53 (1948); *see also* The U.S. Judge Advocate General's School, *Legal Aspects of Civil Affairs* 104 n. 10 (1960), which states that "the belligerent occupant is under no legal obligation to apply laws promulgated by the absent sovereign subsequent to the occupation." The Israeli view is pronounced in Proclamation Concerning Law and Administration (no. 2) of June 7, 1967.

[46] The U.S. Supreme Court held this view with respect to territories occupied by U.S. forces. *Thirty Hogsheads of Sugar v. Boyle, supra* note 2; *United States v. Rice, supra* note 2. *But cf.* the opinion of the U.S. Second Circuit with respect to legislation by the exiled Dutch government in *State of the Netherlands v. Federal Reserve Bank of New York*, 201 F.2d 455 (2d Cir. 1953) ("The legitimate Government should be entitled to legislate over occupied territory insofar as such enactments do not conflict with the legitimate rule of the occupying power.").

[47] *See* 3 C. Hyde, *International Law* 1886 (2d ed. 1945), arguing: "The possession by the belligerent occupant of the right to control, maintain or modify the laws that are to obtain within the occupied area is an exclusive one. The territorial sovereign driven therefrom can not compete with it on an even plane." Dinstein, *supra* note 33, at 113–14, and Stein, *supra* note 45, at 362, suggest that although the occupant has no duty to do so, it might be expedient to respect the new laws in certain circumstances. E. Wolff, *supra* note 40, at 109, mentions operative difficulties: "from a practical point of view such a division of the legislative power between the legitimate government and the occupant would meet with the greatest difficulties. It is hardly possible to draw the border line between measures dictated by 'absolute necessity' and other measures. . . . The second doubt concerns the promulgation. The legitimate government will not be able to comply with the provisions contained in its constitutional law about the promulgation of legislative measures."

[48] *See* Feilchenfeld, *supra* note 26, at 135, asserting that "one goes too far in assuming, as has been done by various authorities, that an absent sovereign is absolutely precluded from legislating for occupied areas. The sovereignty of the absent sovereign over the region remains in existence and, from a more practical point of view, the occupant may and should have no objection to timely alterations of existing laws by the old sovereign in those fields which the occupant has not seen fit to subject to his own legislative power." For similar views, *see* McNair and Watts, *supra* note 29, at 446; von Glahn, *supra* note 8, at 34–36; Debbasch, *supra* note 15, at 229–33.

[49] "[T]he rule [respecting the local laws] freezes the local law for the period of the belligerent occupation. The disseised sovereign cannot, and the Occupying Power may not [with the exception of the necessities of war], interfere with the *status quo ante bellum*. . . . In [matters that are not the legitimate legislative concern of the occupant], the legislation of the disseised sovereign is merely ineffective while the occupation lasts, . . . [and] retroactive application of such legislation [upon the return of the sovereign] is compatible with international law." 2 G. Schwarzenberger, *International Law—The Law of Armed Conflict* 201–2 (1968). "So far as the inhabitants of the occupied territory are concerned, they can invoke legislation-in-exile only in the courts of the restored sovereign after the occupation." Mc-

The Scope of Article 43: Its Applicability to the National Institutions of the Occupying Country

The limitations on the occupant are not restricted to the temporary occupation institutions established to handle the affairs of the occupied territory. They also extend to the national institutions of the occupying country. The occupant may not surpass its limits under international law through extraterritorial prescriptions emanating from its national institutions: the legislature, government, and courts. The reason for this rule is, of course, the functional symmetry, with respect to the occupied territory, among the various lawmaking authorities of the occupying state. Without this symmetry, Article 43 could become almost meaningless as a constraint upon the occupant, since the occupation administration would then choose to operate through extraterritorial prescription of its national institutions. Thus every prescription of policy regarding the occupied territory, every grant of power to act with respect to that area, every general prescription which applies also to the area, and every extension of the courts' jurisdiction will all be subject to the delimiting principle of Article 43.

Support for this proposition is found in one of the earliest decisions of the Israeli Supreme Court.[50] In this case the Court considered whether the national legislature of the occupant state was entitled under international law to prescribe directly with respect to the occupied territory, or whether such a prescription should be promulgated by the occupation administration. The Court approved the arrogation of the powers of the occupant under Article 43 to the occupant's legislature in these words:

> As to the argument that it should have been the military commander and not the State of Israel who legislated for the area, I am of the opinion that if international law recognizes that the military commander has certain powers of legislation, *a fortiori* such power is vested in the legislature of the occupant from which the military commander derives his own authority. . . . Accordingly there is no substance in the assertion that the laws [that were applied to the occupied

Dougal and Feliciano, *supra* note 13, at 771–73. The Swiss Federal Tribunal has held that the enactments of an exiled government were immediately valid in the occupied territory. The court did not qualify this assertion by subjecting it to the legitimate prescriptive powers of the occupant: "Enactments by the [exiled government] are constitutionally laws of the [country] and applied *ab initio* to the territory occupied . . . even though they could not be effectively implemented until the liberation. . . ." *Ammon v. Royal Dutch Co.* 21 ILR 25, 27 (1954).

[50] *Attorney General for Israel v. Sylvester*, [1948] AD Case no. 190 (February 8, 1949). Despite this Israeli precedent of 1948, during the Israeli occupation of the West Bank and Gaza, many important policies were prescribed and applied by the Israeli legislature, government, and even courts, without regard to the delimitations imposed by the Hague Regulations. On these policies *see infra* Chapter 5.

territory] are invalid because they were issued by the State of Israel and not by
the military commander of the occupying forces.[51]

If the national institutions of the occupying army have powers similar to
those of the latter, then they are equally bound by the same constraints on
the use of such powers. Indeed, this equation stems from the bureaucratic
fact that the occupying force is not an actor independent of its own national institutions; rather, it is an implementing arm of those institutions.
There is no point, and no legal basis, for differentiating between them.

Nationals of the Occupying Power: An Exception to the Rule?

A familiar case in which laws are extraterritorially prescribed to the occupied territory occurs with the extension of such laws over nationals of the
occupant who are present in the territory. In this regard, an exception to
the principle of limited prescriptive powers of Article 43 has been recognized in practice and in the literature: the occupant is not bound by the
Hague Regulations in prescribing the internal legal relationships among
the members of its forces and the nationals who accompany the troops
insofar as this does not impinge upon indigenous interests.[52] There is no
international obligation to apply the territorial law of the occupied territory (and hence Article 43) to transactions these nationals have concluded
among themselves, and thus the national law would often be the applicable
law.[53] In practice, the occupant would usually also prevent the local courts

[51] *Israel v. Sylvester, supra* note 50, at 575. The same reasoning is applicable also to under-
takings of the occupying state arising under multilateral conventions. Meron, *supra* note 37.

[52] *See, e.g., The Law of Land Warfare* (U.S. Army Field Manual, FM 27–10, 1956), which
states in Section 374: "Military and civilian personnel of the occupying forces and occupation
administration and persons accompanying them are not subject to the local law or to the
jurisdiction of the local courts of the occupied territory unless expressly made subject thereto
by a competent officer of the occupying forces or the occupation administration." *But cf.*
Greenspan, *supra* note 18, at 254–56 (the troops will not be subject to local law and jurisdiction, but accompanying civilians may be subject to the local law to be applied by the military
tribunals).

According to the British Foreign Marriage Act of 1947, a British ceremony of marriage
will be administered abroad if at least one of the parties is a member of the army. The Law
Commission proposed in 1985 that the same arrangement be extended to civilians who accompany the forces. *See* Cheshire and North, *Private International Law* 565 (11th ed.,
P. North and J. Fawcett, eds., 1987).

[53] Thus acts of marriage between members of Allied occupation forces in occupied Germany and Italy have been held valid by the British Probate Court, which preferred the nationality law on the otherwise applicable *lex loci celebrationis. See, e.g., Merker v. Merker*, [1963]
P 283, [1962] 3 All E.R. 928; *Preston v. Preston*, [1963] P 411, [1963] 2 All E.R. 405 (here
the husband was a member of the occupation forces while the wife, a civilian, lived in the
same army camp).

of the occupied territory from adjudicating claims regarding those nationals.[54]

With regard to nationals of the occupant who are not related to the latter's forces, the legal situation is not as clear. Some authorities support the territorial principle.[55] From the point of view of the law of occupation, it would seem that the test should be whether the application of the national law would have, directly or indirectly, adverse effects on the local public order and on short- and long-term indigenous interests. Usually the application of the nationality principle, in both civil and criminal matters, would not impinge on those concerns, and thus it is arguable that in those cases the nationality principle could replace the territorial principle. But if such measures are liable to affect the indigenous population of the occupied territory, then they ought to pass the scrutiny of international law, including Article 43 of the Hague Regulations. One such external outcome of an application of the nationality principle might be the encouragement of nationals to emigrate to the occupied territory. Such an outcome might impinge on the local "public order and civil life" and therefore be proscribed by international law, particularly by Article 43.

Article 43 and the Duty of the Ousted Government

Ought the ousted government acquiesce to measures taken by the occupant that are deemed lawful under Article 43? Does the law of occupation require it to respect the occupant's valid laws when it resumes authority over the territory? Before reaching these two questions, we have to ask a preliminary question: why are these two questions important to the understanding of the powers and duties of the occupant during the occupation? The occupant has a strong interest in ensuring that its prescriptions and the allocation of entitlements provided by those prescriptions remain effective even after its departure. This probability enhances the inhabitants' incentive to comply with its orders during its rule. A stability in expectations is more likely under such conditions. Moreover, if the occupant's pre-

---

[54] *See, e.g.,* Greenspan, *supra* note 18, at 255.

[55] *See Madsen v. Kinsella,* 93 F. Supp. 319, 323 (S.D. W. Va. 1950), *aff'd,* 188 F.2d 272 (4th Cir. 1951), *aff'd,* 343 U.S. 341 (1952). The case involved a conviction under the German Criminal Code of an American for the murder of her husband. At the relevant time, both had been living in the U.S. occupation zone in Germany, where the husband served as an army officer. Said the court of first instance: "When an American citizen (not a member of the Armed Forces) enters a foreign country, he becomes amenable to the laws of that country, and is triable by its courts. . . ." *See also In re Friess and Ronnenberger,* [1947] AD Case no. 80 (decision after World War II by the French Court of Cassation applying French criminal law to acts of two civilians of German nationality who had resided in France during the occupation).

scriptions that conform with Article 43 are expected to be honored by the ousted government, then the occupant's incentive to comply with Article 43 is strengthened, and this in turn will benefit the occupied population. Conflicting prescriptions by exiled governments (or foreseeable conflicting legislation after liberation) may thus have a substantial adverse impact on civil life during the occupation. Therefore international law recognizes the duty of ousted governments to refrain from issuing prescriptions that would conflict with the occupant's lawful measures,[56] although, of course, such measures are not immune to prospective modifications by the returning government.[57] This standpoint withstood the two world wars, despite the contrasting state practice that accumulated during that period.[58]

Actual practice varies from the proposition endorsed by most scholars. The ample evidence of the conduct of exiled governments and returning governments during and immediately after the two world wars shows that by and large those institutions did not conceive themselves as bound by the international legality test,[59] nor did they always find it expedient to respect the lawful measures of the occupation authorities. Most of the exiled governments issued decrees that conflicted with the policies implemented by the occupants;[60] most of the returning governments sought to

[56] 2 L. Oppenheim, *International Law* 342 (2d ed. 1912), and 3 A. Mérignhac, *Traité de droit public international* 410 (1912), were the first to assert this principle.

[57] Some post–World War II governments held the view that the termination of the occupation implies the automatic lapse of all the occupant's enactments. *See* the views of the French government (with respect to the German but not the Vichy orders) in Delaume, *Enemy Legislation and Judgments in France*, 30 JCLIL 32, 33 (1948); of the Norwegian government in Stabel, *Enemy Legislation and Judgments in Norway*, 31 JCLIL 3, 4 (1949); of the British government with regard to the island of Jersey in Aubin, *Enemy Legislation and Judgments in Jersey*, 31 JCLIL 8, 9. This opinion is not supported by the behavior of other returning governments or by the jurisprudence cited *infra*, which supports the argument that the abrogation of valid occupation laws must be formally expressed.

[58] L. Oppenheim, *International Law* 618 (7th ed., by H. Lauterpacht, 1948); Stone, *supra* note 9, at 721 n.176; Schwarzenberger, *supra* note 49, at 346–47; Greenspan, *supra* note 18, at 213 n.16; Hyde, *supra* note 47, at 1885; J. Spaight, *War Rights on Land* 366–67 (1911); Morgenstern, *supra* note 8, at 299; Feilchenfeld, *supra* note 26, at 147; Debbasch, *supra* note 15, at 176. This overwhelming accumulation of authorities, all concurring in principle, has set aside two other doctrinal propositions. The one, advocated by Belgian authorities and scholars and hence called the Belgian school, denied any legal validity to occupation orders, and conceded to the ousted sovereign absolute power to legislate even retroactively. Thus, when the occupation ends, the occupation orders expire by themselves. 1 A. Rolin, *Le droit moderne de la guerre* 438 (1920). For more on this school, *see infra* Chapter 7, text accompanying notes 13–21. The opposite view required the returning sovereign to refrain from retroactive annulment of even illegal orders. A. Pillet, *Les lois actuelles de la guerre* 255–56 (2d ed. 1901).

[59] The first pronouncement of this test was made by Feilchenfeld, *supra* note 26, at 146. Its most conspicuous advocate was Morgenstern, *supra* note 8, at 291.

[60] Many exiled governments warned their occupied constituencies in advance that only their own prescriptions would be effective upon their return. The king of Belgium made an

undo the outcomes of those policies, whether immediately or gradually.[61] It is difficult to trace any implicit recognition of an international duty to respect lawful occupation measures. Enactments of governments in exile were aimed at disrupting occupation policies regardless of possible hardships caused to the population; enactments of returning governments were intended to reestablish control over resources, to return swiftly to normal life, and to correct injustices. The endorsement of indigenous expectations based on occupation measures was not deemed a consideration commensurate to those goals.[62] The measures of the returning government were

announcement to that effect on April 8, 1917 (*see infra* Chapter 3, text accompanying note 66). During World War II, the Inter-Allied Declaration of January 5, 1943, regarding the validity of acts of dispossession committed in Axis-occupied areas, failed to mention that the occupant had legal authority to modify the law. In that declaration the parties "reserve all their rights to declare invalid any transfers of, or dealings with property, rights and interests of any description. . . ." U.S. Dep't of State Bull., January 9, 1943, at 21. This warning "applie[d] whether such transfers or dealings ha[d] taken the form of open looting or plunder, or transactions apparently legal in form, even when they purport[ed] to be voluntarily effected." *Id.* Some exiled governments also took unilateral initiatives in this respect. On January 10, 1941, the Belgian government provided that all the occupant's measures, those already taken as well as prospective ones, "sont nuls et non avenus." La bulletin législatif Belge, Arrêtés de Londres 18. *See also* the official interpretation of that decree-law by the Belgian cabinet, *id.*: "[Cet Arrêté-loi] proclame la nullité radicale de toutes mesures que prendraient les autorités allemandes d'occupation en Belgique, qu'elles touchent au droit public, a l'organisation administrative, a l'ordre social ou aux droit privés et aux interets des citoyens." (This decree-law proclaims the absolute nullity of all measures issued by the German authorities in Belgium, whether they affect public law, the organization of the administration, the social system, or private rights and citizens' interests.)

[61] The exiled Belgian government proclaimed on May 5, 1944, that most of the measures that had been taken by the Belgian secretaries general who acted within the occupied area were to be considered null and void. La bulletin legislatif Belge, Arrêtés de Londres 157–60. The Dutch government prescribed from London on September 17, 1944, an elaborate order distinguished among various occupation orders, according to principles that seemed to have no correlation with either Article 43 or international law in general. 9 J. Verzijl, *International Law in Historical Perspective* 229 (1978). Other decrees, providing for retroactive annulment of occupation enactments on a general basis, were promulgated by the provisional government of France headed by de Gaulle. Delaume, *supra* note 57, at 33–34. Certain important legislative measures of the Vichy government were explicitly validated. Constitutional acts in Greece after the occupation gave the Greek legislature authority to declare occupation orders void *ab initio*, and the latter made quite an extensive use of this power. Zepos, *Enemy Legislation and Judgments in Liberated Greece*, 30 JCLIL 27, 30–31 (1948). The Norwegian reaction was milder: the relevant law of transition abrogated parts of the occupant's legislation only prospectively, *see* Stabell, *supra* note 57, at 4; the validity of the occupant's laws during the occupation was a matter left to the courts, who were also granted jurisdiction to reopen and revise any court decision that had been rendered during the occupation pursuant to an unlawful enactment, *id.* at 5–6.

[62] *Cf.* McDougal and Feliciano, *supra* note 13, at 744, stating that "the balance between maintaining stability in expectations by honoring acts of the occupant, and permitting the restored territorial sovereign to protect its legitimate exclusive interests which were substantially affected by such acts, tends in many contexts to shift toward the latter."

generally upheld by the local courts, which refrained from scrutinizing their national institutions for conformity with Article 43.[63]

The discrepancy between the demand for sovereigns' respect for the law of occupation, a demand to which the bulk of authorities subscribe, and the actual practice of national institutions may be partly explained by the peculiar circumstances of World War II. But the Belgian government reacted in much the same way during World War I, when the Germans did claim to rule in accordance with the Hague Regulations. The crux of the problem lies in the fact that ousted governments often tend to prefer the protection of their bases of power over the expectations of the population. On the basis of this experience, it would be safe to anticipate similar conduct by other returning sovereigns, motivated by similar goals.

When national courts in liberated territories were asked to determine the validity of a former occupant's prescriptions (lacking clear instruction from the returning government), they did use Article 43 as the test for legality. It seems, however, that this test was so popular largely because of its convenient ambiguity, which provided opportunities to implement policies that served the postoccupation societies. In fact, these decisions stood more for such policies as ensuring market stability in the postoccupation period and preventing unjust enrichment due to the occupation than for the delimitation of the occupant's powers. The courts used this test to solve immediate problems, rather than to redefine the legitimate powers of future occupants. Thus these postoccupation decisions contribute more to the understanding of this transitory period than to the study of the lawfulness of occupation measures: these courts at that period were simply indifferent to the question of international lawfulness.

---

[63] Lawmaking by exiled governments during the occupation period has been recognized after that period as having been immediately applicable within the occupied area in all reported jurisdictions except for Greece. This was the case in Belgium, *see infra* Chapter 7 on post–World War I cases; *see In re Hoogeveen*, [1943–1945] AD Case no. 148 (Court of Cassation, November 6, 1944) for a post–World War II decision, the Netherlands, *Rotterdam Bank Ltd. (Robaver) v. Nederlandsch Beheers-instituut*, [1949] AD Case no. 154 (Supreme Court, January 13, 1950); *Damhof v. State of the Netherlands*, [1949] AD Case no. 155 (Court of Appeal of The Hague, March 3, 1949), Norway, *Public Prosecutor v. Reidar Haaland*, [1943–1945] AD Case no. 154 (Supreme Court, August 9, 1945) (legislation regarding treason); *Public Prosecutor v. Lian*, [1943–1945] AD Case no. 155 (Supreme Court, November 14, 1945), Italy, *Ferrovie dello Stato v. S.A.G.A.*, [1946] AD Case no. 147 (Court of First Instance, Venice, June 21, 1946), and Malaya, *Dominic v. Public Prosecutor*, [1948] AD Case no. 179 (Malayan Union, Court of Criminal Appeal, March 24, 1947). The different jurisprudence of the Greek courts, *Occupation of Cavalla Case*, [1929–1930] AD Case no. 292 (Court of Thrace, 1930); *In re X.Y.*, [1943–1945] AD Case no. 147 (Conseil d'État, 1945), is probably because during the World War II occupation, two distinct bodies, one sitting in London and the other in Cairo, claimed to be the Greek government in exile. The retroactive validation of all enactments of the legal Greek government in exile was finally prescribed in a Constitutional Act of February 8, 1946. Zepos, *supra* note 61, at 31.

The most evident policy of these courts has been the validation of transactions, provided that no unfair advantage could be taken of such validation. Thus, for example, the issuance of new currency by the occupant was generally held to be valid.[64] But when inhabitants tried to take advantage of the steep devaluation of the occupation currency by repaying debts in these valueless notes, the courts intervened on behalf of the payees; by using the international legality test, they held that the introduction of new currency was unlawful and thus void.[65] The consequence of these two applications of the test was, of course, conflicting decisions in different jurisdictions. The policy of validation is evident in two Greek decisions upholding contracts drawn under Bulgarian law during the Bulgarian annexation of parts of Greece.[66] The same policy of validation, with the exception of unfair advantage, was also implemented in questions of status, when courts in various jurisdictions upheld marriage ceremonies conducted under occupation law.[67] The trend to validate commercial and personal transactions

[64] Two such cases were decided by the Philippines Supreme Court. *Haw Pia v. China Banking Corp.* [1951] AD Case no. 203, at 657; *Gibbs et al. v. Rodriguez et al.*, [1951] AD Case no. 204.

[65] This was the position of the Burmese courts in *Taik v. Ariff Moosajee Dooply*, [1948] AD Case no. 191 (High Court), *aff'd*, *Dooply v. Chan Taik*, [1951] AD Case no. 202, and of the Supreme Court of Hong Kong in *Tse Chung v. Lee Yau Chu*, [1951] AD Case no. 200. The district court of Luxembourg reached a similar result in *G. v. B.*, [1951] AD Case no. 198 (emphasizing the unreal exchange rate between occupation and local currency). *Cf. Ko Maung Tin v. U Gon Man*, [1947] AD Case no. 104 (decision of the High Court of Burma declaring occupation currency illegal regardless of specific considerations of unfair advantage).

[66] The requirement under Greek law that a contract for the sale of immovable property be drawn by a Greek notary (not required under the Bulgarian law) was held to be immaterial in those circumstances, and the contracts were declared valid. *L. v. N.*, [1947] AD Case no. 110 (Bulgarian occupation of Greece); *Thrace (Notarial Services) Case*, [1949] AD Case no. 167. Similarly, a will made according to Bulgarian law was held to be valid. *In re P. (Komotini Case)*, [1948] AD Case no. 187.

[67] *See* the following Belgian decisions, regarding marriage in the annexed parts of Belgium. In *Krott v. Merkens*, [1947] 3 Pasicrisie Belge 10 (Tribunal Civil de Verviers, December 9, 1946), *digested in* [1946] AD Case no. 148), despite the illegal annexation and introduction of German laws, a marriage between a Belgian woman and a German man was held valid. The court seemed concerned by the ramifications of a decision to the contrary. It reasoned that the Belgian Decree-Law of 1941 (promulgated by the exiled king) did not intend to render all marriages in these areas during 1940–1944 null and void, and emphasized the fact that such a ceremony was voluntary. As the legal tool for reaching the result, it used the conflicts rule of *locus regit actum*, the law being the German one, that of the temporary de facto sovereign. The same result was reached in *Bourseaux c. Kranz*, [1948] AD Case no. 171 (Court of Appeal of Liège, June 24, 1948). The Belgian law of May 5, 1944, annulling acts "based on the modification of Belgian territory by the enemy" had formally annulled the marriage. Nevertheless, the court held that the couple, in their internal relationship, were precluded from invoking this argument, since the Belgian Civil Code prevented spouses from invoking minor procedural defects for the purpose of relieving themselves of duties related to their status. In the liberated Netherlands East Indies (Indonesia), the court upheld a divorce

was also apparent in cases where the claimant relied not on the occupation laws but on the nonavailability of preoccupation institutions.[68] The policy of validation, as well as judicial expedience, were the considerations that led to the upholding of court decisions from the occupation period, including the decisions of courts that had been set up by the occupant.[69]

In conclusion, the inconsistent application of Article 43 by ousted governments during and after occupation cannot be said to have contributed to the stability of the expectations of the population under occupation. The tendency of local courts after liberation[70] has been to uphold expectations, but only when they would not be required to apply the government's specific laws. The message to the occupant is that Article 43 will not be the sole factor in determining future respect for its laws: the ousted government might not respect lawful acts, and the courts might uphold even illegal acts in the name of stability.

The Concept of Occupation According to Article 43: Past and Present

Early Attitudes

From the exploration of Article 43 and its intellectual environment emerges a picture of the concept of occupations that prevailed at the turn of the century. This concept has been completely changed since.

---

decree despite the fact that the decree was illegally pronounced in the name of the Japanese commander-in-chief. *Mr. P. (Batavia) v. Mrs. S. (Bandoeng)*, [1947] AD Case no. 118 (Netherlands East Indies, 1947).

[68] Thus a testament that lacked one of the formal requirements under the local law (an approval by a notary) was enforced, since under occupation it was impossible to fulfil the formalities. *In re Will of Josef K.*, [1951] ILR 966 (Poland, Supreme Court, 1949). A marriage ceremony performed clandestinely according to local tribal rites was held valid, *Lee v. Lau*, [1964] 2 All E.R. 248, where the validity of marriage celebrated in Hong Kong during the Japanese occupation was examined under the local customary forms, because the civil form was inapplicable during the occupation. Contracts for the transfer of immovable property between Polish nationals during the German occupation were held valid even though they had not been approved by a notarial act (required under Polish law but impossible under occupation). *B. v. T.*, [1957] I.L.R. 962 (Poland Supreme Court, 1949).

[69] See *Mr. P. (Batavia) v. Mrs. S. (Bandoeng)*, *supra* note 67 (the court upheld changes in the judicial organization of the country, which the Editor's Note refers to as "the overthrow of the entire judicial system of Indonesia"); *The King v. Maung Hmin*, [1946] AD Case no. 139 (Burma, High Court, 1946); *Krishna Chettiar v. Subbiya Chettiar*, [1948] AD Case no. 178, at 539–40 (Burma, High Court, 1947); *Woo Chan Shi ad Pak Chuen Woo v. Brown*, [1946] A.D Case no. 156 (Hong Kong Supreme Court, 1946); *Cheang Sunny v. Ramanathan Chettiar and Others*, [1948] AD Case no. 194 (Singapore Supreme Court, 1948); *Endricci v. Eisenmayer*, [1946] AD Case no. 152 (Italy, Court of Appeal of Trent, 1946); *Procurator v. X (Incest Case)*, [1946] AD Case no. 154 (Holland, District Court Almelo, December 1944).

[70] On the practice of these courts during occupation, *see infra* Chapter 7.

The delegates to both Hague Peace Conferences conceived occupation as a transient situation, for the short period between hostilities and the imminent peace treaty, which would translate wartime victories into territorial concessions by the defeated party. The 1870–1871 Franco-Prussian War probably provided a prototype of the envisaged occupation: military victories led to the occupation of French territory, part of which was conceded to the Prussians in the subsequent peace treaty of 1871. This conception was part of a more general theory of war in the nineteenth century, in which war was seen as a legitimate means to achieve national goals. War, in the context of the then-prevailing political theory of social Darwinism, was the means by which the fitter party defeated the weaker, and therefore less worthy, party.[71] War was seen as a match between governments and their armies; civilians were no more than the cheering fans of the fighting teams. Thus the civilians were left out of the war, and kept unharmed as much as possible, both physically and economically. This was the message of the Rousseau-Portales doctrine, which found a succinct expression in the famous statement of King William of Prussia on August 11, 1870: "I conduct war with the French soldiers, not with the French citizens." The limited scope of war implied limited exhaustion of resources. True, during the last decade of the nineteenth century the military budgets of the European Powers increased substantially.[72] Nevertheless, it was still thought that the victor could recoup its expenses from the vanquished party through the forthcoming peace treaty.[73]

This entrenched conception of war was combined with the political and economic philosophy of that period: laissez-faire was the prevailing economic and even moral theory, shared by all the powers. This theory implied minimal intervention of the government in economic life. There were minimal regulatory mechanisms of transactions and other uses of private rights, and the initial entitlements were the ultimate factor in social and economic activity, inspiring a deep reverence, especially by the state, for vested rights.

The minimalist conception of war and the war effort made possible a conception of a laissez-faire type of government even in wartime. The assumption was that the separation of governments from civilians, of public from private interests, would also hold true in times of war. There was not supposed to be any unmanageable conflict between the French citizens and the Prussian king. It was this conception that made the solution of Article

[71] See Mossner, *The Hague Peace Conferences of 1899 and 1907*, in 3 EPIL 204, 205 (1982).

[72] Mossner cites this phenomenon as the background for the convening of the two Hague conferences. *Id.* at 205.

[73] On the payment of reparations secured in a peace treaty, *see, e.g.*, Oppenheim, *supra* note 58, at 592–95. Characteristically, an all-new Article 3 of the 1907 (IV) Hague Convention provided that states may be liable to indemnify the other side under certain circumstances.

43 seemingly possible: the peaceful cohabitation of the local population with the enemy's army, with the minimal necessary interaction between them, and with the continuous immunization of the former's private interests from intervention by the latter.[74] The almost complete separation between governmental and private activity could produce an arrangement that satisfied both stronger states and those weaker ones whose citizens were likely to experience temporary foreign rule. The separation of interests provided room for a simple balancing principle of disengagement: the occupant had no interest in the laws of the area under its control except for the security of its troops and the maintenance of order; the ousted sovereign was ready to concede this much in order to ensure maintenance of its bases of power in the territory against competing internal forces and in order to guarantee the humane treatment of its citizens. This solution was not only well founded in theory; it was supported by the practice of the nineteenth-century occupations. These occupations were of relatively short duration, during which occupants, by and large, retained existing legislation as much as possible.[75]

It has been repeatedly pointed out that the administration of the occupied territory is required to protect two sets of interests: first, to preserve the sovereign rights of the ousted government, and second, to protect the local population from exploitation of both their persons and their property by the occupant.[76] A more detailed analysis of the relationship between the interests of the ousted government and those of the local population reveals that in a possible case of conflict, the occupant was supposed to prefer the interests of the government. Thus, it also had the duty to protect local institutions against indigenous forces that might call for structural changes in the internal body politic.[77] The occupant was expected to fulfil a positive role by filling the vacuum created by the ousting of the local government, and by maintaining its bases of power until the conditions for the latter's return were mutually agreed upon. The local population was similarly under a duty to abide by the occupant's exercise of authority.[78] This point

[74] A vestige of this approach is the separate treatment of the occupant's power to collect taxes (Article 48 of the Hague Regulations) and the immunity of private property from confiscation (Article 46).

[75] Graber, *supra* note 3, at 268–70. The author mentions the pledge made by the Prussians during their occupation of France to reestablish the prewar order and not to modify existing legislation unless military necessity required otherwise. The author also cites both German and French textbooks that affirm that the Prussians abided by their pledge. *Id.* at n.37.

[76] *See, e.g.*, Jennings, *Government in Commission*, 23 BYIL 112, 135 (1946).

[77] This point is emphasized in A. Gerson, *Israel, the West Bank and International Law* 9–10 (1977): "fundamental institutional reform [by the occupant] might be used to stir indigenous rebellion against the ousted sovereign."

[78] Similarly the occupant was granted the power to possess and administer property belonging to the occupied state, subject to the duty to "safeguard the capital of these properties,

was extremely important to the elites of the more powerful participants in the Hague Conferences, such as Austro-Hungary, Russia, the Ottoman Empire and the colonial powers. Indeed, the predominant aspect of this concern is underlined by the one exception to the duty to establish a regime of occupation: the situation of *debellatio*. The doctrine of debellatio asserts that if the enemy state has totally disintegrated and no other power is continuing the struggle on behalf of the defeated sovereign, then occupation transfers sovereignty.[79] The exception of debellatio vividly illustrates the fact that the only relevant political interests (as opposed to economic and social interests) in the Article 43 regime were those of the state elites, not of its citizens. In this sense, Article 43 was a pact between state elites, promising reciprocal guarantees of political continuity, and thus, at least to a certain extent, rendering the decision to resort to arms less profound.

Contemporary Perspectives

Even by the time of the first Hague Conference of 1899, the principles underlying the law of occupation had already been on the decline. Toward the end of the nineteenth century the national governments of some European countries began to show more involvement in their countries' economic and social life. These were the first signs of what would be later termed the welfare state. The armies at the turn of the century had also expanded beyond mid–nineteenth-century proportions: their maintenance demanded vast human and material resources, and the civilian population was called upon to provide those resources. Thus, the distinction between soldier and citizen, between private activity and wartime effort, was gradually eroded.[80] These developments were intensified by World War I, which was the first "total war," by the rise of competing national ideologies concerning the proper functions of the national government in both internal and international affairs, and last, but not at all least, by the advent of the claim for self-determination of peoples and the complementary idea that sovereignty lies in the people and not in its government. Moreover, as

---

and administer them in accordance with the rules of usufruct." Article 55 of the Hague Regulation. As much as this article prevents the occupant from destroying or depleting national resources, it tries to keep other indigenous aspirants from making use of them.

[79] *See, e.g.*, Feilchenfeld, *supra* note 26, at 7 ("If one belligerent conquers the whole territory of an enemy, the war is over, the enemy state ceases to exist, rules on state succession concerning complete annexation apply, and there is no longer any room for the rules governing mere occupation. . . . [But] a phase of mere occupation persists as long as the allies of the conquered state continue to fight. . . ."); Stone, *supra* note 9, at 696 n.13; Schwarzenberger, *supra* note 49, at 167.

[80] *See* Feilchenfeld, *supra* note 26, at 17–21; Stone, *supra* note 9, at 727–32.

it became more difficult to reach accord on the transfer of sovereignty as a result of war, the periods of occupation became longer than before.

As a result of these factors, the balancing mechanism of Article 43 was put under tremendous strain. These factors did not erase the fundamental difference between occupant and sovereign, but the theoretical peaceful coexistence between the former and the local population could not be realistically expected any longer. More and more issues gradually became the objects of unbridgeable conflicts of interest, as the occupant sought to intervene in the affairs of the territory under its control, and at the same time its acts had the potential of causing profound effects in both the public and the private sectors. It was no longer possible to expect the occupant to perform the function of the impartial trustee of the ousted sovereign or the local population; it was no longer feasible to demand that the occupant pay no heed to its own country's interests. As soon as most societies recognized the necessity of some regulation of social and economic activities, policies and goals had to be decided upon and implemented by the central institutions. Thus the mandate to "restore and ensure public order and civil life" has become at best an incomplete instruction to the occupant. Even the simplest function of restoring public order, at a minimal level of intervention, became a profound policy decision, potentially resulting in stagnation of the local economy. Almost every occupation involved a conflict of interests between the occupant and the ousted sovereign, a conflict over policies and goals. Moreover, in some occupations the conflict of interests was further complicated by the appearance of a conflict between the ousted elite and the indigenous community: Article 43's bias in favor of the former was challenged by the emerging principles of self-determination and self-rule. As I will show in the following chapters, relying on the comparative study of occupations and emerging legal principles, these developments contributed to the decline of Article 43's commanding authority.[81]

In the scholarly debate that ensued concerning the legality of occupation measures from World War I until the present, Article 43 was invariably invoked by the advocates of occupants and occupied alike, by impartial tribunals and jurists, by institutions of the occupied entities, and by some—although not the majority—of the occupants. This scholarly debate has by and large sustained Article 43 to this day as the cornerstone of the law of occupation,[82] despite the challenges to the contents of Article 43,

---

[81] Feilchenfeld, in 1942, called the doctrine "a seeming legal paradise." *Supra* note 26, at 24. His concerns were not shared by many others. Only Stone, writing in 1954, reiterated Feilchenfeld's views, adding that the Fourth Geneva Convention had not provided the necessary reform. *Supra* note 9, at 727.

[82] Feilchenfeld and Stone represent a significant minority of scholars who admonished against the precariousness of the status of the Hague law. *Supra* note 81. A recent article expressed similar concerns: Goodman, *The Need for a Fundamental Change in the Law of Bel-*

despite many occupants' disregard of the law of occupation, and despite the introduction of Article 43's successor, Article 64 of the 1949 Fourth Geneva Convention.[83] All these developments contributed to the demise of Article 43, but surprisingly have not been fully acknowledged in legal literature.

---

ligerent Occupation, 37 Stan. L. Rev. 1573 (1985). McDougal and Feliciano, *supra* note 13, have also injected a more realistic view into the study of this issue.

[83] All of these developments will be discussed in later chapters. For the conduct of occupants, *see infra* Chapters 3–6; for Article 64 of the Fourth Geneva Convention, *see infra* Chapter 4; for the other emerging principles of self-determination and human rights, *see infra* Chapter 6.

3

Occupations during and after World War I: Early Challenges to the Traditional Law of Occupation

THE TWO major occupations related to World War I were the German occupation of Belgium from 1914 to 1918 and the Allied occupation of the German Rhineland area pursuant to the Armistice Agreement of November 11, 1918. The relationship between these two occupations is illuminating. When the Armistice Agreement was signed, the occupant and occupied changed their respective roles: part of the territory of the previous occupant became occupied by the former occupied states and their allies. Interestingly, the change transformed both sides' conception of the legal powers and duties of the occupant.

The German Occupation of Belgium, 1914–1918

For more than four years, from the end of August 1914 until the German surrender on November 11, 1918, Germany occupied most of Belgium and parts of France.[1] On August 26, 1914, The German Imperial Cabinet established what it called a "Government General" in most of the occupied area.[2] The constitutive norm of this Government General, an order called "Directions for the Conduct of the Government General in Belgium," pro-

---

[1] The most extensive descriptions of the German administration of Belgium appear in the following works: L. von Köhler, *The Administration of the Occupied Territories* (W. Dittmar trans. 1942, 1927). Professor von Köhler served as chief of the Commerce and Industry Department attached to the Government General in Belgium, and his presentation seems to correspond to the official German point of view. A Belgian point of view is expressed in J. Pirenne and M. Vauthier, *La législation et l'administration Allemandes en Belgique* (1925). A more intermediate approach appears in A. Solansky, *German Administration in Belgium* (1928).

The French version of the occupation orders and decrees of the German Government General (starting from the order of December 15, 1914) appears in volumes 4–9 of the fifth series of the Pasinomie (J. Servais ed. and annot. 1915–1918). This publication, which regularly reproduces the complete collection of Belgian laws on a yearly basis, carried during the occupation the occupant's orders and the Belgian Royal Decree-Laws side by side.

[2] The Etappen Gebiet (area in rear of combat zone), which included parts of Belgium very close to the fighting zone, was separated administratively from the area of the Government General, and was assigned to the military commanders of the German army in the region. *See* Solansky, *supra* note 1, at 18.

vided that "the Regulations respecting the Laws and Customs of War on Land, annexed to the Hague Convention of 1907, be taken into account."[3] Throughout the occupation period, the official German position recognized the duty to observe the law of occupation. According to statements of German officials,[4] many of them did in fact believe that their administration followed the Hague Regulations. According to one of them,

> Everyone who held a responsible position in the German administration in Belgium was thoroughly convinced that the German administration earnestly attempted to live up to the provisions of the Hague Regulations concerning Warfare on Land and to act in its spirit in cases not covered by it. Naturally, in view of the elasticity of the Regulations, opinions differed even among German officials as to whether this or that measure was within their limitations.[5]

According to the German interpretation of the position of the occupant under the Hague Regulations, the transfer of "authority," as mentioned in Article 43, from the sovereign to the occupant, amounted to the total elimination of any subsequent legislative competence of the sovereign. Thus legislation passed by the Belgian king would have no legal effect within the occupied territory.[6] The Belgian law of August 4, 1914, delegating legislative powers to local authorities in case of invasion,[7] which had been promulgated in the eventuality of the defeat or the exile of the Belgian king, was abrogated, and thus the German Government General claimed exclusive prescriptive powers within occupied Belgium.[8] The consolidation of administrative control was achieved by the replacement of the Bel-

[3] Translated in von Köhler, *supra* note 1, at 1.

[4] One such statement is attributed to Governor General von Bissing himself. Pirenne and Vauthier, *supra* note 1, at 56, cite von Bissing's opposition to the transfer of unemployed Belgian workers to Germany, an opposition, which he articulated during an internal debate over the issue in which he noted his duty to take into consideration the stipulations of the Hague Regulations, arguing that the forced transfer contradicted these regulations.

[5] *Id.* at 12.

[6] This standpoint was made clear in an order dated January 4, 1915, 5 Pasinomie 2 (1915): "Il est rappelé que dans les parties de la Belgique soumises au gouvernement allemand et depuis le jour de l'institution de ce gouvernement, seules les ordonnances du gouverneur général et des autorités qui lui sont subordonnées, ont force de loi. Les arrêtés pris depuis ce jour ou encore a prendre par le Roi des Belges et les ministres belges n'ont aucune force de loi dans le domaine du gouvernement allemand en Belgique." ("It is recalled that within the areas of Belgium under German administration and since the day of the establishment of that administration, only the orders of the Government General and of the authorities subject to it have the force of law. The decrees issued since that day and afterwards by the Belgian king and the Belgian ministers have no force of law in the area of the Government General of Belgium.")

[7] 4 Pasinomie 456 (1914).

[8] *See* 2 J. Garner, *International Law and the World Order* 63 (1920).

gian provincial governors and other heads of local authorities by German military governors.[9]

The German authorities extensively modified the Belgian law by abrogating or amending existing laws or by introducing new prescriptions to regulate new areas.[10] The legislation covered almost all branches of the law, including not only the political, penal, and administrative spheres but also the regulation of commercial, monetary, and other economic and social domains. In order to examine the tension between the mandate of Article 43 to restore and ensure public order and civil life, and the actual interests involved in the occupation of Belgium, I shall discuss the German involvement in the following spheres: the reorganization and regulation of the Belgian economy, welfare legislation, changes in the court system, and the restructuring of the Belgian body politic.

Reorganization and Regulation of the Belgian Economy

To grasp fully the importance of the occupant's measures in the economic sector, attention must be given to the Germans' crucial interests in Belgium. Belgium was a highly industrialized country, rich in coal deposits. Its resources and output were all the more crucial to the Germans during the war as a consequence of the economic blockade imposed by Britain. This blockade created severe shortages in Germany in important resources. The occupation of Belgium provided an opportunity to alleviate Germany's strained economy. Indeed, Belgium was considered by the occupant as a bounty to be utilized to support the German war effort.[11] Although one of Germany's official claims was that its acts were justifiable as improving the Belgian economy and benefiting the Belgian population,[12] its main goal in fact was to utilize the Belgian economy as far as possible for its own needs. In an attempt to justify this policy under the Hague Regulations, it claimed that such a goal was commensurate with the Hague Regulations' recognition of the occupant's military concerns:

> [T]he Hague Regulations expressly permit . . . also the economic utilization of the occupied territory, in so far as military necessities so demand. . . . [T]he ever-increasing economic utilization of [Belgium] for the benefit of the occupant . . . grew out of urgent necessity and the long duration of the war.[13]

[9] von Köhler, *supra* note 1, at 39–41.

[10] *See* Garner, *supra* note 8, at 64; von Köhler, *supra* note 1, at 60 ("The number of [statutory rules] . . . was, commensurate with the numerous fields of administration, very large indeed.").

[11] *See* J. Massart, *Belgians under the German Eagle* 297–98 (1916).

[12] *Id.* Massart reproduces a declaration of the governor general dated December 15, 1915, in which the latter asserts his duty to "assist the weak in Belgium, and to encourage them."

[13] von Köhler, *supra* note 1, at 10, 74–75.

The war, the occupation, and the British blockade[14] had severe ramifications for the Belgian economy, which relied on importation of food supplies and raw materials and exportation of coal and manufactured goods. Belgian industry came to a standstill. Factories were closed, and hundreds of thousands of workers became unemployed. The German practices of levying contributions and systematic requisitions, largely of foodstuffs, weakened the already exhausted Belgian economy. Confronted with severe economic problems of both German and Belgian economies, the occupant moved first to control immediate shortages, and then to exploit the economy of the occupied territory to meet the demands of the German war machine.

One policy was clear at the outset: the German economy would not assist the Belgian one. Belgium, like all other occupied countries, "must become self-sufficient, and all goods not needed in enemy countries were eventually to be shipped to the hard-pressed homeland."[15]

REGULATION OF FOOD SUPPLIES AND AGRICULTURE

Soon after the outbreak of the war, a severe food shortage set in both in Germany and in Belgium. The Belgians initially sought to handle the shortage problems on their own. On August 14, the Belgian king issued an ordinance establishing maximum retail prices for several food articles and empowering the provincial governors or mayors to requisition these goods at the fixed prices for distribution to the public.[16] On September 1, 1914, several Belgians took the initiative and organized a committee, the "Comité national de secours et d'alimentation," that coordinated food supplies and demands first in the Brussels area and soon afterwards across Belgium. The occupant had to cope with the food problem immediately upon establishing its rule.

The German regulation of supply and demand involved control over four aspects: prices, procurement, distribution, and consumption. The first aspect was soon treated by abrogating the abovementioned ordinance (on the last day of 1914) and conferring the power to impose maximal prices on the German military governors. In controlling the supply and distribution policies, the occupant had to share authority with indigenous and foreign entities. Since the Belgian economy could not supply its demands for certain foodstuffs from internal sources, and since Germany was not will-

[14] The blockade was extended to Belgium since there was no way to prevent imported goods or foodstuffs (or locally produced foodstuffs) from reaching the Germans. Special arrangements were agreed upon in order to permit certain imported foodstuffs to pass through the blockade. *See* Solansky, *supra* note 1, at 71–73; Garner, *supra* note 8, at 340–41.

[15] von Köhler, *supra* note 1, at 81–82.

[16] 4 Pasinomie 466 (1914).

ing to furnish these from its sources, an international relief system was organized in 1915 to meet the Belgian needs.[17]

Before the commencement of these relief imports (and with regard to domestically grown foodstuffs, even afterwards) the Germans exerted exclusive control in regulating both the procurement and the distribution of foodstuffs. For this purpose they established special agencies that supervised the activities each within its own area. Thus, for example, the Central Harvest Commission (under the direct control of the governor general) had exclusive control over stocks of bread grains, supervised their seizure, maintained their inventory, and determined the quantities to be released and distributed to the local consumers, as well as their price. Similar powers were given to bodies established to treat other crops, such as the Central Barley office, the Potato Supply Bureau, the Sugar Distribution Bureau, the Tobacco Utilization Bureau, and the Central Alcohol Office. The control of marketing fruit and vegetables was allotted to a private German company situated in Brussels.[18] Other crops were regulated merely by fixing prices and creating private monopolies by way of issuing transport permits, as in the distribution of meat and butter.

Limits were also imposed on consumption. Military orders rationed flour on a per capita per day basis; bakeries were forbidden to bake cakes except on Wednesdays and Saturdays; restaurants were forbidden to peel potatoes or to serve meat or fat on the declared meatless and fatless days.

REGULATION OF ENERGY RESOURCES AND OF INDUSTRIAL
PRODUCTION

In addition to the supplies of foodstuffs, the Germans established control over the coal and oil markets in Belgium. On April 26, 1915, the Central Coal Office was founded to take charge of the procurement and distribution of coal.[19] The price of coal was determined by the governor general. The Central Coal Office would remit the proceeds of the sale to the coal producers, minus the office's commission. The controlled price and orientation of the export shipments accommodated the German war effort.[20] In 1917, the same office was put in charge of internal allotment of coal to the various industries within Belgium, giving the occupant the ultimate control over Belgian production. On June 3, 1915, a Central Oil Office was

---

[17] *See* Pirenne and Vauthier, *supra* note 1, at 32–33; von Köhler, *supra* note 1, at 96–97.

[18] The sale of crops prior to their harvest was forbidden, a measure that facilitated the monopoly of the German company, and lowered the farmers' bargaining power.

[19] 5 Pasinomie 18 (1915).

[20] Pirenne and Vauthier, *supra* note 1, at 43, maintain that in 1917 about half of the coal produced was consumed by the German army, and considerable amounts were exported to Switzerland, Scandinavia, and the Netherlands. As Belgium has never produced enough coal for internal consumption, they say, the quantities distributed to the Belgian population were entirely inadequate.

established.[21] This office was initially concerned with procurement of oil lubricants, much needed for the German army. Soon its authority was extended to meet other demands, such as that for fats for industrial purposes. Pirenne and Vauthier claim that the activity of this monopolistic office brought millions of francs to the treasury of the Government General.[22] The third regulating office was the Main Office for Gas, Water and Electricity, to control the distribution and use of these essential commodities.

The German policy with regard to the Belgian production was succinctly outlined by Governor General von Bissing at the first session of the German Economic Committee for Belgium[23] on June 19, 1915:

> I have . . . two tasks of equal importance. As administrator of this country, I am responsible for its welfare and prosperity. I am of the opinion that a lemon squeezed dry has no value and that a dead cow no longer gives milk. Therefore it is so important and necessary that a country which is economically and in other respects of such importance to Germany, be kept alive. . . . But in relation thereto, I am simultaneously obligated to weigh the advantages and disadvantages for Germany. We want to avoid any harm to German industry through our restoration of the Belgian industry.[24]

With these goals in mind, the governor general could still couch his policies under the "elastic" formula of Article 43. With consolidated control over the industry, facilitated by the means previously described, as well as by intricate transport, movement, and export permit systems established by them, the Germans could shape the industrial output of the Belgian economy precisely to their needs. The policing of the Belgian industrial output was motivated by the needs of the German economy, with emphasis on the immediate needs of the army. The combined effect of these measures was to give the occupant exclusive and immediate control of every facet of public and private enterprise in Belgium.

MONETARY MEASURES

Banks

One of the first areas regulated by the Government General was control over the banks. An order dated September 4, 1914, provided that Belgian branches of non-Belgian banks, or Belgian banks controlled by residents of states at war with Germany, were not allowed to enter into any new trans-

---

[21] 5 Pasinomie 58 (1915).

[22] *Supra* note 1, at 44.

[23] This committee was an advisory body, composed of representatives of the General Government, the Imperial Chancellor, the War Committee of German Industry and German industries. It convened on a permanent basis to coordinate the activities of the occupation authorities with the German economy. *See* von Köhler, *supra* note 1, at 24.

[24] *Reproduced in* von Köhler, *supra* note 1, at 134.

actions except for the purpose of liquidating old transactions or discharging their obligations. All other Belgian banks were instructed not to transfer payments to Germany's enemies, and generally to coordinate their activities with the interests of the occupant. A commissioner general for banks, appointed by the governor general, ensured compliance with the ordinance, using the various measures granted to him by the ordinance.[25] It later became apparent that this arrangement was not sufficient, and therefore the occupation authorities imposed a regime of "compulsory administration" upon all Belgian banks, as well as on other businesses that were suspected of being under the influence of nationals or residents of enemy countries or whose operations could impinge on German interests.[26] Specially trained German administrators took over the management of these businesses.[27]

Legal Tender

The German reichsmark became legal tender in Belgium along with the Belgian franc. The exchange rate was determined by the Government General.[28] After the German administration discovered that the Belgian National Bank had shipped its cash, note plates, and stamps to London, it suspended that bank's authority and conferred it on another Belgian bank. Provisions were made to prevent notes issued in London from circulating within Belgium.

Moratoria

The Belgian king, expecting the German occupation, promulgated during August 1914 a series of measures that were intended to aid Belgian absentees and to eliminate recourse to courts during the occupation. The measures included a moratorium on several types of debts and suspension of the statute of limitations with respect to claims of persons who fled the country. The Germans soon undid these measures, annulling the moratorium in certain cases and establishing prescriptive periods regarding claims of local nonmerchant purchasers of goods. They did not, however, lift the moratorium with regard to creditors residing in enemy countries, or to debtors of German nationality or those who were nationals of neutral states.[29]

---

[25] von Köhler, *supra* note 1, at 174–75.

[26] Order dated February 17, 1915, 5 Pasinomie 10 (1915).

[27] *Id*. at 176–77.

[28] Orders dated October 3, 1914, *described in* Pirenne and Vauthier, *supra* note 1, at 145–46. On November 15 of the same year it was provided that payees in every private transaction would be obliged to accept marks if offered, at least at the rate of 1.25 francs to 1 mark (that is, the mark could be strengthened but not weakened). *See also* von Köhler, *supra* note 1, at 139–40.

[29] von Köhler, *supra* note 1, at 143–47.

TAXATION

On November 12, 1914, the governor general announced that pursuant to Article 48 of the Hague Regulations, the occupant would collect the existing taxes for the benefit of the Belgian population and that this source of revenue would be used to defray the administration's expenses. Customs duties on exports from Germany were to be collected according to the pre-war rates.[30] However, the occupation administration soon had to compensate for insufficient revenues by raising rates of existing taxes and introducing new ones. Among the new taxes, the first was the much criticized *decouple tax*, or "absence tax," proclaimed January 16, 1915.[31] It seems that this measure was intended more to induce wealthy refugees to return to their homes in Belgium than to raise revenues. According to this order, Belgians who had left the country since the outbreak of the war and had not returned within six weeks from the date of promulgation were to pay ten times the tax liability imposed on them in the fiscal year of 1914. Half of the revenues would go to the treasury of the Government General, and the other half to the Belgian local administrations, the *communes*. During 1916, new taxes were imposed on landowners (both on the property itself and on the revenues from it) and on revenues from patents. Corporation executives were subjected to additional income tax. On July 29, 1917, a general annual tax on movable property was introduced.[32] In addition, customs duties and other indirect levies were altered. Substantial additional revenues were raised through surcharges on certain commodities for private consumption, such as matches and sugar.

Taxation was only one type of economic burden imposed by the Government General. In addition, it levied contributions on the local population through the Belgian provinces or cities.[33] Another burden was the requisition of agricultural produce for German consumption and of supplies and machines for transportation to Germany.[34]

---

[30] *Id.* at 71. An order dated January 3, 1915, 5 *Pasinomie* 2 (1915), applied Belgian custom duties to the occupied part of France and thus created a single customs zone within the occupied territory.

[31] 5 Pasinomie 5 (1915).

[32] 8 Pasinomie 190 (1917). This tax had a progressive scale, ranging from 15 francs on property worth 20,000 to 35,000 francs to one quarter of a percent on property valued at more than 1.5 million francs.

[33] *See* Solansky, *supra* note 1, at 117–20. Article 49 of the Hague Regulations states: "If, in addition to the taxes . . . , the occupant levies other money contributions in the occupied territory, this shall be for the needs of the army or of the administration of the territory in question."

[34] *See* Solansky, *supra* note 1, at 110–17. Article 52 of the Hague Regulations allows for "[r]equisitions in kind and services . . . for the needs of the army of occupation [and] in proportion to the resources of the country."

Welfare Legislation

The Government General introduced important changes in Belgian labor laws. The Belgian legislature had begun just before the war to take the initiative in regulating the labor of women and children, as well as in advancing workers' compensation schemes. A Woman and Child Labor Law had been enacted by the Belgian legislature in May 1914. However, it was to enter into effect by a royal decree, which had not been issued prior to the occupation. The Germans introduced their own version of that law on December 15, 1914, a version influenced by a similar German law. Another order of a later period imposed maximum weekly hours on workers in certain industries.[35] It should be pointed out that the massive unemployment of the Belgian workers was an important reason for these measures. These orders had the effect of reducing, albeit only slightly, the supply of workers.

Another measure, which on the face of it could seem a far-reaching reform, concerned benefits for retired workers. The Sickness, Disability and Old Age Insurance order of March 14, 1918,[36] sounded very promising. In fact, it seems quite certain that this measure served only as a maneuver for public-relations purposes. Its ceremonial promulgation coincided precisely with the elections to the much-detested Council of Flanders,[37] and it was never put into effect.

The Government General also took important initiatives in the field of education. Starting on February 25, 1916,[38] it required obligatory attendance in elementary schools. This measure and others that followed also provided a process for determining the students' primary language in order to direct them to the proper schools.

Changes in the Court System

Throughout most of the occupation period, the Belgian judicial system continued to function as before the war. The occupant did not encroach upon the activity of the courts, and the courts by and large respected the occupant's authority.[39] Nevertheless, in matters involving German interests, the occupant established other tribunals of exclusive jurisdiction.

[35] 7 Pasinomie 3 (1916).

[36] 9 Pasinomie 17 (1918). It was based on a similar German law. *See* von Köhler, *supra* note 1, at 222–23; D. Graber, *The Development of the Law of Belligerent Occupation 1863–1914* 67 (1949).

[37] *See infra* text accompanying note 63.

[38] 7 Pasinomie 13 (1916).

[39] On the jurisprudence of the Belgian courts during the occupation, *see infra* Chapter 7, text accompanying notes 3–12.

Military courts were established in the large towns, according to a German Imperial Order dating from 1899.[40] These tribunals handled charges against both Belgian inhabitants and Germans (soldiers and civilians) for violations of the Penal Military Code of Germany of 1872.[41] These courts were granted exclusive jurisdiction with regard to any violations of the enactments issued by the occupation administration.[42]

On February 10, 1915, a new tribunal was created to adjudicate between landlords and tenants.[43] The German contention was that this measure was necessary to overcome expensive and slow proceedings in ordinary courts at a period when many tenants, because of the war, were prevented from using their premises.[44] The Belgian advocates, who, like other lawyers, were barred from representing clients in these tribunals, protested against their establishment.[45] But, as one of the lawyers conceded, the tribunals operated "satisfactorily."[46] During the occupation, the Belgian Court of Cassation refrained from declaring their illegality. Another set of tribunals was created to determine the amount of damages the *communes* owed the Germans because of acts of violence committed by the local population.[47] Later the jurisdiction of these tribunals was extended to handle disputes concerning the regulation of the distribution of barley, alcohol, and potatoes.[48] As to personal jurisdiction, Belgian courts were prohibited from conducting a trial or reaching decisions against members of the German army or officials of the occupation administration.[49]

Toward the end of the occupation period, a major rift between the Government General and the Belgian Court of Cassation resulted in the complete dissolution of the indigenous court system. After the court had voluntarily suspended its session until further notice, for reasons outlined

[40] *See* Laval, *German Law in the Occupied Territories of Belgium*, 1916 ILN 20.

[41] This code served also as the constitutive norm upon which the enactment of orders in security matters was based. *See id.* at 21.

[42] Garner, *supra* note 8, at 81. An order dated May 25, 1916, 7 Pasinomie 91 (1916), provided that in case violations of the occupation orders were also unlawful under the Belgian law, the German military courts would decide whether the complaint should be filed in the Belgian or the German military courts.

[43] 6 Pasinomie 9–10 (1915). The local justice of the peace presided over these tribunals, with the assistance of two assessors, a landlord and a tenant. The appeal was limited to awards of over a thousand francs.

[44] von Köhler, *supra* note 1, at 63. It should be added that another order simplified the procedure and lowered the cost of lease transactions.

[45] *See* Leurquin, *The German Occupation of Belgium and Article 43 of the Hague Regulation of the 18th October, 1907*, 1916 ILN 55.

[46] *Id.* at 56. The author was a Belgian advocate in the Court of Appeals in Brussels.

[47] Order of February 3, 1915, 6 Pasinomie 6–7 (1915). This order was found illegal by the Mixed Arbitral Tribunal in *Ville d'Anvers v. État Allemand*, 5 Rec. Dec. Trib. Arb. Mixtes 712 (1925).

[48] *See* Garner, *supra* note 8, at 83; von Köhler, *supra* note 1, at 63–65.

[49] Von Köhler, *supra* note 1, at 146.

below,[50] the Germans, invoking their power and duty under Article 43 to provide for public order, extended the jurisdiction of the military courts to cover violations of the Belgian Criminal Code, and established German courts to handle civil suits of Germans against Belgians.[51]

Restructuring the Belgian Body Politic

Belgium's strategic position had long been important for the European Powers. Viewed as a crucial component of the nineteenth-century European balance of powers, Belgium was declared in the treaty of 1831 among the European Powers to be "an independent and perpetually neutral State."[52] Belgium's population was not homogeneous. It was composed of two peoples, the Flemings and the Walloons, each with its own culture and language.[53] The two peoples occupied more or less distinct parts of the country. The German occupants, seeking a long-term change in the delicate European balance by acquiring influence in the region, tried to split Belgium into two distinct territorial units, Flanders and Wallonia. For that purpose, the occupant discriminated in favor of the Flemish population, invoking pan-Germanic claims emphasizing the Flemish links to the "Lower German race."

Prewar Belgium had had to confront tensions between the two communities, but these were channeled through the political process. No one challenged national unity, and the two major political parties in Belgium drew support from both communities. The conflict was focused mainly on the issue of language. Attempts of Flemings to secure equal status for their language achieved only modest results. For example, the language used in the national government's communications was French, even when it dealt with Flemings who could not speak that language. Intensive prewar public debate on the language issue had focused on the question of a Flemish university. The universities in Belgium used only French. Some Flemings advocated the transformation of one of the four state universities, the University of Ghent, into a Flemish-speaking institution. After many initiatives of Flemish deputies, in November 1912, the Belgian Chamber of Deputies adopted in principle a proposal to transform the University of

[50] *See infra* text accompanying note 64.

[51] On this issue, *see* Garner, *supra* note 8, at 89–92; Pirenne and Vauthier, *supra* note 1, at 110–18; von Köhler, *supra* note 1, at 66–70.

[52] On this issue, *see* Garner, *supra* note 8, at 186–87.

[53] For background on the relations between these two elements *see* Solansky, *supra* note 1, at 148–65.

Ghent gradually into a Flemish institution. Details, however, were not agreed upon, and no further action was taken until the war broke out.[54]

As an occupant, Germany invoked the Flemish sentiments, boasting that its acts were aimed at removing legal, economic, and cultural injustices suffered by the majority of Belgians.[55] As such, the Germans argued, their measures were compatible with the powers and duties of the belligerent occupant.[56] Their first concern was education. In early 1916, a series of decrees provided that the instruction in elementary schools in the Flemish part be in Flemish, and that in certain areas near the German border, the German language should be used.[57] Higher education was their next target. The goal was to transform the University of Ghent into a respectable Flemish institution.[58] For this purpose, considerable resources were allocated from the Belgian budget for investments in the infrastructure of the university. At the same time, it was provided that the language of instruction in the university be Flemish.[59] In 1916, its first year as a Flemish institution, the university drew about one hundred students. By 1918, about four hundred students were enrolled.[60]

In the sphere of public administration, the Germans also made use of the language issue. In an order of September 2, 1916,[61] the governor general instructed all public officials to communicate with residents in the Flemish provinces in Flemish instead of French.

The ultimate and bluntest phase in the policy of dividing the Belgian body-politic came in the spring of 1917, with the creation of separate administrations for Flanders and Wallonia, with Brussels as the capital of Flanders. The existing bureaucratic apparatus, including all the ministries, was to serve Flanders, while new ministries were established for Wallonia in Namur.[62] The occupation administration was also separated. The majority of the Flemings opposed the separation, but the supporters, some of whom were organized in a group of "Flemish Activists," were nurtured

[54] Garner, *supra* note 8, at 75.

[55] von Köhler, *supra* note 1, at 46.

[56] *Id.* at 50.

[57] Garner, *supra* note 8, at 72–73; von Köhler, *supra* note 1, at 232–34; Pirenne and Vauthier, *supra* note 1, at 87.

[58] On this issue, *see* Garner, *supra* note 8, at 74–75; Pirenne and Vauthier, *supra* note 1, at 88; von Köhler, *supra* note 1, at 235–40; Solansky, *supra* note 1, at 156–63.

[59] Order dated March 15, 1916, 7 Pasinomie 21 (1916). This was inconsistent with the Belgian Royal Decree-Law of December 9, 1849, which provided that the language of instruction in universities be French, unless authorized otherwise by the minister of education.

[60] After the war, the debate concerning the transformation of the University of Ghent into a Flemish-speaking institution resumed, and a law promulgated in 1923 approved the move. Solansky, *supra* note 1, at 160–62.

[61] 7 Pasinomie 21 (1916).

[62] Many Belgian civil servants who were required to move to Namur refused, and the occupant imported Germans to fill their places. von Köhler, *supra* note 1, at 52.

and encouraged by the Germans. These activists elected the Council of Flanders, a body that claimed to represent an autonomous Flanders and was officially given the title of advisory body to the Government General.[63]

In the winter of 1918, the Court of Appeals in Brussels, at the initiative of a group of Belgian senators and deputies, directed the state's attorney general to institute proceedings against the members of the Council of Flanders on charges of treason. The attorney general arrested some of the Flemish Activists. The German reaction was to deport some of the judges, and to relieve the rest from their posts. Thereupon the Court of Cassation denounced the German interference with the independence of the courts, and suspended its sessions until further notice. The rest of the courts soon followed with similar decisions, and as a result, the Germans replaced them with courts of their own creation, which operated until the end of the war.[64]

Reactions to the German Occupation Measures

During and after the war, the Belgian government and courts formed their idiosyncratic interpretation of Article 43 in their stern reaction to the occupant's enactments. This reaction contributed its share to the growing instability of the law of occupation.

Albert I, the king of Belgium, stationed with the Belgian army outside the occupied territory, continued to issue decrees, using emergency provisions that gave these decrees the status of Belgian law. Some of the King's decrees were aimed at the population under occupation. Not only Belgian nationals were expected to abide by these decrees. The king made no distinction between Belgians and other nationals, including Germans, who were present in the occupied territory.[65]

The decrees with respect to the occupied area were concerned, *inter alia*, with the imposition of criminal sanctions against certain actions viewed as being against Belgian interests, and with civil matters, such as the decree-law that provided for the indefinite extension of time limits for the purposes of the statute of limitations and civil procedure.

On April 8, 1917, the king pronounced explicitly his position regarding the force of his decrees relative to the occupant's orders:

[63] *See id.* at 48–53; Garner, *supra* note 8, at 78–80; Pirenne and Vauthier, *supra* note 1, at 93–105.

[64] On these courts, *see supra* text accompanying note 50.

[65] *Kauhelen Case*, [1919–1922] AD Case no. 323 (Court of Cassation, October 19, 1920) ("The Decree-Law of 8 April, 1917 [proscribing malicious denunciation to the enemy], applies to the person who gives the information whatever his nationality, even if he belongs to the army of occupation.").

1. Les mesures prises par l'occupant sont tenues pour abrogées de plain droit au fur et a mesure de la liberation du territoire.

2. Sauf disposition contraire, [toutes les décrets du roi] sont obligatoires dans toute l'entendue du Royaume. Les autoritées administratives et judicaires en poursuivront l'application au fur et a mesure de la liberation du territoire et sans nouvelle publication.[66]

This decree-law does not refer to the provisions of Article 43. It asserts the immediate applicability of the ousted sovereign's laws in the occupied territory, even during the occupation, and denies the legal effect of the occupant's prescriptions.[67] As may be imagined, this position put the Belgian courts operating inside the occupied territory in an awkward position. Upon resuming control in late 1918, the Belgian government undid all the German prescriptions retroactively, reiterating its assertion that all the occupant's decrees had, under international law, no effect whatsoever.[68] The Belgian courts in liberated Belgium accepted their government's position without demur.[69]

Not only Belgian officials and lawyers were adamantly opposed to the German measures. Anglo-American scholars of the period have also flatly rejected all the German claims. Although these scholars did not subscribe to the claim of the Belgian school, which totally denied the legality of all occupation measures,[70] nevertheless they invariably chose a minimalistic approach with respect to the occupant's legitimate prescriptive powers. Garner, one of the leading authorities on the legal aspects of this occupation, led quite a blunt attack on the German measures. For him, the very fact that the occupant was involved in trade, education, health, etc., seems a blatant violation of international law.[71] Garner, Oppenheim, and Hyde reiterate the outdated conception of the occupant's status: according to them the occupant was entitled to prescribe only in case of military neces-

---

[66] 8 Pasinomie 14 (1917). "1. The measures taken by the occupant are to be considered null and void by the operation of law upon the gradual liberation of any part of the territory. 2. Unless otherwise provided, [all the king's decrees] are obligatory throughout the kingdom. The administrative and judicial authorities shall enforce them upon the gradual liberation of the territory without further publication."

[67] The legal position expressed in that decree-law was supported by Belgian lawyers, who maintained that the Hague Regulations did not confer on the occupant any legal authority and the latter was therefore precluded from making any modifications in the local law. On this theory of "the Belgian school," *see infra* Chapter 7, text accompanying notes 13–21. This view was rejected as incompatible with Article 43 by the Mixed Arbitral Tribunal in *Herwyn v. Muller*, 2 Rec. Dec. Trib. Arb. Mixtes 368 (1923).

[68] On the theory behind this position, *see infra* Chapter 7, text accompanying note 14.

[69] *See infra* Chapter 7, text accompanying notes 13–21.

[70] This attitude was rejected by the Mixed Arbitral Tribunal in *Herwyn v. Muller, supra* note 67.

[71] Garner, *supra* note 8, at 88–89.

sity.[72] A similar conservative approach was offered by the Germano-Belge Mixed Arbitral Tribunal in the case of *Ville d'Anvers v. Germany*.[73] In short, instead of elaborating on the modern needs of the law of occupation in light of recent experience, most authorities treated the new fields of interest of the modern occupant as mere aberrations.[74]

The Law of Occupation in Light of the Occupation of Belgium

Only seven years after the 1907 Hague Peace Conference reconfirmed the nineteenth-century concepts of belligerent occupation, their underlying assumptions proved inadequate. The occupation in Belgium showed that the interests of the modern occupant covered many aspects of daily life, that these interests could often clash with those of the local community, and that occupant and occupied could be competing for the same scarce resources. It also showed that in such situations the occupant was not likely to adopt an impartial stance. During the four years of occupation in Belgium, Article 43 was invoked as justification for minor, though important, social reforms, but it also served to cover acts that were aimed at the dissolution of the Belgian nation and the impoverishment of its resources and industrial infrastructure. Article 43 also was relied upon for the purpose of interfering with private transactions (through changes in the debt moratorium law, changes in the statute of limitations, and the establishment of special rent control courts). According to the German claim, the occupant did have full authority to prescribe all those measures. The text of Article 43 was so worded that it could even bear an interpretation that justified the implementation of measures to serve German economic or military interests, to address and encourage the "indigenous sentiments" of one segment of the local population, and to counter the hostile reaction of the other segment.

While the German claim was undoubtedly exaggerated, the Belgian counterclaim, which denied the validity of all the occupation measures, was also extreme. In their total denial of any legal validity to any occupation order, the Belgian government and courts failed to employ the Hague Regulations as meaningful instructions for the authorities involved, both during and after the occupation.

[72] *Id.* at 87; 2 L. Oppenheim, *International Law* 237 (3d ed. 1921); 2 C. Hyde, *International Law* 367–68 (1922).

[73] *See supra* note 47.

[74] E. Feilchenfeld, *The International Economic Law of Belligerent Occupation* 22 n.2 (1942). "During and after the War of 1914–18, most authorities were in the habit of treating major deviations from established rules and practices merely as delinquencies and of ascribing their occurrence to a criminal spirit on the part of their national enemies. While there was undoubtedly a constant increase in international lawlessness, it was superficial to disregard the profound effect which fundamental changes in essential factors were bound to have." *Id.*

At that time, the Belgian experience may have seemed unique. It was thought that not every occupant would engage in such an extensive exploitation of the country under its control and that only rarely would an occupant attempt to achieve substantial long-term results during a limited presence in the occupied territory. This was probably the assumption of Garner and other international lawyers of that period who failed to perceive the need for updating the law of occupation. Today, however, in light of other instances of occupation, one is more likely to agree that the German occupation of Belgium was, on the whole, a representative rather than a unique experience. Not only have economic measures been the subject of extensive regulation by almost all modern occupants; crucial measures of a political nature also have frequently been implemented. Take, for example, one of the most criticized policies of the Germans, namely, the attempted separation between Flanders and Wallonia. Many other occupants subsequently tried, for whatever purposes, to divide existing states and separate peoples. Such was the attempt by France in the occupied Rhineland after that war;[75] after World War II, the British tried to separate Libya into two political units, Cyrenaica and Tripolitania;[76] in 1971, India stripped Pakistan of its eastern provinces, when its occupation forces created an independent Bangladesh.[77]

Two fundamental problems surfaced in this occupation. The modern occupant, it was found, can no longer be considered the impartial trustee of indigenous private interests, as the framers of the Hague Convention had envisioned. Rather, the occupant is more likely to be an interested party, with short- and long-term objectives, with effective power to implement those objectives, and with the opportunity to couch them within the language of Article 43. With vital interests at stake, the occupant would hardly be discouraged from making use of the effectively exclusive control over the occupied territory. Indeed, by invoking expansive interpretations of the law of occupation, some occupants would effectively assume full-fledged governmental powers in the area under their control.

This brings us to the other problem, that of the delineation of the occupant's powers under the Hague Regulations. The Germans had their own interpretation of the law; the Belgians and their allies read the text differently. Indeed, a narrow reading of the Hague Regulations, similar to the Belgian interpretation, was the one that reflected the actual intentions of the framers of those regulations. But while the German interpretation of Article 43 was too broad, the other reading was impossibly narrow, too severe in the restrictions it imposed on the modification of the local law. The occupation of Belgium was the first to prove that modern occupations cannot—and, indeed, ought not—be conducted under the overriding prin-

---

[75] See infra text accompanying notes 94–95.
[76] See infra Chapter 4.
[77] See infra Chapter 6.

ciple of stability, with minimal involvement of the occupying authorities. However, aside from the emphasis on stability, Article 43 provided little guidance as to the lawful intervention by the occupant and the modification of the status quo. The text of the Hague Regulations does not suggest internationally accepted goals for the occupation administration to pursue. Instead, one must find a way across vague concepts, which technically can support both narrow and wide propositions. Indeed, the law of occupation in the nineteenth century, which culminated in the Hague Regulations, did not envision the need for such guidelines, but in this century their want was painfully felt.

Only in the 1949 Fourth Geneva Convention would such goals be delineated. Until then, the room for idiosyncratic interpretations was great. Each side, occupant and occupied, could advance its own interpretation of the Hague Regulations, justifying its acts and accusing the other of infringement of the law.

The Armistice Occupation of the Rhineland

The Armistice Occupation was an occupation of an enemy territory as a result of a war, pending a peace treaty.[78] Although the actual occupation of the Rhineland was not achieved through invasion, but rather by agreement with the sovereign, the occupant was expected to comply with the law of occupation. According to that agreement, troops of Belgium, Britain, the United States, and France moved eastward on December 1, 1918, to occupy the German territory west of the river Rhine (including three bridgeheads on the right bank). The Armistice Occupation lasted until January 10, 1920, when it was replaced by the "peaceful occupation" pursuant to the peace treaty of Versailles.[79]

The Armistice Agreement, signed on November 11, 1918, did not provide for any derogations from the relevant Hague Regulations concerning

---

[78] Detailed accounts of the legal aspects of the Armistice Occupation appear in U.S. Army, *American Military Government of Occupied Germany 1918–1920* (1943); Imperial War Museum, *The Occupation of the Rhineland 1918–1929* (1944, facsimile ed. 1987); E. Fraenkel, *Military Occupation and the Rule of Law* (1944).

[79] The occupation under the Treaty of Versailles, which entered into force on January 10, 1920, had a specific arrangement, "The Rhineland Agreement," regarding the occupation regime. On that arrangement, *see* Fraenkel, *supra* note 78, at 71 *et seq*. This occupation was intended to be a guarantee for the execution of the peace treaty, that is, the German payments of reparations to the victors. Article 3(a) of the Rhineland Agreement provided that the occupation authorities "shall have the power to issue Ordinances so far as may be necessary for securing the maintenance, safety and requirements of the Allied and Associated forces. . . . [T]hey shall have the force of law and shall be recognized as such by all the Allies . . . and by the German civil authorities."

the law of occupation.[80] The supreme commander of this operation, Marshal Foch of France, acknowledged the applicability of the Hague Regulations. In a note of instruction to the Allied commanders-in-chief, he urged them to "adhere to the principles laid down with regard to cases of occupation by the Hague Convention."[81] This overriding principle was reiterated in Marshal Foch's proclamation addressed to the Rhineland population. The proclamation provided that "the rules and regulations in force at the time of the occupation will be guaranteed by us in so far as they do not prejudice our rights and our safety."[82]

Despite the initial acceptance of the applicability of the Hague law of occupation, both proponents and opponents of the Armistice Occupation ultimately tended to emphasize its consensual origins. For both sides, this shift was necessary to justify claims that were inconsistent with assertions with respect to German policies in occupied Belgium and France. The Allies, especially the French and Belgians, tended during the war to interpret the occupant's powers narrowly. However, once they became occupants, they asserted claims for wide discretionary powers. At the same time, the German views changed in the opposite direction: having part of their country under occupation, they reversed their broad reading of the occupant's power, although only with respect to the Rhineland occupation. Both sides sought to avoid the charge of being inconsistent with their former legal arguments, by attributing their new positions to the unique nature of this occupation, namely, its consensual basis.

Occupation Policies

From its inception, the occupation of the Rhineland was oriented first and foremost toward the future allocation of military powers and economic resources within postwar Europe. The following account will examine the

[80] The text of the treaty appears in C. Parry, ed., 224 *The Consolidated Treaty Series* 286 (1918–19). On the relationship between the Hague Regulations and armistice agreements in general, *see, e.g.*, Roberts, *What Is a Military Occupation?* 55 BYIL 249, 265–67 (1985), arguing that armistice occupation "is quite widely viewed as one form of belligerent occupation. . . . It is widely accepted that the Hague Regulations apply to armistice occupations. . . . The Hague Regulations remain important, at the very least, as a set of minimum standards." Feilchenfeld, *supra* note 74, at 110–11, maintains that the parties to the treaty may mutually agree to disregard the Hague Regulations. On this subject, *see also* G. von Glahn, *The Occupation of Enemy Territory* 28 (1957); Schwarzenberger, *The Law of Belligerent Occupation: Basic Issues*, 30 Nordisk Tidsskrift for International Ret 10, 18 (1960); Bothe, *Occupation after Armistice, in* 4 EPIL 63.

[81] Official English translation of the Note of November 15, 1918, *reproduced in* Imperial War Museum, *The Occupation of the Rhineland, supra* note 78, at 62.

[82] Proclamation of November 15, 1918, reproduced in *id.* at 66–67.

reflections of this concern in the occupants' policies and assess their compatibility with international law.

France and Belgium took possession of areas contiguous to their eastern borders. Belgium controlled the northernmost part, an area rich in coal and highly industrialized. France held the southern part, which was the largest and in which important factories were found.[83] Britain and the United States administered two other zones, which were situated between the Belgian and French zones. The different occupants had different stakes in the Rhineland. France conceived its zone as a buffer between Germany and its eastern border, the only meaningful protection from a renewed German offensive.[84] Sentiments of revenge were not missing in the Belgian and French administrations, in which demands were put forward to exploit the rich resources put at their disposal, and control the industries that competed with their own. Britain, meanwhile, was more worried about France and was interested mainly in restricting French power. The sole concern of the U.S. forces stationed there was to stabilize the area.[85] These different interests were reflected in the measures adopted by the various occupants in their respective zones.

All occupants, no matter what their interests were, had to regulate private activities. Soon after gaining control, they had to confront an impoverished economy, massive unemployment, and social unrest.[86] The measures aimed at raising the inhabitants' standard of living were coordinated by the Inter-Allied Rhineland Commission, a body that soon after its inception became the center of administrative activities. Issues of distribu-

---

[83] France considered its control over Alsace-Lorraine an exercise of sovereign rights, despite the fact that it had ceded this territory to Germany in 1871. France applied its laws, administration, and court system in Alsace-Lorraine fifteen months before the Treaty of Versailles retroactively recognized French sovereignty there. *See* Niboyet, *Question de droit international privé en Alsace-Lorraine durant l'armistice*, 16 Revue droit int'l privé et droit pénal int'l 78 (1920) [hereinafter Niboyet, *Alsace-Lorraine*]. On November 13, 1919, the French Court of Cassation, in a case regarding proceedings against a violation in Alsace-Lorraine of a French law concerning exchange rates, ruled that French law applied in that area. Its reasoning mixed the powers of the occupant under international law, and those of the annexationist. It referred to that area as having been "reunited" with France and placed under the authority of the French prime minister, who had jurisdiction to prescribe orders for the security of the army and the maintenance of public order. *In re Weber*, [1919–1922] AD Case no. 313. *See also In re Ziwi*, [1931–1932] AD Case no. 231 (Conseil d'État, November 4, 1932) (upholding a French decree annulling a German law in Alsace-Lorraine).

The internal political pressure to treat Alsace-Lorraine as having been immediately incorporated—"reunited"—into France was overpowering. In another similar type of occupation during this war, the Italian occupation of Triest, about to revert to Italian sovereignty, the practice of the Italian authorities was comparable. *See* Feilchenfeld, *supra* note 74, at 120–21.

[84] Mordacq, *L'evacuation anticipée de la Rhenanie*, 51 Revue des deux mondes 761, 768 (1929).

[85] *See* H. Allen, *The Rhineland Occupation* 216 (1923).

[86] Fraenkel, *supra* note 78, at 13.

tion of foodstuffs and raw materials within the four zones of occupation were, however, left to the discretion of each of the occupants.

TRADE

Trade among the countries of the occupying powers, the occupied zones, and Germany was one of the major issues in the economic power struggle. Soon after occupation, all the German statutes concerning trade with the enemy were annulled with respect to trade between the Rhineland and the Allied countries. The German cartels were rendered powerless with respect to the trade between local and Allied merchants. Customs control, although entrusted to German bureaucrats,[87] was also controlled by the Allies.[88] Export and import provisions were enacted by each occupant in its respective zone; all conflicting German laws were suspended. These provisions allowed the free flow of goods across the border to and from France and Belgium.[89]

Trade between the Rhineland and the rest of Germany was controlled by the Inter-Allied Economic Committee, headed by a French national. The Americans soon realized that that committee's policies "would . . . result . . . in the closing of factories, the throwing of men out of employment and unrest and consequent disturbance," and that "the tendency of th[is] Committee, in its early operation, was to throttle trade."[90] Implementing their own measures, the Americans managed to decrease unemployment and to alleviate the economic situation in their zone.

The French used the occupation, mainly through the prominent positions held by French officials in the central occupation institutions, to strengthen French industry, and to strengthen the economic relationship between the occupied area and France. The French Trading with the Enemy Act was suspended on January 15, 1919, with regard to trade with the Rhineland.[91] At the same time, the commercial contacts between the two banks of the Rhine were further restricted by the French military forces, which imposed a de facto blockade of the unoccupied part of Germany through their supervision of financial institutions and other com-

[87] The border between France and the occupied area was not controlled by German customs officials until November 15, 1919. *Id.* at 41.

[88] The Allies refused to recognize a German statute of July 1919 that required custom officials to collect custom duties on the gold standard instead of in paper money. *Id.* at 40.

[89] *See* Ireton, *The Rhineland Commission at Work*, 17 AJIL 460, 464 (1923).

[90] 3 U.S. Army, *American Military Government*, *supra* note 78, at 452.

[91] Even before that suspension, trading with the enemy was widespread, to the point where Niboyet suggested that the French statute had fallen into *desuetude*. Niboyet, *L'occupation du Palatinat durant l'armistice*, 16 Revue droit int'l. privé et de droit pénal int'l. 46 (1920) [hereinafter Niboyet, *Palatinat*].

mercial enterprises.[92] The *sections économiques*, the agencies entrusted by the French military administration with control over various aspects of economic policies, were put in charge of the licensing of German local businesses. These agencies accumulated detailed information about the German businesses, to the extent that the latter protested against what they thought was commercial espionage by French industrialists.

POLITICAL CHANGES

In addition to the economic initiatives, the French planned some political moves to implement their long-term political interests in the region. Alsace-Lorraine, which had been ceded to Germany after the 1870–1871 war, was treated from the outset of the French occupation, and well before the area was formally returned to France, as French territory, "reunited" with the rest of France.[93] In the Palatinate, a region close to the French eastern border, attempts were made to arouse local secessionist sentiments. The French authorities set up a Council of Notables, a body that was to represent the local population on economic and political issues before the administration.[94] A parallel—and unsuccessful—effort was made to effect a secession of the Palatinate from Germany, by supporting a local separatist movement, which attempted a coup d'état.[95]

THE COURT SYSTEM

The occupants left the jurisdiction of the local courts largely intact. They even retained the link between those courts and the appellate courts situated in the unoccupied part of Germany. Thus the Reichsgericht, the German Supreme Court sitting in Leipzig, had the opportunity to define German judicial policies with respect to the occupation measures. The occupants, in their turn, could prevent the implementation of these policies on the left bank of the Rhine by disallowing the execution of the former's judgment.

From the jurisdictional point of view, it should be noted that German courts adjudicated only cases involving German nationals in matters that did not involve the interests of the occupants. The subject matter jurisdic-

---

[92] Fraenkel, *supra* note 78, at 21.

[93] *See supra* note 83.

[94] Fraenkel, *supra* note 78, at 36.

[95] The failure of the coup can be attributed in large part to the reluctance of the U.S. army commanders to comply with French requests for assistance to the coup. *U.S. Army, supra* note 78, at 291–315. *See* especially the account of the events on the eve of the attempted coup. *Id.* at 300–302.

tion of the local courts did not include violations of occupation law or crimes committed against the personnel of the occupation forces. The criminal law applicable to these matters was the national law of the occupant in each zone.[96] These matters were submitted to tribunals set up by the occupants.[97] The controversy that arose regarding the jurisdiction of the local courts to adjudicate German nationals for aiding the secessionist movement in the Palatinate was a mirror image of the German-Belgian confrontation of 1918 over the arrest of the Flemish Activists: an order on January 29, 1919, deprived local courts of the jurisdiction to handle charges against such secessionist activists, and a recalcitrant judge, who prosecuted one of the participants in a French-sponsored coup, was arrested.[98]

Limitations *ratione personae* on the court's civil jurisdiction extended to the members of the occupation authorities and their families.[99] The local courts were not prevented from adjudicating civil disputes between locals and other nationals of the Allied powers, but in fact their authority was quite limited. The French, for example, who were the national group most involved in transactions with the local population enjoyed both the immunity granted to them by Article 15 of their national Civil Code, which had been interpreted in France as rendering exclusive jurisdiction to French courts to entertain suits against French nationals, and Article 14 of the same code, which extended to French courts the jurisdiction to adjudicate any claims of French nationals against foreigners.[100] Judgments rendered in Germany against French nationals would have in any case been subject to the French *exequatur*, which could become in fact a retrial. Although authorities are not clear on this issue, it seems that judgments rendered in French courts against locals were executed directly by the occupation authorities.[101]

[96] B. de Jaer *L'armée Belge d'occupation et son droit de jurisdiction* 78 (1928).

[97] *See id.* at 75–83.

[98] Fraenkel, *supra* note 78, at 45.

[99] Vanard, *La jurisdiction civile des tribunaux Allemands en territoire occupé*, 19 Revue de droit int'l. privé 205, 209 (1923–1924). The author was attached to the legal advisor's unit of the Inter-Allied High Commission.

[100] *See, e.g., id.* at 210–13.

[101] Niboyet, *Alsace-Lorraine, supra* note 83, at 57. The author does not mention the requirement under the local German law that any foreign judgment, in order to have effect, be subject to the grant of recognition or enforcement order by a German court. Apparently, the occupation authorities enforced the foreign judgment without involving the local German courts. According to Niboyet, Article 14 of the French Civil Code "laissait sous-entendre que la decision rendue sur ce point par un tribunal civil de France serait exécutée par les soins de l'autorité militaire dans les pays occupés." *Id.* It should be noted that according to the German law, a French judgment under Article 14 is not enforceable in Germany. Vanard, *supra* note 99, at 212.

The German Reaction

The German Reichsgericht, situated outside the occupied territory, and still having appellate jurisdiction over local Geman courts in the occupied region, was the most authoritative German institution to reflect on the legality of the occupation measures. It was in a position both to declare new German legislation automatically obligatory in the occupied area and to assert that various occupation enactments were illegal and thus null and void.[102]

The German Supreme Court's first decision on the subject was not critical of the occupation measure under consideration. The Court reiterated the German contention from the days of the occupation of Belgium, namely, that the occupant is the sole power entitled to legislate within the occupied territory during the occupation, and that the occupant's enactments may not be reviewed by local courts under Article 43 of the Hague Regulations.[103] Subsequent decisions, however, and the only ones to be communicated to the general public at that time, adopted the opposite view. In these cases the Court consistently held that German statutory legislation was immediately obligatory in the Rhineland,[104] and that the Court was entitled indirectly to pass judgment on the international legality of the occupation laws, in the course of deciding civil or criminal suits.[105]

---

[102] Theoretically, the German courts in the Rhineland could have also reviewed the legality of occupation measures and even declared the applicability of new German laws. In practice, however, local courts hesitated to do so. In the French zone, such a possibility was, in fact, prevented: the authorities, through a representative who attended court sessions, oversaw the decisionmaking process, and influenced its outcome. Fraenkel, *supra* note 78, at 45–46.

[103] The "Uhlmann case," of October 25, 1920, *reported in* V. Bruns, ed., 1 Fontes Juris Gentium [FJG] Case no. 205, at 575 (1931). The Court held: "Mit der Besetzung deutscher Gebiete durch die alliierten Mächte fiel lätzteren die Ausübung der Staatgewalt in diesen Gebieten zu. Die Ausübung der Staatsgewalt umfasste auch die Ausübung der gesezgebenden Gewalt, welche nur ein Bestandteil der Staatsgewalt bildet. . . . [D]ie Gerichte des besetzten Gebiets [sind] nicht in der Lage, zu prüfen und zu entsscheiden, ob die alliierten Mächte bei Ausübung der Staatsgewalt im besetzten Gebiet über die grenzen ihrer [völkerrechtlicher] Befugnisse hinausgegangen sind." ("With the occupation of German areas by the Allied powers, the administration of state power in those areas was lost to them. The administration of state power included also the authority to issue laws, being only part of state power. The judges in the occupied area are not in the position to examine and decide whether the Allied powers, in administering state authority in the occupied zone, acted beyond their competence as delineated by international law.") *Id.* at 577–78. The decision was not published in Germany until 1931. (*See* Fraenkel, *supra* note 78, at 210).

[104] *Rhineland (German Decrees) Case*, [1919–1922] AD Case no. 315 (September 29, 1921). The Court made no distinction between new and already existing local laws: all were obligatory unless objected to by the occupant. In a decision of March 7, 1922, 1 FJG Case no. 253, the court held as immediately applicable a pricing order from November 1919.

[105] Judgment of November 14, 1923, *cited in* Fraenkel, *supra* note 78, at 187–88. In this

In justifying its new position, the Court relied on the fact that "it was a contractual, not a war[time] occupation."[106] The only recognized restrictions on German sovereignty, maintained the Court, must therefore be based on the Armistice Agreement (which said nothing explicit in this respect). Thus, by using what it deemed to be different bases for review, the Court could treat, for example, the French introduction of its currency in Alsace as illegal and void,[107] and at the same time uphold similar wartime German measures in occupied Belgium[108] and Poland[109] as legally valid. The Court's double standard was all the more apparent when it upheld the validity under international law of the seizure and transfer to Germany of Belgian machines during the war, claiming that "a state may in case of necessity depart from the Hague Regulations."[110]

Despite its self-asserted competence to review occupation measures, the Court generally stopped short of reaching the consequences that its position could have led to. Maybe out of concern for the welfare of the population in the Rhineland, or because of the fact that anyhow such decisions would not have been enforced there, the Court subordinated legal principles to reality. In doing so, the Court relied on what it conceived as the acquiescence of the German authorities, their "tacit toleration" of the occupation measures.[111] In a series of decisions it solved the conflict between occupation law and German law by giving precedence to the former whenever it was actually enforced in the occupied territory.[112] The Court also exonerated a defaulting party to a contract, the performance of which was rendered illegal by the occupation authorities, despite its prior holding that none of the occupation enactments could qualify under the German law, the Bürgerlichen Gesetzbuch (BGB), as laws that could void conflicting contractual liabilities.[113] The local population was given the instruction to

case the Court declared that the introduction of French currency into then-occupied Alsace was illegal and void.

[106] *Rhineland Case, supra* note 104. *See also* Judgment of March 7, 1922, 1 FJG Case no. 253; Judgment of May 12, 1922, 1 FJG Case no. 262 ("content of the Armistice Agreement is alone decisive").

[107] *See* Judgment of November 14, 1923, *supra* note 105.

[108] Judgment of November 20, 1924, 1 FJG Case no. 335; Judgment of April 22, 1922, 1 FJG Case no. 259.

[109] Judgment of November 11, 1921, 1 FJG Case no. 245.

[110] Judgment of November 5, 1924, 1 FJG Case no. 332.

[111] Judgment of March 9, 1929, 1 FJG Case no. 407; Judgment of November 10, 1926, 1 FJG Case no. 375.

[112] *See, e.g.*, Judgment of November 10, 1926, 1 FJG Case no. 375 (abolition of the German foreign currency ordinance held effective); Judgment of June 7, 1921, 1 FJG Case no. 228; Judgment of May 10, 1921, 1 FJG Case no. 225 (trade with occupied territory not subject to German import and export laws).

[113] Judgment of May 2, 1923, 1 FJG Case no. 287. The occupation order involved was the

observe "those valid ordinances of the Reich authorities whose observance [was] possible,"[114] but were reassured that a "legal situation which the German authorities tacitly tolerate, even though forced to do so, may be adopted by the individual as his standard of conduct without acting *contra bonos mores*."[115]

To conclude, the challenge posed by the Reichsgericht's jurisdiction and legal doctrine was not a substantial one after all. The cases reviewed here show that the Court in fact acquiesced to the effective control of the occupant. Its recognition of its jurisdiction to review Allied occupation measures, and the circumscribed authority it was ready to concede to them under the Armistice Agreement, may have served internal political needs and as a faint admonition to the occupants to abide by their international obligations, but it was not translated into concrete directives to the Rhineland population to disobey the occupation authorities.

Occupants in subsequent cases suspended the local population's right of appeal to higher courts situated outside the occupied territory.[116] Such an appeal procedure was probably judged too risky for the occupant to tolerate. In weighing the justification for suspending the appeal procedure, one might consider this unique German experience. Did it serve the values that underlie the law of occupation? Clearly, the interplay between occupants and an appellate court outside the territory was an awkward experience for all parties involved. It is debatable whether the Reichsgericht's curtailed opportunity to discuss occupation measures had any positive effects on life under occupation. If it did have effects, they are not evident from those cases referred to above, cases that show a tendency to endorse occupation policies. On the other hand, the Reichsgericht's acquiescence could be explained by the soundness of the challenged occupation measures. It is possible that another position would have been taken against other, more offensive measures. The Court's position kept open an option for a stronger reaction against such measures.

The Law of Occupation in Light of the Armistice Occupation

The Armistice Occupation demonstrates the marked difference between interested and the impartial occupants. For those who wanted to take ad-

---

prohibition in the American zone on the sale of wine, which subjected the offenders to severe criminal penalties. The court did not consider this order "arbitrary."

[114] Judgment of February 22, 1922, 1 FJG Case no. 251.

[115] Judgment of November 10, 1926, *supra* note 111.

[116] This was done by the Allies during the 1945–1947 occupation of Venezia Giulia (Italy), *see* Section 2 of General Order no. 6, The Civil Courts for the Occupied Territories, of July 12, 1945, AMG Gazette, no. 1, at 32, by Britain during the occupation of Cyrenaica (Libya), *see infra* Chapter 4, text accompanying note 73, and by Israel with respect to the West Bank, *see infra* Chapter 5, text accompanying note 54.

vantage of their temporary control, the law of occupation was not a significant restraint. The French, for example, struggling to rebuild their country after the disastrous war, pursued economic and political objectives that were clearly incompatible with the Hague Regulations. Other occupants did respect the limited role granted to them by international law. The U.S. and British administrations did not capitalize on their temporary control: they were simply not interested in the economic exploitation of Germany. The different practices of the Rhineland occupants indicate that the occupant with the least territorial and economic demands and expectations will adhere more to the principles of the Hague Regulations, while the occupant who stands to gain more is liable to exploit the vague language of Article 43.

In the two major World War I occupations, occupation was seen as an opportunity to achieve long-lasting economic and political gains, to the disadvantage of the occupied population. This phenomenon would be present in many of the later occupations as well. The Armistice Occupation, as much as the German occupation of Belgium, demonstrates that modern occupants may be called upon to regulate a wide array of public and private interests. The prevailing understanding of the Hague Regulations in the postwar era, however, recognized only very limited powers of the occupant.[117] There was no effort to settle this discrepancy, for two related reasons: first, the Rhineland occupation was treated as being outside the scope of the Hague Regulations, because of its consensual origins,[118] and second, recognition of greater authority of the occupant would have cast a more favorable light on the German occupation of Belgium, and might have even reduced the reparations from Germany. As a result of this rejection of the applicability of the Hague Regulations, the international law of occupation on the eve of World War II was as conservative as in the nineteenth century, and as out of date as in 1914.

The Armistice Occupation was the first significant case in which an occupant invoked an authority that was not based on the law of occupation. In this case, the consensual origins of the occupation, namely, the Armistice Agreement, provided a specific source of legitimacy to the occupation. Invoking the 1918 agreement, the occupants justified their acts without recourse to the Hague Regulations, and thus deflected contentions about their alleged illegal behavior.[119] As we shall see in subsequent occupations, this tactic of making up exemptions from the duty to respect the law of occupation has been chosen by many occupants, and at times even endorsed by scholars. In World War II the argument in vogue would be

[117] *See supra* text accompanying notes 71–74.

[118] Feilchenfeld, *supra* note 74, at 22, points out that the Hague Regulations survived the Armistice Occupation because of the Allies' theory of the uniqueness of their status.

[119] For the French and Belgian use of the argument of contractual versus wartime occupation, *see, e.g.*, B. de Jaer, *L'armée Belge d'occupation, supra* note 96, at 14, 29–34.

the debellatio doctrine, according to which the complete dissolution of the occupied state confers sovereignty on the occupant.[120] Other occupants would take pains to demonstrate indigenous endorsement of their measures, at times even indigenous consent to formal annexation. As I shall later argue, these claims do not discharge occupants from their international obligations. These tactics do, however, call for clarification of the scope of the law of occupation.

[120] This argument was used by Italian scholars to justify the 1935 annexation of Ethiopia and by Anglo-American officials and scholars to explain the Allies' measures in occupied Axis territories. *See infra* Chapter 4.

4

The Second Phase: The Law of Occupation in the Wake of World War II

THE OCCUPATIONS during World War II signify a new phase in the law of occupation. The new phase is characterized not by occupants' adaptation of the 1907 Hague law to modern exigencies, but rather by most occupants' disregard of this law. Ultimately, this phase culminates with the introduction of the 1949 Geneva Convention Relative to the Protection of Civilian Persons in Time of War, which reformulated several aspects of the law of occupation in response to the experience of the recent war.

On the eve of World War II, the Hague Regulations were in critical need of adjustment to modern conditions, but at the same time, they were still the prevailing law, and their framework was generally accepted by occupants. In contrast, most of the occupants in World War II did not operate within the constraints of the Hague law. In most instances during this war, the framework for belligerent administration of occupied territories, as prescribed by the Hague Regulations, was not applied. The first part of this chapter outlines the practice of the Axis powers and of the Soviet Union prior to its invasion by Germany in 1941. This is a tale of total disrespect for the basic demands of the law of occupation. This account will be followed by the description of the measures taken by the Western Allies. They, too, in their more important occupations, of Italy, Germany, and Japan, claimed exceptions to the applicability of the Hague Regulations. In light of these assertions, the question became not only the interpretation of the Hague Regulations, but also the conditions for their applicability to certain types of foreign rule. Moreover, the poor record of adherence to this law compromised the status of the Hague Regulations as customary law. Indeed, there is sufficient ground to claim that in light of the recurring disregard of the law of occupation, the Hague Regulations had lost their legal authority by the end of the war.

After the war, a new body of law replaced the by then defunct Hague Regulations. The 1949 Fourth Geneva Convention prescribed a new set of guidelines for the modern occupant. The last part of this chapter describes this new law.

Occupations by the Axis Powers

The three Axis powers, Germany, Italy, and Japan, completely ignored the basic tenets of the law of occupation. Italy annexed Ethiopia and Albania, Japan set up puppet states throughout southeast Asia, and Germany did both, in addition to other illegal forms of foreign rule.

Japanese Occupations

Japan embarked on its East Asia campaign motivated by economic, security, and ideological considerations.[1] East and Southeast Asia were perceived as indispensable to Japan's economy, being both a solid source of raw materials and energy resources and large consumption markets. Japanese interests were deemed to be threatened by Western influence over China and control over the colonies and other territories in Southeast Asia. Japan had no intention of being the temporary administrator of the territories it would occupy. Rather, it strove to create a new order in East Asia—the so-called Greater East Asia Co-Prosperity Sphere—in which Japan would replace the West as the dominant actor. The clever slogan "Asia for the Asiatics" challenged the moral and legal claims of the Western colonialists, and implied—indeed, sought to justify—Japanese rejection of the applicability of the law of occupation to East Asia.

The precursor of the Japanese expansion into Asia was the occupation of Manchuria in 1931–1932. The chosen mode of governance was the innovative idea of a puppet state. The prototype for puppet states consisted of two elements: the constitution of a fictitious indigenous government, which was supervised by Japanese consultants, and the assurance of Japanese interests through a "bilateral agreement" in which the local entity conceded practically everything the former wanted. In the Japanese-created "State of Manchukuo," which asserted its independence in the territory of Manchuria in 1932, both elements existed.

Japan had learned from its 1910 annexation of Korea that annexation was not always the best method of foreign rule. The Korean annexation had confronted the homogeneous Japanese society with the problems of restraining the flow of Korean workers into mainland Japan and controlling their activities once they were present in Japan. In addition, the animosity of the Koreans toward Japan was attributed to the annexation. In the 1930s, Japan would seek to avoid—or, at any rate, lessen—such prob-

---

[1] A comprehensive overview of Japan's policies and practices in East Asia is found in J. Lebra, ed., *Japan's Greater East Asia Co-Prosperity Sphere in World War II* (1975).

lems by avoiding outright annexation. No longer would Japan annex newly occupied territories. Rather, it would create new vassal states. The creation of these new "entities" enabled the occupant to exploit indigenous nationalistic sentiments (especially in the colonies and other Western-dominated territories of Southeast Asia), to differentiate easily between native inhabitants and Japanese, and to seek international recognition of its acts.[2] Japan implemented its modified policy in the first phase of the establishment of the new order, that is, the occupation of Northeast China in the beginning of the 1930s.

The "state" of Manchukuo and other, similar creations of the Japanese Empire were never taken seriously by the international community. Manchukuo was denounced by the Lytton Commission, which referred to it as territory occupied by Japan,[3] and by the League of Nations, which endorsed the conclusions of the Lytton Commission's report and recommended that its members not recognize the new entity.[4] Moreover, the vast majority of states refused to recognize it as a state.[5] It goes without saying that this "state" was completely run by the Japanese, who also exploited its natural resources extensively.[6] To solidify the ties with Japan, the Japanese language was declared the official language of the country, and the Japanese Shinto religion (linked to the Japanese state) was imposed as the national religion of Manchukou.

The official assertion of the Greater East Asia Co-Prosperity Sphere preceded the military campaign in Southeast Asia in 1940–1942.[7] The prom-

---

[2] See K. Kawakami, *Manchukuo—Child of Conflict* 190–91 (1933), for a Japanese point of view of the conflict.

[3] See *Report of the Commission of Enquiry into the Sino-Japanese Dispute*, in *1932 League of Nations Publications*, VII Political, 1932.VII.12, 1, at 97 [hereinafter Lytton Commission Report].

[4] Resolution of the League of Nations Assembly of February 24, 1933 [hereinafter League of Nations Resolution].

[5] It was recognized by the Axis powers, El Salvador, Finland, Hungary, Poland, Romania and Spain. See R. Langer, *Seizure of Territory*, 123–25 (1957), Q. Wright, *The Existing Legal Situation as It Relates to the Conflict in the Far East* 58 (1939).

[6] See Lytton Commission Report, *supra* note 3; League of Nations Resolution, *supra* note 4. Kawakami, *supra* note 2, at 144–45, gives the Japanese view, according to which the laws of Manchukuo were drafted by Manchurian figures "assisted by Japanese jurists." A personal account of Henry Pu-Yi, the puppet head of Manchukou and the last emperor of China, which affirms the report of the Lytton Commission, appears in Ch'ing Hsuan-T'ung, *The Last Manchu* (1967).

[7] Before the beginning of World War II, in addition to its rule over "Manchukuo," Japan occupied Inner Mongolia, North China, and parts of central China (1937). These territories were organized as one "independent" entity, dubbed the "Reformed Government of Central China," whose capital was Nanking. On the Japanese methods of government in these territories *see* Q. Wright, *supra* note 5, at 38–40; C. Buss, *War and Diplomacy in Eastern Asia* 69–74, 105–7 (1941).

ise to "deliver Greater East Asia from the fetters of America and Britain"[8] bolstered Japan's military efforts in occupying and administering the colonies. The Japanese promised independence to the invaded territories, and for many, frustrated by Western domination, this seemed a momentous opportunity. At its peak, the Japanese sphere of influence covered almost all of Southeast Asia. On October 30, 1943, the "Greater East Asia Conference" opened in Tokyo, with the participation of delegates from the "free states" of China, Thailand, Manchukuo, Burma, and Free India (the last as observers).[9] Other puppet states were Malaya (including Singapore), and the "Second Republic of the Philippines." In 1945, after the Allies invaded France, Japan assumed control over the French colonial territories in Indochina by establishing indigenous governments in Cambodia, Luang Prabang (part of Laos), and Vietnam.

Although the Manchukou-style "independence" was nothing more than a change of foreign rulers, the Japanese promise raised nationalistic expectations in the occupied colonies. The promise of independence was enthusiastically accepted by many, even though this aspect was played down after the war. Several prominent leaders of these countries participated in the construction of the new entities. Some of these leaders continued to enjoy massive public support even after the return of the Western powers.[10] Other indications of indigenous support for this wave of nationalism were the participation of local forces in the defense against the reoccupying Allies, the conciliatory policies of the returning colonialists toward the locals who had sided with Japan and toward the legal changes initiated by the Japanese,[11] and ultimately the subsequent swift end of the colonial regimes in this part of the world.[12]

---

[8] From Japan's Prime Minister Tojo's speech before the Greater East Asia Conference of November 1943, *reproduced in* Lebra, *supra* note 1, at 92.

[9] *See* 2 A. Hartendorf, *The Japanese Occupation of the Philippines* 91 (1967).

[10] T. Agoncillo, *Filipino Nationalism 1872–1970* 308 (1974). On the Japanese occupation of the Philippines *see* the handbook of the U.S. army, *Japanese Administration of Occupied Areas—Philippine Islands* (1944). Among the authors of the Constitution of the Third Philippino Republic (after the war) were "many outstanding figures in Philippine political life during the past twenty years . . . certainly some of them were known to have pro-Japanese leanings." *Id.* at 6. The history of the Japanese occupation of the Philippines is documented in A. Hartendorf, *The Japanese Occupation of the Philippines* (2 vols., 1967).

[11] The local courts after the war also treated the Japanese legislation quite respectfully. By and large, they upheld the occupation laws even when the latter manifested none of the permitted grounds for legal changes under Article 43 of the Hague Regulations. Thus, for example, the establishment of a new civil court system in Burma was held legal by the court that had rejected the Crown's contrary position, *see, e.g., The King v. Maung Hmin et al.*, [1946] AD Case no. 139; for a similar Indonesian case, *see Mr. P. (Batavia) v. Mrs. S. (Bandoeng)*, [1947] AD Case no. 118.

[12] On the reoccupation of the colonies in Southeast Asia and the challenges of Japanese-

Even during the period between invasion and the establishment of the so-called republics, the Japanese refrained from invoking the Hague Regulations, nor did they otherwise indicate their intention to abide by them.[13] Similar disregard of the Hague law was shown in those territories to which the Japanese did not "grant independence," such as the Netherlands East Indies (later Indonesia) and Hong Kong. The official policy with respect to territories under military administration, announced in November 1941, suggested that "existing governmental organizations [in occupied territories] be utilized as much as possible, with due respect for past organizational structure and native practices."[14] This limited deference to local practices was limited in time as well: the text emphasized that "[t]he ultimate status of the occupied areas and their future disposition shall be separately determined by the Central Authorities," and provided for the utilization of the local economies for Japanese interests.[15] The military administrations made extensive changes in the local law of these jurisdictions, introducing their civil code, changing the judicial system, and regulating economic activities to their advantage. The introduction throughout "Greater East Asia" of the Imperial Japanese Calendar is a symbol of the kind of control the Japanese set as their goal in occupied Southeast Asia.

Italian Occupations

At the same time that Japan was setting up new entities in China, Italy was pursuing the ancient practice of annexing conquered territories. The Italians began with the invasion and subsequent annexation of Ethiopia in the spring of 1936, and three years later (before the outbreak of the war) continued with the annexation of Albania and replacement of its 1928 constitution.[16] On the eve of World War II, the king of Italy possessed a new

---

sponsored nationalism, *see* F. Donnison, *British Military Administration in the Far East 1943–46* (1956).

[13] Japan had signed and ratified both 1899 and the 1907 Hague conventions. *See* D. Schindler and J. Toman, eds., *The Laws of Armed Conflicts* 88, 90 (2d. ed. 1981). On the legislation in occupied Malaya, *see* S. K. Das, *Japanese Occupation and Ex Post Facto Legislation in Malaya* (1960). A rare documentation of the legislation in Malaya during the occupation is 1 Perak State Laws (1944). On the situation in Singapore, *see* Lyons, *The Courts of Singapore under the Japanese Occupation*, 30 BYIL 507 (1953). Other occupation prescriptions may be culled from court decisions reported in the *Annual Digest*.

[14] Principles for Administration of Southern Areas, adopted by the Liaison Conference, November 20, 1941, *translated in* H. Benda et al., *Japanese Military Administration in Indonesia: Selected Documents* (1965), *reproduced in* Lebra, *supra* note 1, at 111–16.

[15] *Id.* at 114.

[16] *See* Basic Statute of the Kingdom of Albania, imposed from Rome on June 3, 1939. For the text, *see* R. Lemkin, *Axis Rule in Occupied Europe* 267 (1944).

title: "the King of Italy and Albania, the Emperor of Ethiopia."[17] Some Italian scholars put forward explanations for their government's total disregard of the law of occupation. They relied on the total defeat of the forces of both Ethiopia and Albania, and argued that according to the doctrine of debellatio, sovereignty was now vested in the power that controlled these territories.[18] Indeed, at that time, debellatio was still an arguable doctrine, and it was subsequently used also by the Allied powers.[19] But there is ample evidence that the Italian forces had no intention of respecting the law of occupation from the start of the campaign, when they were still facing the resisting Ethiopian forces and therefore when there was still no situation of debellatio.[20]

German Occupations

Europe during World War II experienced annexations as well as many other types of foreign domination. The Axis occupants did not invoke the Hague Regulations with regard to the administration of occupied territories.[21] Advancing their claim for a New Order in Europe, they tailored the political organization of the different occupied countries to provide the Axis occupant with the most potent mode of governance.[22] Some areas

[17] *See* Law no. 580 Regarding Acceptance of the Crown of Albania by the King of Italy, Emperor of Ethiopia, April 16, 1939, *reproduced in id.* at 267.

[18] On these legal arguments, *see* M. G. Scelle, *Le conflit italo-éthiopien devant le droit international* 207–11 (1938). *See also* Langer, *supra* note 5, at 132–54, 245–53.

[19] *See infra* text accompanying notes 136–44. On the demise of the doctrine of debellatio, *see infra* text accompanying notes 145–51.

[20] Upon occupying the provinces of Tigre and Agam, the military proclamation issued conveyed the message of a new colonialist, not of a temporary occupant. The ordinance opens with the indication of the authority of the new regime ("In the name of His Majesty the King, I assume government over this country"), and ends with specific policies of integration into the Italian structure ("The tolls and custom duties [with Italian Eritrea] are abolished"). *Reproduced in* Scelle, *supra* note 18, at 200. Upon the entry of Italian forces into the Ethiopian capital, the Italian prime minister declared that Roman civilization had triumphed over barbarism, and therefore "Ethiopia is Italian." *Reproduced in id* at 204–5).

[21] One notable exception is the occupation regime established in the British Channel Islands, where the Germans invoked the Hague Regulations, though not consistently. One possible reason is the fact that the occupant wished to maintain good relations with the local community in this strategically important region. On this policy, *see* C. Cruickshank, *The German Occupation of the Channel Islands* 111 *et seq.* (1975).

[22] A general survey of the occupations by the Axis powers in Europe is found in Lemkin, *supra* note 16. A detailed description of the administration of eastern Europe is found in A. Dallin, *German Rule in Russia* (1957). Specific descriptions of occupation regimes in Belgium, Czechoslovakia, France, Greece, The Netherlands, Norway, and Poland were prepared by the U.S. Army and published in 1944 in a series of handbooks entitled *German Military Government—Belgium, German Military Government—Czechoslovakia,*" etc. Extensive discus-

were incorporated into the Axis states: Germany absorbed Alsace-Lorraine, Luxembourg, eastern Belgium, the free city of Danzig, western Poland, and the Sudeten; Bulgaria annexed parts of Greece; part of the Western Ukraine was assigned to Romania. Puppet states were created in Slovakia and Croatia. Puppet governments were set up in Norway and in parts of France and Greece. In Denmark, the local government retained administrative powers throughout most of the occupation period, with only minor concessions to the Germans. Occupation regimes as such, that is, rule by a foreign military power, without the fiction of a so-called independent government, were practiced in Belgium, the Netherlands, part of France, part of the Soviet Union (including areas that the Soviet Union had occupied in 1939–1940), and part of Greece. However, in none of these cases did the occupants invoke their powers under the international law of occupation, nor did they abide by it. Upon gaining control over a territory, the occupant would announce that the existing laws would remain in force as far as would be compatible with the goals of the occupation or with the orders issued by the occupant.[23] The basic premise of the Hague Regulations, namely, the inviolability of the sovereignty of the ousted power, was not accepted by the authors of the European New Order, as it was rejected by the champions of Greater East Asia.[24] The occupant claimed to possess all the powers of the ousted sovereign, including its plenary legislative powers.[25]

In addition to the various forms of foreign rule, the Axis occupants used

---

sion on these occupations appears also in 9 J. Verzijl, *International Law in Historical Perspective* 194–289 (1978). On the status of Denmark, *see* Ross, *Denmark's Legal Status during the Occupation*, 1 Jus Gentium 1 (1949).

[23] The military proclamations failed to mention the Hague Regulations, and their contents were incompatible with the latter's rules. *See, e.g.*, the notice of the military governor of occupied France, dated May 10, 1940: "The general orders and regulations issued by the German Military Commanders take precedence over the law of the land. Local law not in conflict with these orders and regulations remain in force unless incompatible with the purposes of the occupation." Lemkin, *supra* note 16, at 389. The German decree of May 18, 1940, regarding the establishment of an occupation regime in the Netherlands, declared: "The law, heretofore in force, shall remain in effect in so far as compatible with the purposes of the occupation. The Reich Commissioner [vested with "supreme civil authority"] may, by order, promulgate laws." *Id.* at 446.

[24] *Id.* at 25.

[25] *See, e.g.*, Section 1 of the order of the Reich commissioner for the occupied Netherlands, concerning the Exercise of Governmental Authority in the Netherlands, May 29, 1940: "(1) To the extent required for the fulfillment of his duties, the Reich Commissioner for the occupied Netherlands territories assumes all powers, privileges, and rights heretofore vested in the King and the government in accordance with the Constitution and the laws of the Netherlands. (2) Should the interests of the Greater German Reich or the safeguarding of public order or life in the Netherlands so require, the Reich Commissioner may take appropriate measures, including the issuance of general orders. These orders of the Reich Commissioner shall have the force of laws." *Id.* at 448.

diverse methods for modifying the legal systems of the occupied territories. Not every annexation entailed the comprehensive transformation of the local legal system. While in some areas, such as Danzig, Memel, and the eastern districts of Belgium (all of which had been ceded by Germany after World War I), the entire legal system was replaced with the German one, in Austria and the Sudeten, the transformation was phased. In the latter cases, it was provided that German laws promulgated after the annexation would automatically apply, while prior legislation would be applied specifically. In western Poland, Alsace-Lorraine, and Luxembourg, the German laws had to be individually introduced in order to take effect, but this method by no means signified a less extensive prescription of German law. In these areas, the occupant introduced, among other laws, and in addition to many political and administrative laws (including the duty to be conscripted into the German army), the German Commercial Code, the law concerning organization of the courts, the Lawyers' Code, and in Poland, the Criminal Code.[26] The Bulgarian annexation of parts of Greece included a policy of complete eradication of any vestige of Greek nationality, and the legal system was changed entirely.[27]

In the territories not annexed by the Germans, the amount of occupant legislation was still very extensive.[28] In Belgium the Germans took advantage of a local law that delegated to the secretaries-general of the governmental ministries the competence to issue laws in times of national emergency. The Germans controlled the activities of these ministries and were able to implement their policies through these functionaries.[29] To supplement these measures, the occupation authorities issued orders consolidating their control over the country's industry and banking system. In the Netherlands the Germans changed the constitutive framework of the local law by creating a system similar to the one in Belgium, in which legislative powers were delegated to the responsive secretaries-general of the various ministries. This system was complemented by decrees of the German Civil Administration.[30]

[26] *Id.* at 25–26.

[27] *See* the description in the postwar decision of the Greek Court of First Instance of Rhodope, *In re P. (Komotini Case)*, [1948] AD Case no. 187.

[28] Excerpts from Axis orders outlining the various prescriptions promulgated by the Axis powers in Europe are compiled in Lemkin, *supra* note 16, at 267–635. The legislation in occupied France is described in P. Jacob, *Les lois de l'occupation en France* (1942).

[29] A joint decree by the secretaries general, the "Order Concerning the Organization of the National Economy" of April 24, 1941, established a regulatory regime, which was the most potent tool to achieve the integration of the Belgian economy with that of Germany (excerpts of the order are reproduced in Lemkin, *supra* note 16, at 323–25).

[30] The Dutch Special Court of Cassation, established after the war, held that the creation of the civil administration by the occupation forces to manage the country's affairs was incon-

Occupations by the Soviet Union, 1939–1940

From the point of view of the law of occupation, the Soviet occupations during the first year of World War II did not fare better than those of the Axis powers. The Soviet expansionist policies, like those of the Axis states, were in complete contradiction to the basic principle underlying the Hague Regulations, the principle of inalienability of sovereignty through the use of force. The annexations effected by the Red Army were accompanied by a clear ideological statement justifying certain armed conflicts in pursuance of communist ideals. Most disturbing from a legal point of view was the fact that while at the end of the war the Axis practices could be considered as passing aberrations, the Soviet claims remained to a large extent in effect and had to be reconciled with the postwar law of occupation.

The Communists' idiosyncratic version of international law was elaborated by leading Soviet lawyers. That version injected political criteria into the otherwise neutral principles of the law of occupation:

> [T]he task of Soviet lawyers consists in giving a learned justification of the legality of partisan wars on territories occupied by the imperialist aggressors, having in mind the Leninist-Stalinist teachings on just and unjust wars.[31]

World War II gave the Soviet Union the opportunity to implement those Leninist-Stalinist teachings. The Soviet occupations proceeded in two steps. The Molotov-Ribbentrop Agreement enabled the Soviet Union to invade Poland in September 1939 (after officially declaring that "the Polish State and its government have virtually ceased to exist" because of the German invasion).[32] Within six weeks of this invasion, the national assemblies of the Western Ukraine and Western Byelo-Russia, formerly parts of Poland, whose delegations had been "elected" by at least 90 percent of the local population, unanimously voted for their incorporation into the Soviet Union, and their wish was promptly granted.[33] A similar scenario took place in the summer of 1940, when shortly after the Soviet

---

sistent with the Hague Regulations. *In re Rauter*, [1949] AD (Case no. 193, at 540 (January 12, 1949).

[31] Excerpt from a discussion at the Theory of State and Law section of the (Soviet) Academy of Social Sciences, April 20, 1950. *See* translated excerpts of the report of the discussion in Kulski, *Some Soviet Comments on International Law*, 45 AJIL 347, 349 (1951).

[32] *See* the note delivered by Molotov to the Polish ambassador in Moscow on September 17, 1939, *translated in* M. Laserson, *International Conciliation—Documents for the Year 1943*, at 87–88. For an account of the Soviet expansion *see* Langer, *supra* note 5, at 254–84.

[33] *See* the Proclamation of the National Assembly of Western Ukraine of October 27, 1939, and the decision of the Supreme Soviet in Moscow of November 1, 1939, officially admitting these entities, *translated in id.* at 91–92.

invasion of the Baltic republics of Estonia, Latvia, and Lithuania, newly elected national assemblies unanimously voted for their incorporation into the USSR.[34] Two other republics that were similarly incorporated into the USSR during 1940 were Moldavia (formerly part of Romania) and the Karelo-Finnish Republic (detached from Finland).[35]

After initial defeats by the German army, which forced the temporary retreat of the occupant, the Soviets reoccupied those "lost" territories, and resumed control over them as inseperable parts of the USSR. The international community acquiesced to the Soviet resurrection of the 1940 international borders, although formal recognition of the incorporation was generally witheld. Only in autumn 1991 was the independence of the Baltic republics reestablished.

The Relevance of the Axis and Soviet Occupations to the Law of Occupation: The Status of Unlawful Occupations

The occupations by the Axis powers before and during World War II were part of megalomaniac plans to establish a New Order of the entire world. The Soviet agenda called for another type of new order. These occupants rejected the basic tenets of the law of occupation by seeking perpetual and exclusive control over the territories they occupied. The control was to be wielded either directly, through annexation or military administration, or indirectly, through puppet regimes. Preoccupation law was not accorded any intrinsic moral or legal value, and the sole motivation for its retention, in those few cases in which it was retained, was the occupant's convenience.

The Axis and early Soviet occupations were illegal in another aspect, which stemmed from the emerging prohibition on the use of force. These occupations were the first to take effect after the illegality of wars of aggression had become widely regarded as binding law, and they were effected through the Axis powers' aggression.

These occupations were therefore illegal on two grounds: first, illegality predicated on the aggression that led to the occupation, and second, the illegal mode of governance chosen by the occupying army upon assuming control. There can, of course, be other situations in which only one of these two grounds of illegality exists. And the question with respect to each of these situations is Do the Hague Regulations apply to those occupations as if they were "legal" occupations?

---

[34] Report by Foreign Minister Molotov to the Supreme Soviet on August 1, 1940, *translated in id.* at 93–94.

[35] *Id.* at 95.

Ample attention has been given to the first aspect of illegal occupation, namely, occupation through aggression. Some scholars have argued that an aggressor is not entitled to all the powers that international law confers upon the occupant. Since the Axis powers were aggressors, the claim goes, none of their acts merits respect.[36] The bulk of authority rejects this position, holding that the law of occupation, like the law of war, applies equally to lawful and unlawful armies.[37] Indeed, there are cogent reasons to disregard the prior aggression of the occupant that led to the occupation. Ultimately, this is a question of incentives: if we want the occupant to respect the law of occupation, we must recognize the validity of its measures. The occupant is given the opportunity to invoke the Hague Regulations in return for the setting up of an occupation administration abiding by the same rules.[38]

The second aspect of illegal occupation merits, I submit, a different approach. Here, the question is not whether or not the occupant can be relieved from international obligations by setting up administrations not according to the framework of the Hague Regulations. The occupant may not escape these duties, notwithstanding the type of government established.[39] The important question concerns the occupant's legal powers:

---

[36] *See* Harvard Research in International Law, *Draft Convention on the Rights and Duties of States in Case of Aggression*, 33 AJIL (Supp.) 827, 844 (1939) (suggests depriving the aggressor of its rights, but not of its duties, as an occupant); Wright, *The Outlawry of War and the Law of War*, 47 AJIL 365, 370–71 (1953).

[37] *See, e.g., In re List (Hostages Trial)*, [1948] AD Case no. 215, at 637 (U.S. Military Tribunal at Nuremberg, February 19, 1948); Morgenstern, *Validity of Acts of the Belligerent Occupant*, 28 BYIL 291, 321 n.1 (1951); Lord McNair and A. Watts, *The Legal Effects of War* 372 (4th ed. 1966); J. Stone, *Legal Controls of International Conflicts* 695 and n.10a (1954).

[38] Ross, *Denmark's Legal Status during the Occupation*, 1 Jus Gentium 1, 7 (1949), arguing that "[t]o go on [emphasizing only the illegal invasion] amounts to leaving everything to the arbitrary sway of the invader"; Morgenstern, *supra* note 37, at 321 n.1, mentioning that otherwise the occupant "would, in effect, be freed of the obligation to treat the population in accordance with international law"; Lauterpacht, *The Limits of the Operation of the Law of War*, 30 BYIL 206, 231 (1953), noting that "[a]ny legal theory which denies to the aggressor . . . the rights usually associated with the conduct of war may act as an inducement for him to depart from the obligations imposed by that part of the laws of war"; *see also* A. Gerson, *Israel, the West Bank and International Law* 12 (1977).

Others emphasize another concern, the possibility of lawlessness. *See, e.g., Aboitz v. Price*, 99 F. Supp. 602, 611–12 (D. Utah 1951), in which the court held that "dangerous as it may be to recognize any authority in [the occupant], it is better to encourage some proper government than none at all. Without some kind of order, the whole social and economic life of a community would be paralyzed." Wolff, *Municipal Courts in Enemy Occupied Territory*, 29 TGS 99, 100 (1944), agrees, warning that otherwise "[g]eneral disorder would ensue, and the first to suffer would be the inhabitants of the occupied territory."

[39] *See, e.g., In re Greifelt and Others*, [1948] AD Case no. 216, at 655 (U.S. Military Tribunal at Nuremberg, March 10, 1948); *Tsemel v. The Minister of Defence and Others*, 37 (3) PD 365 (Israeli Supreme Court, 1982) (the law of occupation applies to the Israeli presence

does an illegally established regime taint *all* its measures, rendering them null and void, or is the occupant entitled to expect that those measures that would have conformed with the law of occupation had it established a lawful administration be respected despite its denial of that law? Would other actors, such as the ousted government or its national courts, be obliged to examine the occupant's measures under the Hague law? Or do they have discretion to form whatever policies they find suitable in light of the fact that an illegal regime was established?

The reaction of the governments ousted by these occupants was straight-forward. During the war or upon their return to power, these governments did not consider their prescriptive powers constrained by the Hague Reg-ulations. Implicitly they refused to recognize the validity of the occupation measures that would have been in line with the law of occupation had a lawful regime of occupation been established.[40] A few national courts re-ferred to this issue, holding that the initial violation of the Hague Regu-lations tainted all other measures.[41] But as mentioned in Chapter 2,[42] the bulk of national courts in postoccupation countries have taken a more practical approach, often invoking the Hague Regulations as the criteria for judging the legal effects of the occupants' measures.

It would seem that measures taken by an annexationist state, or by any other regime that illegally attempts to alienate permanently an occupied territory from its lawful sovereign, do not mandate any deference under international law.[43] The occupant who establishes such a regime does not seek international protection for its interests, and, indeed, is not entitled

---

in Lebanon during the 1982 war, despite the lack of a declaration to that effect by the Israeli army).

[40] However, there is no indication that their reaction would have been different had the occupant established a regime according to the Hague Regulations. The conduct of the Bel-gian government during World War I is an example of an ousted government's tending not to respect prescriptions of a formally legal occupation regime.

[41] In one case decided by the Polish Supreme National Tribunal on July 7, 1946, the court based its declaration of the inapplicability of the Hague Regulations to western Poland, which had been annexed by Germany, both on the illegality of the war and on the "criminal" incorporation of that territory. *In re Greiser*, [1946] AD Case no. 166, at 388. Not in con-nection with World War II occupations, the Egyptian court of Port Said refused to enforce a judgment rendered in the Jordanian-occupied West Bank since, *inter alia*, Jordan's annexation was illegal, and therefore "the judgement [was] rendered by a tribunal without legal exis-tence." [1950] ILR Case no. 98 (November 26, 1950). Wolff, *Municipal Courts in Enemy Occupied Territory*, 29 TGS 99, 103–04 (1944), was of the opinion that judgments of courts established under a regime inconsistent with the Hague Regulations have no legal effect whatsoever.

[42] *See infra* text accompanying notes 64–70.

[43] This is, however, subject to the possibility that a territorial unit, illegally alienated from the former sovereign, might qualify as entitled to independence under the principle of self-determination. This seems to be the case of Bangladesh. This issue is discussed in Chapter 6.

to it. There is no point in trying to encourage this occupant's observance of the law: this occupant is indifferent to the reaction of the ousted sovereign simply because it has no intention of relinquishing its hold. As it fails to share power with the lawful government under the auspices of international law, the latter is not precluded by the same law from taking whatever countermeasures it can in order to protect its interests during and after the occupation. Under such circumstances, the ousted government, from exile or upon its return, is under no obligation to respect those measures that would have been lawful had the occupant respected the basic norm of international occupation law. The message to the occupant, upon its assumption of power, is that there is but one way of receiving recognition of its measures, and that is by administering the territory in accordance with the framework of the law of occupation. For this message to be effective, it is required that third-party states also refuse to recognize such measures.

This position is backed not only by the conduct of ousted and returning governments. It can also be inferred from the international principles regarding recognition of states.[44] Most of the forms of unlawful foreign domination would be through either annexation or the creation of puppet states or governments (as in most of the Axis occupations). Thus the international norms regarding recognition become relevant, as they, from their perspective, concur in the result: under customary international law, there is a duty not to recognize such entities or give legal effect to their prescriptions.[45] In fact, this duty was first enunciated by the League of Nations with respect to the Japanese occupation of Manchuria and the creation of so-called Manchukou.[46]

[44] The laws of occupation and those of recognition are closely linked. In fact, as Schwarzenberger has observed, the basic principle of occupation law, the inalienability of territory through conquest, has been derived from the practice of not recognizing the conqueror's title over such areas. G. Schwarzenberger, *International Law—The Law of Armed Conflict* 167 (1968). *See also* J. Dugard, *Recognition and the United Nations* (1987).

[45] Ian Brownlie showed that this principle, often referred to as the Stimson doctrine, has been widely accepted by states, and enunciated in international instruments: I. Brownlie, *International Law and the Use of Force by States* 410–19 (1963). J. Crawford, *The Creation of States in International Law* 122–23 (1979), is of the opinion that this rule is a substantive one, which may be considered as *jus cogens*. The 1970 consensual Declaration on Principles of International Law Concerning Friendly Relations and Cooperation among States in Accordance with the Charter of the United Nations states in Article 1(11): "No territorial acquisition resulting from the threat or use of force shall be recognized as legal." Resolution 2625(XXV) of October 24, 1970.

[46] Note, however, that the text of the Resolution of the Assembly of the League of March 11, 1932, emphasized the illegality of the resort to aggression, rather than the illegal establishment of a puppet regime. The relevant part states "that it is incumbent upon the Members of the League of Nations not to recognize any situation, treaty or agreement which may be brought about by means contrary to the Covenant of the League of Nations or the Pact of Paris." *League of Nations Official Journal*, Spec. Supp. 101, at 87–88 (1932).

Of course, the sovereign government may, upon its return to power, uphold certain unlawful occupation measures. Other governments, however, do not have the same prerogative, and hence they are not entitled to derogate from the strict rule of nonrecognition described above. This difference between sovereign and third states is also relevant to the conduct of national courts. National courts have often encountered the plea to recognize acts of an illegal actor, be it an insurgent faction in a civil war or an illegal annexing power in an international conflict. Thus, the U.S. Supreme Court was ready to recognize certain enactments of the Confederate states after the Civil War.[47] That Court exercised the prerogative of the sovereign. Courts in other jurisdictions, however, are not entitled to derogate from the principle of nonrecognition of regimes that defy the law of occupation.[48]

Allied Occupations during World War II

Many instances of occupations by Allied powers took place during the war. Each occupation had its own distinctive traits, determined mainly by the principal power among the Allies that took charge of the area, the stage of war at the time of occupation, and the local conditions in each territory.

British Occupation of African Territories

British forces completed the occupation of French and Italian colonies in Africa prior to the joint Allied invasion of Sicily in 1943. The following is an account of those occupations, in chronological order.[49]

---

[47] *Texas v. White*, 74 U.S. (7 Wall.) 700, 733 (1868), in which the Court held that "acts necessary to peace and good order among citizens, such, for example, as acts sanctioning and protecting marriage and the domestic relations, governing the course of descents, regulating the conveyance of property, real and personal, and providing remedies for injuries to persons and estates, and other similar acts, which would be valid if emanating from a lawful government, must be regarded in general as valid when proceeding from an actual, though unlawful government."

[48] *But see* the opinion of Lord Denning in the case of *Hesperides Hotels v. Aegean Turkish Holidays Ltd.*, [1978] QB 205, [1978] 1 All E.R. 277, in which he applied the approach of *Texas v. White* to the Turkish occupation of Northern Cyprus.

[49] A comprehensive account of those occupations appears in Lord Rennell of Rodd, *British Military Administration of Occupied Territories in Africa* (1948). The author participated in this administration in various prominent roles. Another British source is War Office, *British Military Administration of Occupied Territories in Africa during the Years 1941–43* (Cmd 6589, 1945).

ERITREA

Eritrea was an Italian colony adjacent to Ethiopia, along the coast of the Red Sea. It was occupied in 1941, in one of the early phases of the British offensive in eastern Africa.

The instructions to the military administration of Eritrea called for the retention of Italian laws "in so far as military exigencies shall permit and in so far as they are not deemed to be contrary to natural justice or equality."[50] Although not formally in line with Article 43 of the Hague Regulations, this policy seems to be well within the legal powers of the occupant. With respect to the local administration personnel, the basic strategy of the occupant was to replace most senior Italian executive officials, while judges were to be permitted to carry on with their duties.[51] The occupant was in no hurry to eradicate Fascist institutions, which were to be "progressively broken up or taken over."[52] Only in December 1942, apparently in connection with the growing concern over a possible Japanese invasion and the rekindled hopes of local Fascist elements, did the authorities arrest the Italian secretary general, a professed Fascist who had been the titular head of the local Italian administrative personnel.

As the Italian provincial machinery proved impracticable, Eritrea was divided into seven administrative divisions. In each district the echelon of authority conformed with British colonial experience. One important province, however, Tigrai, which had been part of the Eritrean colony, was detached by the British and handed over to Ethiopia. This move, which was a violation of the Hague Regulations, was the fulfillment of a promise to local leaders in exchange for their assistance in fighting the Italians.[53]

SOMALIA (ITALIAN SOMALILAND)

Like Eritrea, Somalia, which the British called Italian Somaliland, had been an Italian colony. It bordered British Somaliland, part of which was occupied by the Italians in earlier stages of the war. The local population, the Somali tribes, were generally nomads.

While the occupation of Eritrea followed to a large extent the guidelines of the Hague Regulations, the experience in Somalia was much different. Indeed, formally, the military administration of Somalia followed the

---

[50] Section 2 of the *Instructions to the Military Administration in Eritrea and Somalia*, August 1, 1941, *reproduced in* Rennell, *supra* note 49, at 116.

[51] Rennel, *supra* note 49, at 51–2.

[52] *Id.* at 131.

[53] *Id.* at 143–44. This violation of the law of occupation was not a single incident of that sort: later, a similar motive would encourage Britain to divide Libya, and to create the independent state of Cyrenaica.

guidelines of the administration in Eritrea. The occupant, however, set up in effect a colonial administration, according to the British practice regarding areas inhabited by nomads. This administration and the administration of reoccupied British Somaliland were both under the command of the same headquarters.

Lord Rennell maintains that the local administrative system collapsed and the occupant had to establish new systems, including the judicial system, "from first principles."[54] In addition, "the inherent lawlessness of the Somali [people]"[55] necessitated an efficient military government, and as a result "[t]he Legal Department's work was not so much concerned with international law or wide issues as with efforts to reinstate internal law and order."[56] About a year after the occupation, the British took over the affairs of the Italian colony, after dissolving the last remnants of Italian administration, which consisted of the municipality of Mogadishu, the capital, where most of the small Italian community resided.

ETHIOPIA

As a background to the British occupation of Ethiopia, the following facts are pertinent. Britain's policy of appeasement had led to its 1938 de jure recognition of Italy's illegal annexation of Ethiopia.[57] After the outbreak of the war, and in pursuance of covert military operations inside the area, His Majesty's government withdrew its recognition of the Italian title, and recognized the claim of the ousted emperor to regain his throne. This very transfer of recognition allowed the British forces to assert that the territory about to be invaded would not be enemy territory subject to the Hague Regulations, but rather a liberated territory subject to the sole authority of the Emperor Haile Selassie the First. The official British policy regarding the administration of Ethiopia, pronounced just four days after the change of attitude stated that

> [a]s His Majesty's Government have withdrawn their recognition of the Italian conquest, it may be correct to say that *de jure* any part of Ethiopia which is wholly cleared of the enemy comes *ipso facto* and at once under the rule of the Emperor, who will be present in person to claim it and to give it effective administration.[58]

---

[54] *Id.* at 333.

[55] *Id.*

[56] *Id.*

[57] On that annexation, *see supra* text accompanying notes 17–20.

[58] *Reproduced in* Rennell, *supra* note 49, at 45. The memo goes on to assert British "guidance and control" until a formal transfer of authority to the emperor under agreed-upon terms.

The arrangements for the administration of Ethiopia were agreed upon informally prior to the invasion by the British officials and the emperor, and a formal agreement was signed on January 31, 1942, by the United Kingdom and Ethiopia. That agreement prescribed the framework for the administration of the affairs of the country.[59] It should be noted that the Italian civil and criminal laws were immediately suspended, and pre-Italian law was resurrected.[60]

These events give us the opportunity to examine another aspect of the links between the international norms concerning recognition of states or governments and the law of occupation.[61] The applicability of the law of occupation to a certain area is, of course, always predicated on the initial assignment of sovereign title over that area. The case of Ethiopia is a clear example of the immediate consequence of the recognition of sovereign title upon the claims regarding the applicability of the law of occupation. In this case, Emperor Haile Selassie had a valid claim to sovereignty, a claim that was not diminished by the illegal Italian annexation.[62] Therefore the administration set up by the emperor and the British forces that operated under his authority were not subject to the constraints of the Hague Regulations.[63] However, the problem with the British shift of positions regarding the recognition of sovereigns is that it might set an example to be used by future occupants, who would try to avoid the duty to abide by the law of occupation by shifting their recognition of sovereignty from an enemy to an ally prior to the actual occupation. It is therefore suggested that a strong presumption be established against the legality of such a "preemptive" recognition.

MADAGASCAR

The occupation of the French colony on the island of Madagascar raises a similar question regarding the relationship between occupation and recognition laws. In this case the problem was to decide which government was entitled to control the island, the Vichy government or the one led by General de Gaulle, and consequently, whose claim the British occupant was required to uphold.

[59] The agreement is reproduced in *id*. at 539–58.

[60] *See* Sections 12 and 13 of the memo, *supra* note 58, at 48–49. The Ethiopians claimed title to Italian property, both public and private. The British were of the opinion that it was their responsibility to safeguard Italian private property, and took the necessary steps for that purpose.

[61] One aspect already discussed was the recognition of illegal regimes established in violation of the law of occupation. *See supra* text accompanying notes 44–46.

[62] On the Italian annexation, *see infra* text accompanying notes 14–17.

[63] On the occupation of an allied territory, *see* Roberts, *What Is a Military Occupation?* 55 BYIL 249, 263–65 (1985).

The British army invaded the island in September 1942, without the aid of the Free French forces. The plan in London had been to set up a Free French administration in Madagascar as soon as possible.[64] However, this plan had to be delayed until the terms of an agreement between de Gaulle and the British government could be settled. In the meantime, a British military administration was set up. Only on December 17, 1942, did the British government and General de Gaulle sign an agreement regarding the transfer of authority over the island to the latter and delineating the responsibilities of the British forces in the island.[65] On the day it entered into force, January 8, 1943, the British administration of the island was taken over by the Free French administration.

The three months of British administration can be characterized as cooperative with, and to a great extent dependent on, the largely intact local French (Vichy) administration. This cooperation was reached after the two highest French officials who had been loyal to Marshal Petain had been removed from office, and their place taken by a local official appointed as secretary general. The latter served as the titular head of the local administration, and all the enactments were promulgated through his authority.

Was the transfer of authority to a Free French administration a permissible act under the Hague Regulations? To answer the question one must first determine which was the lawful French government. Only the transfer of control to the lawful government would be deemed legal under the Hague Regulations. But how can one determine the identity of the legal government under such circumstances? In the case of Madagascar, for example, a considerable portion of the local French population was loyal to the Vichy government. It actively opposed the Allied invasion and rejected General de Gaulle's authority. Should the recognition of the lawful government in such cases be determined by popular support? In circumstances where foreign occupation is involved, any unilateral determinations by the occupant should be taken with a grain of salt since the occupant could effortlessly portray its ally's government, or a puppet "indigenous" one, as the lawful one, thus claiming exemption from the application of the law of occupation. Therefore, the law of occupation must delimit occupants' power to transfer authority from one government to another, and persist in treating the territory as occupied until the actual withdrawal of the occupation forces or, in exceptional cases, until authority is transferred to an indigenous government that enjoys the support of the majority of the occupied community constituting a self-determination unit.

[64] Rennell, *supra* note 49, at 215.
[65] The agreement is reprinted in *id.* at 233–37.

LIBYA

Until the Allied invasion of Libya in November 1942, the territory had been an Italian colony. It had been treated by the Italians as one territorial unit, divided only for administrative purposes. The Allied invasion, however, effected, for the period of occupation, a political and economic division of the country into three parts: Cyrenaica, Tripolitania, and the Fazzan. If the occupants could have had their way, three different states would have emerged from that occupation. Indeed, it would seem difficult to reconcile this treatment with the Hague Regulations. Yet the fiction of conformity by the Allied occupants with international law was retained by the portrayal of their acts as having been motivated solely by considerations of administrative expediency.[66]

Cyrenaica

The British military occupation of Cyrenaica was proclaimed on November 11, 1942. The occupant promulgated a series of basic proclamations establishing the basis for the Military Government of Cyrenaica. Together with those proclamations, General Montgomery published a message to the people of Cyrenaica, outlining the basic British policy toward that territory. Perhaps the most important part of the message was the following promise:

> The British Government has thanked Sayed Mohammed Idris el Senussi for the assistance he has given to the Allied cause and has promised that the Senussis will not again be subject to Italian rule.[67]

This promise was the outcome of the close cooperation throughout the war between the British forces and the Senussi leaders of Cyrenaica. While the leaders of the Tripolitanian community believed in an Axis victory, the Senussis, longtime foes of Italy, supported the Allies.[68] Sayed Idris, the revered Senussi leader, exiled in Egypt, had urged his people to take part in military operations against the Axis powers and, in return, managed to elicit, before the occupation, the British promise not to return Cyrenaica

---

[66] *See* Watts, *The British Military Occupation of Cyrenaica, 1942–1949*, 37 TGS 69, 72–73 (1951). On the long-term aims of the occupation of Libya, *see* British Foreign Office Brief for the British Delegation to the Potsdam Conference (May–July 1945), *reproduced in* 3 L. Woodward, *British Foreign Policy in the Second World War* 487 (1971); M. Khadduri, *Modern Libya—A Study in Political Development* (1963).

[67] *Reproduced in* Rennel, *supra* note 49, at 251.

[68] On the background to the local power struggle, and the relationships among Cyrenaican and Tripolitanian leaders *see* Khadduri, *supra* note 66, especially 28–37.

to Italian domination, in addition to oral promises of Cyrenaican independence.[69]

Upon gaining control, the British administration was confronted by the indigenous claim for participation in governance, as a prelude to the promised independence. Britain, however, wanted to stay in charge of the administration and to ensure its future influence over that country well beyond the period of occupation. Here the Hague Regulations came to the aid of the occupant, who explained to the Senussis that international law prevented it from relinquishing control.

Italian law remained theoretically in force; in fact, however, that law was impossible to implement, for all the Italian judges and lawyers had fled the country before the invading army arrived.[70] Thus the military administration became both the source of extensive legislation in substantive law (through, for example, the promulgation of an entirely new criminal code)[71] and instrumental in the establishing of new criminal and civil judicial systems.[72]

To implement British policy with respect to the future separate status of Cyrenaica, a political and economic border between Cyrenaica and Tripolitania was established. In concert with the (separate) occupation administration of Tripolitania, the movement of people and goods across this border was restricted. Trading was at first subject to customs, but later an agreement on a customs union between the two provinces was reached. The judicial system of Libya was separated into two independent systems, with a separate Shari'a Court of Appeal in Benghazi, Cyrenaica.[73] In 1943, a separate native civil service was organized in Cyrenaica.[74]

The British administration of Cyrenaica remained in force even after the 1947 peace treaty with Italy, in which the latter renounced the title to its African colonies. The British administration remained until the independence of (unified) Libya. Britain sought to prevent the emergence of that unified entity. In pursuit of that goal, the British administration unilaterally allowed, after the peace treaty of 1947, self-rule in Cyrenaica, with extensive powers over all internal affairs, including the power to enact a

[69] A statement of Secretary of State for Foreign Affairs A. Eden, announced in the House of Commons, January 8, 1942, 377 *House of Commons Debates* 77–78 (1942), *reproduced in* Khadduri, *supra* note 66, at 35.

[70] Watts, *supra* note 66, at 76. Rennel, *supra* note 49, at 252: "It was too much to expect the Administration to administer Italian Law in full: hardly a legal book remained and the number of officers capable of interpreting was necessarily small."

[71] Watts, *supra* note 66, at 76. According to Watts, it was not necessary to change the laws in civil matters, since the population had become accustomed to their "simpler provisions."

[72] *Id.* at 76–80.

[73] Rennell, *supra* note 49, at 341. Before that there was one appeals court for all of Libya, situated in Tripoli.

[74] Khadduri, *supra* note 66, at 45.

constitution.[75] Finally, however, the British plan was defeated by the United Nation's 1949 decision to grant independence to a unified Libya.[76]

In summing up the Cyrenaican experience, I would like to draw attention not to the seeming infringement of the principles of the law of occupation by the unique treatment given to that province, but rather to the use made by the British of the Hague Regulations. The British occupation is another example of the manipulation of the Hague Regulations to the occupant's advantage. In particular, it shows that occupants who enjoy democratic processes at home would appreciate the occupation regime as an extremely advantageous tool for exclusive control. Such a regime enables the implementation of long-term policies in the occupied area, without having to be accountable to locally elected elected representatives. The Hague Regulations do not provide any institutionalized way for the ousted government or the local population to participate in the process of making and implementing policies. In fact, in the Cyrenaican occupation, the occupant invoked international law for the very purpose of denying indigenous access to that process. Since the occupant ostensibly followed "international law," it was not open to the criticism of being despotic or colonialistic. The occupant's claim of being constrained by "international law" probably sounded respectable, but for the local population, their demands for change rejected, it was hardly convincing. It is small wonder that the latter, as Lord Rennell later recalled, "came to treat 'International Law' as a poor joke which they could not understand."[77]

Tripolitania

Britain had no long-term interests in Tripolitania. This fact was the cornerstone for its policy towards the occupied province. An administration for Tripolitania, separate from the one in charge of Cyrenaica, was established upon the December 1942 invasion. According to Lord Rennell, the "objective of the Administration followed the text-book."[78] Indeed, in contrast to the direct rule exercised in Cyrenaica, the British administration of Tripolitania became much less involved in actually running the affairs of that province. Its scope of interests was quite limited: "It was frequently stressed that all thought must be in terms of war-time economics and the

[75] See the Transitional Powers Proclamation of September 16, 1949, cited in Khadduri, supra note 66, at 74. The British retained authority over matters of foreign affairs, defense, and Italian property.

[76] The UN General Assembly defeated a joint Anglo-Italian initiative—the so-called Bevin-Sforza Plan—according to which Britain would have UN Trusteeship over Cyrenaica, and Italy would have similar control over Tripolitania. See Khadduri, supra note 66, at 128–29.

[77] Rennell, supra note 49, at 252–53.

[78] Id. at 270.

security of the Allied forces."[79] Many Italian employees of the former colonial administration had stayed in the country, and the British found it
"possible and desirable" to keep them in their posts.[80] Italian courts were
reopened and worked side by side with British military courts.[81] Religious
courts of limited jurisdiction, the Shari'a and rabbinical courts, continued
their operation. Indigenous petitions for reforming the local administration to enable local participation in it were rejected by the occupant, who
invoked its limited powers under international law.

The lack of interest of the British occupant was evident in the very conservative treatment of the affairs of Tripolitania. This is another example
that shows that the Hague Regulations suit the occupant who has no interests in the territory under its control.[82] But the Tripolitanian occupation
also shows the possible undesirable consequences that "administration by
the book" may bring about. A disinterested occupant has no incentives of
its own to invest in improving the condition of the occupied territory.
Thus stagnation of the local economy, such as that which occurred in Tripolitania, is a likely outcome of indifferent administration. Neglect in other
areas, such as health and education, is also probable. The Tripolitanian
experience is a strong case for the recognition of the affirmative duties of
the occupant, to improve the standard of living whenever necessary.

The Fazzan

The third part of Libya was assigned to the control of the Free French
forces. This territory, which lies in southern Libya, was occupied by these
forces in January 1943. The goal of the French—clearly incompatible with
the requirements of the Hague Regulations—was to retain permanent
control over this piece of land, as an integral part of their African colonies.
To achieve this goal, they put two Fazzanese regions under the authority
of the French administration in Algeria and Tunisia, encouraged the trade
with Algeria, and discouraged Fazzanese commercial ties with the rest of
Libya.[83] They also used a local family, the al-Nasr family, as an intermediary through which they implemented their policies.

The French did not give up hope even after the UN General Assembly
decided in November 1949 to grant independence to an undivided Libya.
A year later they set up a new political arrangement, with a Fazzanese Representative Assembly, and a chief of Fazzan. This effort was aimed at the

[79] *Id.* at 284.

[80] *Id.* at 271.

[81] *Id.* at 273 and 342 ("The work done by the [Italian] courts was generally excellent; their
co-operation helped considerably to the establishment and maintenance of good order.").

[82] The other examples are the U.S. and British zones of occupation during the Armistice
Occupation of the Rhineland.

[83] Khadduri, *supra* note 66, at 107.

inclusion of Fazzan as one of the three provinces of a future loosely federated state of Libya, in which France would maintain limited influence. But
the postwar decolonization process, already under way, changed this plan,
along with the parallel British plan with respect to Cyrenaica.

The First U.S. Occupation of the War: French North Africa

EARLY OCCUPATION POLICIES

The United States forces were initially quite apprehensive about their involvement in managing the civil affairs of alien communities. Their concerned attitude is reflected in the policy of minimal involvement they
adopted in French North Africa. This was to be the only occupation in
which such a policy would be followed. Later, with increased confidence,
U.S. forces assumed a more active role as occupants.

In the fall of 1942, U.S. forces occupied Algeria, Morocco, and Tunisia,
at that time under the colonial rule of the Vichy government of France.
The Americans sought to keep their involvement at a minimum with respect to the administration of these territories. The underlying motivation
of the U.S. government in forming this policy was to reduce to the minimum the number of personnel from the armed forces employed in civil
administration.[84] It was thought that the local French authorities, because
of their loyalty to the Vichy government, would cooperate with the U.S.
army only if the local administration remained intact. Accordingly, President Roosevelt directed the designated chief of civil administration to inform the local "reliable" French nationals that "[n]o change in the existing
French Civil Administration is contemplated by the United States."[85]

Indeed, no change in the administrative and legal system in these territories was effected. In November 1942 one of the highest-ranking Vichy
officials, Admiral Darlan, following an agreement with General Eisenhower and approval from Marshal Petain, assumed authority over the local
French military and civilian institutions as the high commissioner of all
French North Africa.[86] Even the French armed forces in the region were

[84] AFHQ GO 5, October 12, 1942, OPD Files, 381, *reproduced in* H. Coles and A. Weinberg, *Civil Affairs: Soldiers Become Governors* 34 (1964). This policy was consistent with the
then-existing U.S. Army Field Manual. *See The Rules of Land Warfare*, Section 9(d) (U.S.
Army Field Manual, FM 27-5, 1940).

[85] The message also included promises of remuneration, and of the exclusion from the Allied forces of the forces of General de Gaulle. Directive of September 22, 1942, *reproduced in*
Coles and Weinberg, *supra* note 84, at 32–33.

[86] An interesting account of the events that led to the agreement with Darlan and the hesitant British reservations is found in 2 L. Woodward, *British Foreign Policy in the Second World
War* 360–85 (1971).

not dissolved. Under the agreement with Admiral Darlan, this Vichy-associated administration was entrusted with the responsibility to "take such measures as [were] necessary for the maintenance of order and public administrative services throughout the territory in consultation with the Commanding General of the United States Army."[87] Indeed, General Eisenhower's apprehensions concerning the necessity of interfering with issues of civil administration were so great that he acquiesced even in the continuance of the oppressive and racial policies of the Nazi-influenced Vichy government. Thus, out of fear of the "explosive possibilities" of the "local Jewish-Moslem problem," the Vichy anti-Semitic laws were not abolished.[88] Nor did the administration release the prisoners who had been arrested for aiding the Allied cause. This untenable position would not be followed in subsequent occupations; instead, the occupant would assert that it was "absolutely prevented," in the sense of Article 43 of the Hague Regulations, from maintaining such racial laws.

Despite the original intent, the timidity of the U.S. occupant could not last long. The Americans soon found that they could not renounce all authority, and that they ought to engage the problems of public administration. In this context, General Eisenhower's complaint is worth citing. In a letter to General Marshall dated November 30, 1942, he laments the burden of the management of the nonmilitary affairs, a burden that was not alleviated by the functioning of the local French government:

> [T]he sooner I can get rid of all these questions that are outside the military in scope, the happier I will be! Sometimes I think I live ten years each week, of which at least nine are absorbed in political and economic matters.[89]

AFTERMATH: THE CHANGING U.S. ATTITUDE TOWARD THE ADMINISTRATION OF OCCUPIED TERRITORIES

The shortcomings of the U.S. administration in French North Africa prompted the U.S. government to train military personnel as future administrators of occupied territories.[90] In preparing for this training and for a new version of the Field Manual, many officials discussed the proper nature of such an administration. Before the invasion, in March 1942, the prospectus of the School of Military Government took the minimalistic view:

---

[87] Agreement of November 22, 1942, *reproduced in* Coles and Weinberg, *supra* note 84, at 36.

[88] *See* Eisenhower's message to Marshall of December 8, 1942, *reproduced in id.*, at 46.

[89] The letter is reproduced in *id.* at 45.

[90] Coles and Weinberg, reproduce a selection of internal U.S. correspondence, which, in a hesitant and somewhat reluctant decisionmaking process, finally led to the realization of the necessity to establish military administrations in occupied territories and to the creation, for that purpose, of a school of military government. *Id.* at 63–113.

The ideal type of military government is one which, coming into being amid the utter chaos of a civilian population whose armed forces have just been subjected to military defeat, can restore order and stability with dispatch and at the same time integrate the local institutions and psychology of the occupied area and the superimposed military authority with a minimum of change in the former and a maximum of control by the latter.[91]

This minimalistic attitude was criticized a year later, after the first experience in North Africa. Here we can benefit from a nonlegal opinion, but an experienced and insightful one:

It is . . . quite certain that any planning for military government, based on the assumption that the legal *status quo* in the territory occupied should be supported and the existing local personnel utilized, is on dangerously weak foundations. It will not always be easy to define the legal *status quo* and it may be highly undesirable to support it when it is defined. Shall we, for example, wish to give military sanction to the legal *status quo* in Nazi Germany . . . ? Shall we want to endorse the Nazi educational system? Analogous questions will arise in other countries, some very difficult questions in confused areas like Alsace and Lorraine. They will have to be answered by the military governor with the uncomfortable feeling that the answer he gives will itself establish a *status quo* which will tend to perpetuate itself and profoundly influence the pattern of ultimate peace. . . . These are not the kinds of problems which can be solved out of military government books. The areas likely to be occupied must be studied intensively, the local personnel must be checked, the realities of the *status quo* as distinguished from the textbook version of it must be carefully appraised.[92]

The next version of the military Field Manual, published in December 1943, although still cautious, gives the occupant more leeway regarding existing local laws and institutions. Echoing contemporary experience as occupants, and expecting the need to administer vast areas in the near future, the relevant provision asserted:

[I]t is advisable that local laws, customs, and institutions of government be retained, except where they conflict with the aims of military government or are inimical to its best interests.[93]

Yet already at that period, even this recognized leeway still fell short of the goals of the Allies in occupied Europe. With the invasion of the first European territory about to commence, the U.S. government, together with the other Allies, asserted its intention to eradicate the existing Fascist

---

[91] *Reproduced in id.* at 145.

[92] This memo was sent by W. Donovan, the director of the Office of Strategic Services to the secretary of the Joint Chiefs of Staff, in April 1943. *Reproduced in id.* at 145–46.

[93] *Military Government and Civil Affairs* at Section 9(h) (U.S. Army field Manual, FM 27-5, (1943).

and Nazi regimes and institutions. But these goals were not expressed in the 1943 Field Manual. The discrepancy between the then-prevailing views of scholars regarding the law of occupation and the political aims of the Allies was thought to be unbridgeable.[94] In this sense, the 1943 Field Manual did not reflect the actual policies of the U.S. forces in the territories occupied by them. The apparent contradiction between the Hague Regulations and the Allied goals would be solved later, essentially by denying the applicability of the Hague law to most of the Axis territories.[95]

Thus, one can detect a constant shift of U.S. policy regarding occupations, from the timid approach practiced in North Africa in 1942 to the very active role played in occupied Germany and Japan. The change may be attributed to the increasingly better position of the Allies vis-à-vis the Axis powers in the battlefields; their growing self-confidence as occupants; their improving interaction with local inhabitants, who had come to realize which power would prevail; and their formulation of more detailed long-term goals for the occupied territories in the postwar era. The U.S. attitude toward the law of occupation was being adjusted to accommodate actual developments. Indeed, it seems that in many cases, including those of North Africa, Germany, and Japan, the justification under the law of occupation for measures taken (or not taken), came only as an afterthought.

The Joint Allied Occupation of Italy

The U.S. preparations for the occupation of Italy were inadequate, despite the lessons of French North Africa.[96] There was still a reluctance to form and implement clear guidelines regarding the objectives of the administration of the areas about to be occupied. As a consequence, the officers who were entrusted with setting up AMGOT (Allied Military Government of Occupied Territories, later to be changed to AMG) had not received prior to the invasion of Sicily any instructions regarding the policies to be pursued. The historians of the U.S. occupation in Italy, Coles and Weinberg, noted:

> Of the initial assumptions concerning civil affairs in World War II none was more fallacious than the idea that there is a distinct boundary line between the

[94] Coles and Weinberg, *supra* note 84, at 146 n.4, point out that the doctrine of the Hague Regulations "was not longer adhered to in the expressed political aims of the United Nations, but international law as interpreted by conservative jurists had not kept pace with the recent changes in ideology and practice."

[95] *See infra* text accompanying notes 133–51.

[96] Two comprehensive accounts of the occupation of Italy, from the point of view of the Allies, are Coles and Weinberg, *supra* note 84, at 157–652; C.R.S. Harris, *Allied Military Administration of Italy 1943–1945* (1957).

military and the political. . . . The only hope for civil affairs officers abroad lay in quickly realizing the falsity of all the indoctrination about their non-political role in Italy and in trying to lift themselves by their own bootstraps. Since they had not been taught the politics of civil affairs they would have to learn it themselves, the hard way.[97]

Another fundamental flaw in the Allied scheme was the choice of a co-equal Anglo-American command to supervise the military administration. Such a joint administration might have been feasible had the occupation been a purely nonpolitical task, or had both powers had similar interests in the area. But there was a conflict of long-term interests between the two Allies, each seeking lasting exclusive influence over postwar Italy. Disagreements also arose regarding the nature of the administration: should army officers replace local functionaries in a "direct" type of administration (as the Americans suggested), or would it suffice to conduct an "indirect" rule, through supervision over indigenous officials (the British suggestion).[98]

One example of political decisions inevitably entering into seemingly nonpolitical matters, and thus an example of the insurmountable difficulties of running a co-equal occupation administration, occurred well before the actual invasion. In preparing for the occupation, the future occupants had to resolve the question of the exchange rate between the Italian lire and the military currency about to be introduced (military notes of both dollar and sterling). While the British suggested a "realistic" rate, that is, close to the putative market rate (which had also been the exchange rate in British-occupied Italian colonies), the Americans proposed a "benevolent" rate, close to what they thought was commensurate with the expectations of the local population. The rate suggested by the British was *double* the Americans' rate.[99]

SICILY

Only about a fortnight before the actual invasion of Sicily, in early July of 1943, did the Allies reach a common understanding regarding the nature and goals of the occupation of the island. There was a compromise regarding the exchange rate between the lire and the military currencies. The decision whether to employ a "direct" or an "indirect" mode of governance was relegated to the military commander in the field.[100]

[97] Coles and Weinberg, *supra* note 84, at 158.
[98] *See id.* at 170–73.
[99] Memo of the Civil Affairs Division of May 1943, *reproduced in id.* at 176.
[100] *See* the Directive of the Combined Chiefs of Staff of June 28 1943, Sections I(5), I(6), and II(1), *in id.* at 177–80.

AMGOT was designed according to the principles of the Hague Regulations.[101] A set of thirteen proclamations and two general orders was drafted in preparation for the occupation. Most of them dealt with routine measures taken by a new occupation administration upon assuming control over hostile territory, such as the proscription of crimes against the invading army, the establishment of military courts, the temporary closure of financial institutions and the control of supply and distribution of foodstuffs.

Conspicuous among the proclamations was Proclamation no. 7, entitled "Dissolution of Fascist Organizations and Repeal of Laws." The Allied policy with regard to the Fascist laws and institutions was clear at the outset: the Directive of June 28, 1943, instructed AMGOT to dissolve the entire Fascist organization, remove its members from any post of authority, and abolish forthwith all laws that discriminated on the basis of race, creed, or color.[102] The preamble to Proclamation no. 7 based the prescribed measures on "the purpose of the Allied Powers to deliver the people of Italy from the Fascist Regime."[103] The text did not invoke the claim that the Allies were "absolutely prevented" from maintaining these laws and institutions. Indeed, such a claim would have been questionable since in American-occupied French North Africa similar racial laws had been left intact.[104] Nor could the claim for greater latitude in eradicating laws and institutions under conditions of debellatio be invoked at the time of the occupation of Sicily.[105] It seems, therefore, that the policy of de-Fascification was incompatible with the then-prevailing conservative reading of the Hague Regulations. Indeed, the occupants' own doubt about the compatibility of this policy with the Hague Regulations is reflected in the texts of both the Directive of June 28 and the preamble of Proclamation no. 7.[106]

---

[101] AMGOT Plan for Military Government of Sicily, Part I(A)(3), *in* U.S. Army Service Forces, *Civil Affairs Handbook: Italy* 2 (1943).

[102] *Id.* at Section I(6), at 177.

[103] *Id.* at 56.

[104] *See supra*, text accompanying note 88.

[105] For this type of claim, argued with respect to the "postsurrender" occupation of Germany and Japan, *see infra* text accompanying notes 136–44.

[106] The implementation of this policy of de-Fascistication was not as resolute as the texts had foreseen. The actual promulgation of Proclamation no. 7 was postponed, and a more realistic approach toward the Fascist institutions and personnel was adopted. The Fascist party was, indeed, dissolved, but the Italian (Fascist) administration continued to function. The General Administrative Instructions for Guidance of AMG Personnel, which still appeared in the November 1943 edition of the *Civil Affairs Handbook: Italy, supra* note 101, at 80, stated that in order to economize on "manpower," the maintenance of the Italian administration, nearly all of whose officials were Fascists or members of the Fascist party, would be secured for the time being. The complete eradication of Fascism was postponed to a later stage.

SOUTHERN AND CENTRAL ITALY

The administration of southern and central Italy did not follow the Sicilian example. As the Allied forces were preparing for the invasion of mainland Italy, political developments within Italy changed the Allies' original plans to set up an occupation administration. On July 26, 1943, Mussolini fell from power and in his place the king appointed Marshal Badoglio, who was not averse to the idea of an armistice with the Allies. The Allies seized this opportunity and brought Badoglio to sign a capitulation agreement just a few days before the planned invasion of the mainland. About a month later, the king declared war on Germany. According to the Armistice Agreement, the commander in chief of the allied forces was empowered to "establish Allied Military Government over such parts of Italian Territory as he may deem necessary in the military interests of the Allied Nations."[107] Allied domination over the rest of the Italian territories was legally secured through the commitment of the Italian government to bind itself to take such measures as the Allied commander-in-chief might require.[108] In a subsequent Armistice instrument, the Long Term Armistice (*Armistizio Lungo*) of September 29, 1943, the Badoglio government undertook to disband all Fascist institutions, and rescind all laws involving discrimination on grounds of race, color, creed, or political opinion.[109]

The Badoglio administration consisted of little more than himself and the king, who had both fled Rome to the south. In order not to destroy their prestige, military government was not declared in four southern provinces, later referred to as the "King's Italy," where the king and the Badoglio government exercised authority (with the aid and supervision of Allied officers). This Italian government was no more independent than any puppet government. It formed no policies of its own, nor did it have the means to carry out any measures. This government was little more than a rubber stamp used to bestow legality upon Allied measures without referring to international law.[110] As General Eisenhower remarked, "The importance of the Badoglio administration [was] its unchallenged claim to legality."[111]

The Allied policy was to extend the nominal jurisdiction of the Badoglio

[107] Article 10 of the "Short Term" Armistice Agreement of September 3, 1943, *reproduced in* Coles and Weinberg, *supra* note 84, at 227.

[108] *Id.*

[109] Articles 30 and 31 of the Additional Conditions of the Armistice, *reproduced in id.* at 235.

[110] For example, the introduction of military currency and the establishment of the same exchange rate as existed in Sicily were effected not through military orders but through a proclamation made by Badoglio in the king's name, *reproduced in id.* at 229.

[111] From a message to the Combined Chiefs of Staff, September 18, 1943, *reproduced in id.* at 231.

government as much as possible. However, because of the latter's weakness, certain areas recovered from the Germans were initially controlled through military administration. On February 9, 1944, the authority of the Italian government over the areas under military administration, including Sicily, was formally restored. However, a secret agreement with Badoglio provided that the Allied would retain the powers they had been exercising in these regions.

NORTHERN ITALY—VAL D'AOSTA, BOLZANO, AND VENEZIA GIULIA

The occupation of the northern provinces was laden with sensitive political problems. The very establishment of an occupation administration was a political decision. Three countries were contesting Italy's title to these provinces, namely, France, Austria, and Yugoslavia, and it was foreseen that the identity of the occupant would determine the subsequent sovereignty over the occupied territory. The British and U.S. occupants sought continued Italian sovereignty over the provinces, but because of local hostility toward the Italian government, it was impossible to reintroduce the Italian administration there at that stage.

In the northwestern part of Italy, France coveted the Val d'Aosta. The French army invaded the province under Allied instructions, but in defiance of the Allied orders, it then refused to evacuate the area and hand it over to the Allied Military Government.[112] Only after communications at the highest level did the French troops withdraw and allow the establishment of the Allied Military Government.[113]

In Bolzano the conflicting claim was asserted by the South Tirolese population, which consisted of at least two-thirds of the population in this province. Their newly constituted South Tirolese party invoked the right to self-determination and demanded the creation of a new republic independent of Italy. The Allied Military Government's policy was to maintain the territory within the jurisdiction of Italy, but at the same time to encourage local self-government.[114] Both Val d'Aosta and Bolzano had reverted to the control of the Italian government by the end of 1945.

Venezia Giulia posed the most difficult problem for the Allies, and as a result, remained under Allied occupation until 1947.[115] Long before actual occupation, the Yugoslav Liberation Army announced its intention to annex this northeastern province, which had been ceded to Italy at the end of

[112] Harris, *supra* note 96, at 317; Coles and Weinberg, *supra* note 84, at 552.

[113] In a communication from President Truman to General de Gaulle the former threatened that no military equipment and munitions would be issued to the recalcitrant French army. De Gaulle acquiesced immediately. Coles and Weinberg, *supra* note 84, at 570.

[114] *Id.* at 571.

[115] On this issue *see* Coles and Weinberg, *id.* at 587–613; Harris, *supra* note 96, at 328–50.

World War I. The invasion of the province developed into a race between the Allied and the Yugoslav forces. The two armies succeeded in conquering parts of the province, and the city of Trieste was separated into two zones of control. In this case the Allied lacked the leverage they had over the French forces in the south: they could not force Marshal Tito's army out of the area without a military showdown, which was not desirable. Subsequently, the province was divided between the two armies, and ultimately this division became the demarcation line between Italy and Yugoslavia.

Even before an official agreement on the division of sovereignties was signed, Yugoslavia had begun treating the territory under its control as part of its own, with no consideration of international duties.[116] The Allied Military Government, on the other hand, was cautious, and refrained until the peace treaty with Italy, in which the new borders were defined, from its otherwise applicable policy (in Italian territory under AMG authority) of implementing laws passed by the Italian legislature. Instead, it promulgated occupation proclamations and other enactments for this region. These enactments, according to the Hague Regulations, referred to the Italian law as it had been on September 8, 1943, the date when the Armistice Agreement with Italy was announced.[117]

The fact that in Venezia Giulia the Allied Military Government chose to promulgate enactments directly, and not through the Italian institutions,[118] provides a rare opportunity to examine how a modern military occupant used its prescriptive powers under the Hague Regulations with respect to a relatively highly developed area.[119]

[116] The Yugoslav forces did not lose time in transforming the administrative system in the areas under their control. *See* Harris, *supra* note 96, at 344. Years after the Yugoslav occupation, the Italian Court of Cassation ruled that the extension of the Yugoslav law to the occupied Italian territories, and the replacement of local national institutions by the occupant's institutions, was in violation of the "Long Term" Armistice Agreement. The court held the introduction of Yugoslav divorce law to be illegal, and hence declared divorces null and void. *Blecich*, Il foro Italiano, at 234–35 (Court Cass., March 16, 1967); P. Picone and B. Conforti, *La Giurisprudenza Italiana di dirito internationale publico* 638–40 (1988).

[117] Article III of Proclamation no. 1 of the AMG of Venezia Giulia (1 AMG Gazette, no. 1, at 3). The enactments of this AMG are compiled in the AMG Gazette, in two volumes.

[118] The AMG also suspended the right of appeal to the Italian Court of Cassation: Section 2 of General Order no. 6, The Civil Courts for the Occupied Territories, of July 12, 1945, 1 AMG Gazette, no. 1, at 32).

[119] Technically, the occupation administration in this area could have claimed to have received its authority from the Italian government, through the terms of the Armistice Agreement with Italy, and thus been freed from the limits imposed by the Hague Regulations (for similar claims regarding the 1918 Armistice Occupation of the Rhineland, *see supra* Chapter 2). However, no such claim was asserted, and rightly not. The Armistice Agreement with Italy contained no specific arrangement that could be construed as exempting the Allies from the limitations of the Hague Regulations.

As the basis for its administration, the AMG promulgated a set of proclamations, which was similar to the one prepared for the Sicilian administration. One of the dominant policies mentioned in the proclamations was de-Fascification. Among the measures taken were the repeal of anti-Jewish laws on July 3, 1945,[120] and the dissolution of the Fascist party and affiliated organizations on August 18, 1945.[121]

In the two years of AMG rule in Venezia Giulia (1945–1947), the occupant made extensive use of its prescriptive powers under Article 43 of the Hague Regulations, enacting ordinary measures concerning the supply of foodstuffs to the local population and public health, as well as other issues related to the local economy. The authorities extensively modified the labor laws, granting freedom of association,[122] regulating wages,[123] and prescribing provisions for arbitration and mediation in labor disputes.[124] There were even important changes in welfare legislation, amending, inter alia, pension laws,[125] and family allowances.[126] One act of profound demographic significance, whose validity under the Hague Regulations is questionable, was the abolition of Italian laws granting allowances for marriages and births in order to encourage procreation.[127]

Many orders refer to changes in fiscal laws. These changes corresponded to similar measures taken simultaneously in the other parts of Italy. One indication is found in an order which made excise duties subject to the rates published by the Italian government.[128] Changes were introduced in income tax,[129] the motor vehicle tax,[130] and other specific taxes, such as the taxes on registration, mortgages, and estates.[131] The local municipalities were granted the power to impose a consumer tax on certain consumer goods.[132] All these are but examples of the extensive changes introduced by the AMG in the fiscal laws of the territory.

On the whole, this occupation was characterized by extensive interference with preoccupation law in many issues pertaining to the civil life of the occupied community. Looking back at this two-year period, and the heavy volumes of the AMG Gazettes containing the orders promulgated

---

[120] General Order no. 3 of July 3, 1945, 1 AMG Gazette, no. 1, at 25–27.

[121] Proclamation no. 6 of August 18, 1945, 1 AMG Gazette, no. 1, at 19–20.

[122] General Order no. 4 of July 6, 1945, 1 AMG Gazette, no. 1, at 27.

[123] General Order no. 15 of July 1, 1945, 1 AMG Gazette, no. 3, at 8.

[124] Order no. 78 of February 26, 1946, 1 AMG Gazette, no. 16, at 25.

[125] *See* General Orders no. 34 of December 31, 1945, 1 AMG Gazette, no. 21, at 3.

[126] General Order no. 43 of February 11, 1946, 1 AMG Gazette, no. 14, at 3.

[127] Order no. 281 of December 12, 1946, 2 AMG Gazette, 332.

[128] Order no. 267 of November 6, 1946, 2 AMG Gazette, 213.

[129] *See, e.g.*, General Order no. 25c of October 8, 1946, 2 AMG Gazette, 125.

[130] Order no. 24 of November 26, 1945, 1 AMG Gazette, no. 8, at 3.

[131] General Order no. 39 of January 25, 1946, 1 AMG Gazette, no. 16, at 3.

[132] General Order no. 36 of January 16, 1946, 1 AMG Gazette, no. 12, at 3.

during that period, one may wonder to what extent the AMG administration in Venezia Giulia differed from an indigenous regime operating without the constraints of international law. In other words, given the extensive use of prescriptive powers in addressing various aspects of social activities, one may wonder whether Article 43 of the Hague Regulations has had any impact on delimiting the prescriptions of the occupant.

Unconditional Surrender and Debellatio: The Occupations of Germany and Japan

Throughout the war the Allies insisted on the unconditional surrender of Germany and Japan as the requisite condition for the cessation of hostilities.[133] The acceptance of this condition by Germany and later by Japan was the foundation upon which the Allies would base their claim for exemption from the constraints of the Hague Regulations. This exemption was crucial to the Allies because it was generally accepted that the law of occupation did not condone the measures the Allies intended to implement in both Germany and Japan. These measures, which included the eradication of the existing national institutions and the establishment of democratic ones in their stead, were one of the war's main goals. Indeed, the Allies claimed the "supreme authority" to effect these measures long before the hostilities ended. A proclamation to that effect was issued by the Allies immediately upon crossing the German border, when the defending army was still resisting the invasion.[134] Confident in their ultimate victory, the Allies chose to treat Germany as if it were already defeated. In the case of Japan, actual occupation took place only after its surrender. Thus, the Allies never treated the law of occupation as the source of their authority in Germany and Japan, nor did they consider their administrations bound by the Hague Regulations, which they saw as inapplicable in Germany and Japan.[135]

[133] For a recent study of this principle and its relevance to the occupations of Japan and Germany, *see* N. Ando, *Surrender, Occupation, and Private Property in International Law* (1991).

[134] General Eisenhower's proclamation of 1944 called for the obliteration of Nazism, and asserted that "[s]upreme legislative, judicial and executive authority and powers within the occupied territory are vested in me as Supreme Commander of the Allied Forces and as Military Governor. . . . All German courts and educational institutions within the occupied territory are suspended." *Reproduced in Dalldorf and Others v. Director of Prosecutions,* [1949] AD Case no. 159, at 436–37 (British Zone of Germany, Control Commission Court of Appeal).

[135] Other suggestions to justify the Allied measures, this time under the Hague Regulations, explored the term "absolutely prevented" in Article 43. M. McDougal and F. Feliciano, *Law and Minimum World Public Order* 770 (1961), emphasize security concerns: "The Allied belligerent occupants may fairly be said to have been 'absolutely prevented' by their own

APPLICATION OF THE DEBALLATIO DOCTRINE

The legal argument with respect to unconditional surrender draws upon the notion of debellatio.[136] As it is generally understood, "deballatio," also called "subjugation," refers to a situation in which a party to a conflict has been totally defeated in war, its national institutions have disintegrated, and none of its allies continue militarily to challenge the enemy on its behalf.[137] In such a situation the defeated state is considered not to exist any longer. Thus the territory of the previous entity is not "occcupied," the Hague Regulations are inapplicable, and the victorious power is entitled to annex it or otherwise assume sovereign powers over it.[138]

The conditions of debellatio are therefore a purely factual matter.[139] Thus an agreement to cease hostilities in which one party "unconditionally surrenders" would not ipso facto amount to debellatio. The inclusion of that phrase in a legal instrument that provides for an end to hostilities would not relieve the victor of the need to satisfy the factual conditions for debellatio. If there were no debellatio, the law of occupation would still be relevant, subject to the provisions laid down in that instrument. This point was relevant to the occupation of Japan: unlike Germany, whose institutions had completely disintegrated prior to the occupation, the Japanese government still functioned when it signed the Instrument of Surrender. That was hardly a situation of debellatio. Japanese sovereignty was probably retained,[140] and therefore the legal source of Allied authority was the

---

security interests from respecting, for instance, the German laws with respect to the Nazi Party and other Nazi organizations and the 'Nuremberg' racial laws." M. Greenspan, *The Modern Law of Land Warfare* 225 (1959), referred to the declared ideological objectives of the war: "If, in those circumstances [of unconditional surrender], the victors are not 'absolutely prevented' . . . from respecting those institutions, then those words ['absolutely prevented'] have no sensible meaning." The British War Office, *The Law of War on Land, Being Part III of the Manual of Military Law* 143 n.1 (1958) [hereinafter *The Law of War on Land*], explicitly invokes moral arguments: "[I]t is no part of the duty of the Occupant to give effect to a regime which is contemptuous of human rights and of modern notions of legality." However, it is not at all clear whether all of the occupation measures taken in Germany and Japan may qualify under these interpretations of Article 43. *See, e.g.*, Ando, *supra* note 133, at 107–8, with respect to the redistribution of property in Japan.

[136] On prior claims of debellatio, *see* the discussion of the Italian occupation of Ethiopia, *supra* text accompanying notes 18–19.

[137] For recent reiterations of this principle, *see* Roberts, *supra* note 63, at 267–68 and n.67; Ando, *supra* note 133, at 76–80.

[138] *See also* E. Feilchenfeld, *The International Law of Belligerent Occupation* 8 (1942); M. Bothe, *Belligerent Occupation, in* 4 EPIL 65, 66 (1982) (in such cases, "annexation would no longer be unlawful").

[139] An instrument indicating formal surrender is not a prerequisite. A. Gerson, *Israel, the West Bank and International Law* 5 (1977).

[140] Ando, *supra* note 133, at 100. *But cf. Cobb v. United States*, 191 F.2d 604 (9th Cir. 1951), *cert. denied*, 342 U.S. 913 (1952), in which the court held that the United States acquired de facto sovereignty over the formerly Japanese island of Okinawa, but that de jure sovereignty had not passed to the United States, since a formal act of annexation, or at least

Instrument of Surrender, which was based upon the Potsdam Declaration and the Japanese responses to it.[141] Nevertheless, that instrument's terms were sufficiently broad to enable the occupant to implement—mainly through the Japanese government, serving as an intermediary—fundamental changes of Japan's laws and institutions, similar in scope to those effected in vanquished Germany.

It was generally accepted that the conditions for debellatio had been met with respect to Germany and hence the four occupying powers had acquired sovereign title over it. A month after Germany's unconditional surrender and its complete occupation, the Allies acknowledged this fact in their announcement of June 5, 1945, in which they declared that they had assumed "supreme authority with respect to Germany, including all the powers possessed by the German Government, the high command, and any State, municipal or local government or authority."[142]

Most of the authorities link this transfer of sovereignty to what they view as the self-evident outcome, namely, the inapplicability of the law of occupation. The logic behind this claim was that since the Allies had acquired sovereignty, the measures they took within Germany were internal matters not governed by international law. This position was endorsed by courts in many jurisdictions, including those in Germany,[143] and by Western scholars.[144]

---

an intention to annex, had not been communicated. A similar view is expressed by Freeman, *War Crimes by Enemy Nationals Administering Justice in Occupied Territory*, 41 AJIL 579, 606 (1947), who maintains that the situation in Japan was similar to the one in Germany, notwithstanding the continued functioning of the Japanese government.

[141] These instruments are reproduced in Ando, *supra* note 133, at 127–30. The Basic Initial Post-Surrender Directive to the Supreme Commander for the Allied Powers (SCAP) for the Occupation and Control of Japan, of November 3, 1945, Section 2, *Reproduced in id.* at 136 *et seq.*, states that those instruments are the basis for SCAP's authority over Japan as "Supreme Commander." It adds: "In addition to the conventional powers of a military occupant of enemy territory, you have the power to take any steps deemed advisable and proper by you to effectuate the surrender and the provisions of the Potsdam Declaration."

[142] *Reproduced in* Ando, *supra* note 133, appendix 20.

[143] British courts: *Grahame v. Director of Prosecutions*, [1947] AD Case no. 103, at 233 ("The Control Council and the Zone and Sector Commanders in their perspective spheres are neither mere *de facto* authorities set up by a belligerent occupant with limited powers nor are they ruling the occupied territory adversely to any existing German Government, for there is no other German Government; *but they are, for the time being, the supreme organs of government in Germany.*") (My emphasis); *Dalldorf et al. v. Director of Prosecutions*, [1949] AD Case no. 159, at 438. U.S. courts: *In re Altstötter and Others (The Justice Trial)*, [1947] AD Case no. 126 (Nuremberg, U.S. Military Tribunal, December 4, 1947). German courts: *Loss of Requisitioned Motor Car (Germany) Case*, [1952] ILR 621 (Federal Supreme Court); *Recidivist (American Military Tribunal) Case*, [1951] ILR 617 (Frankfurt Federal Court of Appeal). Dutch Courts: *In re Flesche*, [1949] AD Case no. 87 (Special Court of Cassation). French Courts: *In re Bauerle*, [1949] AD Case no. 93, at 292 (Court of Appeal of Colmar).

[144] *See* Kelsen, *The Legal Status of Germany According to the Declaration of Berlin*, 39 AJIL 518 (1945) ("The [Berlin Declaration] means that the German territory, together with the population residing on it, has been placed under the sovereignty of the four powers. It means

CRITIQUE OF THE DEBELLATIO DOCTRINE

While the Allies' title to Germany was not challenged, its logical consequence, namely the inapplicability of the law of occupation to the administration of the territory, was convincingly contested, especially by German
scholars.[145] They emphasized the predicament of the population under
what actually was alien domination. Formal legal principles aside, they argued, international law must not abandon its concern for the local population only because the national institutions had disappeared. Max Huber,
then the president of the International Commission of the Red Cross,
voiced his discomfort with the Allied legal claim in a letter to U.S. Secretary of State Byrnes:

> Unconditional surrender of the German and Japanese forces which resulted in
> their laying down arms without the special reservations usually inserted in ar-
> mistice conventions, does not *ipso facto* imply that the capitulating power aban-
> dons all claim to the benefits of the Hague and Geneva Conventions in favor of
> its nationals.[146]

Note that Huber's argument builds upon the conception that the subjects of international law are states: the rights of the population are implied
by, and dependent solely on, the acts and concessions of their government.
Fifty years later, after witnessing the growth of awareness of human rights
on the international level, one need not deduce the rights of the population
whose government had unconditially surrendered only from the acts of
their government. The local population is the direct bearer of rights, rights
that are embedded in the respectable body of human rights law.

Moreover, an even stronger claim can be made against the notion of
debellatio and its outcome, namely, the purported release of the victor
from any international constraints on its administration. The doctrine of
debellatio is a remnant of an archaic conception that assimilated state into

---

further that the legal status of Germany is not that of 'belligerent occupation'."); Fried, *Transfer of Civilian Manpower from Occupied Territories*, 40 AJIL 303 (1946), at 326–27 ("Germany's military defeat . . . resulted in the transfer of sovereignty over Germany to the Allies. As
a result of the subjugation . . . [t]he [Allied] occupants do no longer act *in lieu* of the 'legitimate sovereign'. They themselves exercise sovereignty. . . . One of the prerogatives of the
Allies resulting from the subjugation is the right to occupy German territory at their discretion."). *See also* Jennings, *Government in Commission*, 23 BYIL 135 (1946); Freeman, *supra*
note 140, at 605–6.

[145] von Laun, *The Legal Status of Germany*, 45 AJIL 267 (1951); Bagge, *The Legal Position
of the Allied Powers in Germany*, 1 Jus Gentium 23 (1949) (English summary at 41–42);
T. Schweisfurth, *Germany, Occupation after World War II, in* 3 EPIL 196–97 (1982). For a
recent critique of this position by a Japanese lawyer, *see* Ando, *supra* note 133, at 76–77.

[146] *Reproduced in* part by Freeman, *supra* note 140, at 605 n.138 (excerpt).

government,[147] a vestige that was revived by the Allies to explain their expanded powers, but whose demise should now be recognized. This conception was buttressed in the realm of the law of war by the Rousseau-Portales doctrine, which conceived of war as a duel between governments.[148] This doctrine has no place in contemporary international law, which has come to recognize the principle that sovereignty lies in a people, not in a political elite. The fall of a government has no effect whatsoever on the sovereign title over the occupied territory, which remains vested in the local population. The fact that their army has been totally defeated cannot divest them of their entitlement. The only lawful change of status (annexation, secession, etc.) may therefore take effect with the consent of the people involved. Otherwise, the territory should continue to be treated as occupied.

The doctrine of debellatio is not only inconsistent with contemporary law and political philosophy. It is also wrong as a policy. If we assume that international law plays a role in the army's decisionmaking process, then the greater latitude granted in the case of complete victory might create an incentive to continue unnecessary fighting.

Earlier evidence for the demise of the doctrine of debellatio is found in state practice regarding those states subjugated by Italy and Germany before the outbreak of World War II. Despite their apparent debellatio, these entities were reconstituted well before peace treaties ended the war. This practice may be treated as one crack in the doctrine, motivated by the maxim *ex injuria jus non oritur*.[149] However, developments in the postwar era reveal a comprehensive rejection of debellatio. In addition to the recognition of the principle of peoples' sovereignty, outlined above, specific rules for wartime conduct rendered the deballatio doctrine irrelevant. Common Article 2 of all four 1949 Geneva conventions, which defines their scope of application, does not make any exception with respect to debellatio. Therefore, it seems that the Fourth Convention Relative to the Protection of Civilians would apply to situations such as that of Germany after 1945.[150] For the duration of the occupation, no change in the insti-

---

[147] *See* 1 D. O'Connell, *State Succession in Municipal Law and International Law* 5–6 (1967), noting that the separation of the two notions—state and government—took place around the middle of the nineteenth century, "[w]ith the abstraction of the concept of sovereignty."

[148] *See supra* Chapter 2, text accompanying notes 71–74.

[149] On this maxim as a consideration in recognizing states, *see* Crawford, *supra* note 45, at 418–19. However, this view would contrast with the principle that legal and illegal occupants enjoy similar powers in their control of occupied territories. Since aggressors invariably make up justifications for their use of force, attempts to differentiate on the basis of legality would only be detrimental to the interests of the occupied population.

[150] *See* Roberts, *supra* note 63, at 270–71. *But cf.* the British military manual, *The Law of War on Land, supra* note 135, at 140 n.2, according to which the applicability of this convention to situations such as that of post–1945 Germany is "doubtful." The fact that the

tutions or government of the territory, or any annexation, may deprive the local population of the benefits prescribed by the Fourth Geneva Convention.[151] To sum up, the Hague Regulations might not have been initially intended to apply to the postsurrender occupations of Germany and Japan. However, subsequent changes, which include those of the 1949 Fourth Geneva Convention, contemporary emphasis on peoples' sovereignty, and moral and practical considerations warrant the recognition of the demise of the doctrine of debellatio and the application of the law of occupation to postsurrender occupations.

The Law of Occupation in the Wake of World War II: The Termination of the Normative Force of the Hague Regulations

The account of the major occupations immediately before and during World War II shows that all the major powers failed to apply the Hague Regulations in most of the foreign territories that came under their control. The ousted governments, from exile or upon their return, also accorded little respect to the law of occupation. The effect of these actions and reactions was to strip the Hague Regulations of their normative command, at least during that period.

The violations by the Axis powers and by the Soviet Union of the law of occupation were described earlier and need no further elaboration here. The ideologies of these powers explicitly contradicted the basic concepts of the law of occupation. The Allied occupations, in contrast, did not demonstrate a total denial of the validity of the Hague Regulations. The Allies professed their adherence to them; moreover, their conduct implied acknowledgment of the continued existence of these regulations. However, too often one can discern efforts to find legal justifications for the failure to abide by them.

Among the bases that the Allies used to claim inapplicability of the Hague Regulations were official recognition of governments other than the acting ones as the lawful governments (in the British occupations of Ethiopia and Madagascar), agreements with local elements (in the American occupations of French North Africa and Italy), and claims of sovereign powers in a postsurrender occupation (in Germany and Japan). To these claims one should add some outright violations of the Hague Regulations:

---

conventions were drafted during the postwar occupations but contained no specific provisions for postsurrender occupations, supports the argument that there was no intention to treat those occupations differently. As Pictet noted, the delegates had in mind the occupations of Germany and Japan. J. Pictet, ed., *Commentary: The Fourth Geneva Convention* 62 (1958).

[151] Article 47, in conjunction with Article 6 of the Fourth Geneva Convention.

the illegal attempts by Britain and France to fragment Libya and the transfer of the province of Tigrai to Ethiopia. Finally, I should mention some
questionable policies in that handful of occupations where the law of occupation was invoked by the occupant. These policies range from almost
complete inaction (by Britain in Tripolitania) to extensive modifications of
the status quo in policy decisions concerning taxation and even procreation
(as in Venezia Giulia, Italy). These different policies point to a self-serving
approach rather than a structured method for treating occupied territories.

   Against this background it would have been surprising if a government
that had been ousted during the war and resumed control after its end were
to pay any attention to the prescriptions of the Hague Regulations. Indeed, at that period these regulations seemed to have lost their authority
as the embodiment of customary international law.

   However, at the same time as the authority of the Hague Regulations
was on the decline, there were enough indications to suggest that the basic
principle of the law of occupation, namely, the inalienability of sovereignty
through the use of force, was still respected at the end of the war, at least
by the Western Allies. The most significant evidence for this proposition is
the treatment of occupied Germany, which had surrendered unconditionally to the Allies. The latter claimed to have assumed supreme authority
with respect to Germany, but never intended to annex or subjugate it.

   This basic principle was extremely important to the Allies in their quest
to regain control over their Southeast Asian colonies, which had attained
"independence" during the Japanese occupation. From 1943 to 1945, the
law of occupation served as a perfect legal justification for the restoration
of the colonial regimes and other dependent territories of the Allies in the
Far East, despite the sometimes violent opposition of considerable parts of
the local population. Under the principle of inalienability of sovereignty
through force, the Allies could return to those colonies as the sovereigns
whose titles remained valid.[152]

   In describing the Japanese practice of unilaterally granting independence
to Far East colonies, I emphasized the fact that this merely ceremonial
independence was enthusiastically accepted by many in the local communities. Indeed, the prospect of recolonization drove many to oppose militarily the invading Allied forces. However, the principles of self-determination and anticolonialism, invoked in some colonies, were not developed
enough at that stage to prevail in the international arena over the Allied

---

[152] Moreover, the law of occupation proved very useful to the reoccupants, who invoked it
in order to allow the military administrations wide discretionary powers unencumbered by
constitutional restraints. *See, e.g.*, for example Donnison's account of the British decision to
apply the law of occupation as the legal basis for their authority in Burma, *supra* note 12, at
38–40.

claim.[153] It was not until 1971, with the Indian invasion of East Pakistan and the worldwide recognition of the new entity of Bangladesh,[154] that the historical sovereignty of the "ousted sovereign" and, in that sense, the entire law of occupation were subordinated for the first time to the principle of self-determination.[155]

The Fourth Geneva Convention and the Status of the Law of Occupation in 1949

The Hague Regulations suffered a major setback from the conduct of World War II occupants. At the same time that the International Military Tribunal in Nuremberg described these rules as being declaratory of customary international law,[156] they effectively lost their normative value. This was the situation on the eve of the 1949 Diplomatic Conference in Geneva, which would produce the Fourth Geneva Convention Relative to the Protection of Civilian Persons in Time of War. The effort to define anew the international law of war in reaction to the atrocities committed during World War II included an attempt to redefine the law of occupation. This was not an easy task, partly because the leaders of the postwar world were at that time, and for an indefinite time thereafter, occupants of the Axis territories and, on the other hand, did not anticipate having any of their own territories being put under alien occupation in the foreseeable future. They were interested in the occupants' having as much latitude as possible. The smaller countries, many of them with fresh memories of the predicament of occupation, were adamantly opposed to such an approach.

Two fundamental issues of occupation law are treated by the Fourth Geneva Convention: the principle of the inalienability of sovereignty through the use of force (Article 47) and delimited control by the occupant over the occupied territory (Articles 64 *et seq.*).

---

[153] In two areas, the anticolonial struggle has been very substantial. In the wake of the Japanese retreat and before the Allies could resume authority, new indigenous nationalistic governments declared their independence: the Republic of Indonesia (August 17, 1945), and the Republic of Viet Nam (August 18, 1945). The preamble of the constitution of the Republic of Indonesia reflects the local attitude toward the colonials: "Since independence is the right of every nation, any colonial system in the world is contrary to humanity and justice and must therefore be abolished." *Reproduced in id.* at 420.

[154] On this incident, *see infra* Chapter 6.

[155] On the tension between the principle of self-determination and the law of occupation, *see infra* Chapter 6.

[156] International Military Tribunal in Nuremberg, *The Trial of the Major War Criminals* 65 (1947). The International Military Tribunal for the Far East (1948) viewed the Hague Regulations as "good evidence" of customary international law. *In re Hirota*, [1948] AD Case no. 118, at 366.

Article 47: Retention of Sovereignty by the Occupied Sovereign

Article 47 states:

> *Inviolability of Rights:* Protected persons who are in occupied territory shall not be deprived, in any case or in any manner whatsoever, of the benefits of the present Convention by any change introduced, as a result of the occupation of a territory, into the institutions or government of the said territory, nor by any agreement concluded between the authorities of the occupied territories and the Occupying Power, nor by any annexation by the latter of the whole or part of the occupied territory.

As the first article in Section 3, which deals with occupied territories, Article 47 provides that an occupied territory shall remain characterized as such notwithstanding any purported changes in its status. Thus, the practices that loomed large during the war, such as the creation of new "states," the appointments of new "governments," and the annexations or other changes of territorial boundaries, would not affect the applicability of the convention. Nor would the passage of time render the convention inapplicable: Article 47, as well as most of the other articles in the section dealing with occupied territories, continues to be effective "for the duration of the occupation."[157]

Note that nowhere in the text is there an indication of the illegality of the enumerated attempts of political change. In fact, the language of the article mentions only the rights of the individuals under alien occupation, with no explicit reference to the issue of sovereignty. The article does not go beyond providing against the deprivation of the "Protected Persons," the nationals of the enemy who remain in the territory.[158] The official commentary of the International Committee of the Red Cross (ICRC) reiterates this limited angle of the article: "The main point, according to the Convention, is that changes made in the internal organization of the State must not lead to protected persons being deprived of the rights and safeguards provided for them."[159]

This formulation is a reflection of the general concept of the Fourth Geneva Convention, apparent in its title: to provide for humanitarian treatment of civilian persons under occupation, without reference to the mode of governance in those territories. This effort is quite distinct from that of the Hague Regulations, which strove to cater to the interests of the gov-

---

[157] Article 6, paragraph 3.

[158] "[T]he text in question is of an essentially humanitarian character; its object is to safeguard human beings and not to protect the political institutions and government machinery of the state as such." Pictet, *supra* note 150, at 274.

[159] *Id.*

ernments involved in the dispute.[160] I would assume that this specific focus
of the Fourth Geneva Convention made possible the international support
it received. It is doubtful whether worldwide consensus would have been
formed around an explicit condemnation of the political changes to which
Article 47 refers. This is not to say that Article 47 recognized even implicitly the legality of such political changes. Indeed, the possibility that the
article would be interpreted in this way was perceived during the preliminary work on the subject, but no explicit provision to counter it was introduced. The Red Cross's commentary asserts that "the reference to annexation in this Article cannot be considered as implying recognition of this
manner of acquiring sovereignty."[161] This conclusion is enhanced by the
continued applicability of the Hague Regulations, as provided by Article
154.[162]

Article 64: The New Constitution for Occupation Administrations

The scope of the prescriptive power of the occupant is delimited by Article
64 of the Fourth Geneva Convention, entitled "Penal Legislation: 1. General Observations." This article is followed by six more articles (65–70),
which prescribe more specific limits on the legislation in penal matters.
Article 64 states:

> The penal laws of the occupied territory shall remain in force, with the excep-
> tion that they may be repealed or suspended by the Occupying Power in cases
> where they constitute a threat to its security or an obstacle to the application of
> the present Convention. Subject to the latter consideration and to the necessity
> for ensuring the effective administration of justice, the tribunals of the occupied
> territory shall continue to function in respect of all offenses covered by the said
> laws.
>
> The Occupying Power may, however, subject the population of the occupied
> territory to provisions which are essential to enable the Occupying Power to
> fulfil its obligations under the present Convention, to maintain the orderly gov-
> ernment of the territory, and to ensure the security of the Occupying Power, of
> the members and property of the occupying forces or administration, and like-
> wise of the establishments and lines of communication used by them.

The commentary of the Red Cross claims that "Article 64 expresses, in
a more precise and detailed form, the terms of Article 43 of the Hague

[160] Cf. id. at 614: "the Hague Regulations . . . are intended above all to serve as a guide to
the armed forces, whereas the Fourth Convention aims principally at the protection of civilians."

[161] Id. at 276.

[162] On the relationship between the Hague Regulations and the Fourth Geneva Convention, see infra note 176 and accompanying text.

Regulations, which lays down that the Occupying Power is to respect the laws in force in the country 'unless absolutely prevented'."[163] I will argue however that in fact Article 64 introduces innovative elements into the law of occupation, and thus represents a departure from Article 43 of the Hague Regulations, rather than a more precise and detailed expression of it.

The first question that comes to mind from reading the text is the apparent lack of reference to nonpenal legislation. The heading of Article 64, and its first paragraph, refer to "penal laws." Similarly, the jurisdiction of local tribunals is to be retained with respect to "offenses covered by the said laws." And what about nonpenal laws? And what about the jurisdiction of courts in civil matters? The Red Cross commentary explains that express reference was made only to penal laws, and not to the civil law, simply because the penal laws "had not been sufficiently observed during past conflicts; [and] there is no reason to infer *a contrario* that the occupation authorities are not also bound to respect the civil law of the country, or even its constitution."[164] This explanation could hardly satisfy the reader of previous chapters: the infringments of international limitations concerning the occupant's legislative powers extended during the war also, if not primarily, to nonpenal legislation.

Is Article 64 silent about nonpenal legislation? Not at all. While the first paragraph of Article 64 commands respect for existing (penal) law, the second paragraph defines the conditions under which the occupant is entitled to change local law. This second paragraph contains no qualification as to the scope of the relevant laws. It is conspicuous that here the legislative powers are not restricted to penal laws. Under this paragraph, the occupant "may . . . subject the population of the occupied territory to *provisions. . . .*" These provisions can be of a penal character, but they could also be of administrative and even civil character, as long as they are essential to the promotion of the ends that the occupant is empowered and obliged to attain under the convention.[165]

It is not a mere coincidence that the adjective "penal" is missing in the second paragraph. From reading the preparatory documents of Drafting Committee no. 2, one can appreciate that on this very issue a strong debate ensued. The drafting committee could not achieve unanimity on the question of whether or not to add the restrictive adjective "penal" to the noun "provisions" in the second paragraph. Therefore it submitted two versions to vote on. While the minority preferred the addition of the adjective "penal," the majority of delegates voted for the version that referred to "pro-

[163] Pictet, *supra* note 150, at 335.

[164] *Id.*

[165] It seems that the poor description of the article's contents in its title (it refers only to penal legislation), is responsible for the insufficient attention this article has received in legal literature.

visions" with no qualifications.[166] Thus, Article 64 should be read as demanding respect for the existing *penal* laws, but permitting modifications (under certain circumstances, to be elaborated below) in *all* types of laws. This conclusion is the only one possible if we consider Article 64 in the context of the other issues dealt with in the Fourth Geneva Convention. Clearly, it would be wrong to assume that the occupant would not be entitled to modify nonpenal law, which could prevent the provision, *inter alia*, of humane treatment of the population. Support for this interpretation of the occupant's prescriptive powers is found in Article 51, which refers to labor conditions, and which commands that "legislation in force in the occupied territory" be applicable to protected persons assigned to work. The Red Cross commentary reads in this respect:

> This does not mean that working conditions must remain unchanged throughout the period of occupation. The Diplomatic Conference recognized, on the contrary, that labor laws would probably be modified from time to time during the occupation, and that wages would in particular be liable to vary if prices increased. . . .

This view necessarily recognizes the authority to modify nonpenal laws.[167]

The next issue to be explored involves the conditions recognized by Article 64 for the modification of existing laws. While Article 43 of the Hague Regulations demands respect for "the laws in force," without exceptions, paragraph 1 of Article 64 mentions only the penal laws as the objects of the occupant's respect. While the condition for lawful modification of existing law under the Hague version is strongly negative ("unless absolutely prevented"), the Geneva formula is positive and milder: the occupant "may subject . . . to provisions which are essential to enable. . . ." It seems that the later formula conveys a more positive approach toward legal changes. The reason for the more permissive approach of Article 64 toward modification of the local law (as opposed to Article 43 of the Hague Regulations) can again be found by looking at the preparatory work. The original draft suggested by the International Red Cross was minimalistic, and unrealistic in its limitation of the occupant's legislative powers only to the security of its forces and their property.[168] This draft soon came under

---

[166] *See* 3 *Final Record of the Diplomatic Conference of Geneva of 1949*, at 139–40 [hereinafter *Final Record*].

[167] *The Law of Land Warfare* (U.S. Army Field Manual, FM 27–10, 1956) gives a much more accurate title to Article 64, which is incorporated verbatim in the Manual as Section 369. This title, "Local Law and New Legislation," does not confine it to penal matters only. *But cf.* the British military manual, *The Law of War on Land, supra* note 135, at 156, which interprets Article 64 as referring solely to criminal legislation.

[168] Article 55 of the draft states: "The penal laws of the occupied Power shall remain in force and the tribunals thereof shall continue to function in respect of all offenses covered by said laws.

attack. While discussing the limits on the occupant's prescriptive powers, the U.S. delegation suggested a text that admitted virtually no limitations to the occupant's discretion:

> *Until changed by the Occupying Power*, the penal laws of the occupied territory shall remain in force and the tribunals thereof shall continue to function in respect of all offenses covered by the said laws.[169]

As the U.S. delegate explained, this suggestion "was prompted by the experience of the American authorities at the time of the occupation of Germany."[170] This suggestion was criticized, *inter alia*, by the USSR delegation as "greatly exceed[ing] the limited right laid down in the Hague Regulations."[171]

As it turned out, the British suggestion was the closest to the final version.[172] The weaker European countries of Belgium and the Netherlands, in keeping with their almost traditional role as representatives of potentially occupied states,[173] appreciated that they could not overcome the stronger nations' wish to increase the occupant's power. Instead of insisting on rephrasing Article 64, they concentrated their efforts on the retention of the Hague Regulations and the clarification of the relationship between the older regulations and the new convention.[174] Indeed, largely through their efforts, it was decided not to relinquish the Hague Regulations altogether, as the original draft had called for.[175] It seems, however, that despite these efforts, the Hague Regulations were replaced, at least with respect to the prescriptive powers of the occupant, by the new Geneva rules.[176]

"The occupying Power may, however, subject the population of the occupied territory to provisions intended to assure the security of the members and property of the forces or administration of the occupying Power, and likewise of the establishments used by the said forces and administration." 1 *Final Record, supra* note 166, at 122.

[169] 3 *id.* at 139 (my emphasis).

[170] 2A *id.* at 670.

[171] *Id.*

[172] For the text of the British suggestion, *see* 3 *id.* at 139.

[173] For their role in the Hague peace conferences, *see supra* Chapter 2, text accompanying note 22.

[174] *See* 2A *Final Record, supra* note 166, at 672 (General Schepers of the Netherlands) ("If Article 55 [the initial number of Article 64] was adopted, what would remain of Article 43 of the Hague Regulation[s] . . . ? It was inadmissible that the new Convention should overrule an existing convention of wider scope."). *See also* the position of Monaco and Norway, *id.* at 670–71. The discussion soon involved the relationship between the two conventions, and the representative of Belgium suggested a version close to the final version of Article 154, which declared the Fourth Geneva Convention as supplementary to the Hague law.

[175] Initially, the Geneva Convention was intended to replace the provisions of the Hague Regulations. *See id.* at 675–76.

[176] Article 154, entitled "Relation with the Hague Conventions," provides that for parties

The major improvement of the Geneva formula over Article 43 of the Hague Regulations, also in the direction of increasing the occupant's powers, was the recognition of the power and the duty of the occupant to modify the existing law "to fulfil its obligations under the present Convention." The other two grants of prescriptive powers—for the maintenance of orderly government and the security of the occupant's forces—had already been recognized in international law. The improvement over the Hague Regulations consisted of a set of internationally accepted guidelines for the modification process, guidelines that the Hague Regulations had failed to address.

The duties of the occupant under the Fourth Geneva Convention are, indeed, numerous, and as a result, the occupant's legislative powers are wide, but at the same time more clearly defined. A synopsis of these duties will demonstrate this point: Article 27 postulates the duty of the occupant to ensure the humane treatment of protected persons, without discriminating among them, and to respect, among other things, the protected persons' honor, family rights, religious convictions and practices, and manners and customs.[177] Article 50 requires the occupant to facilitate the proper working of all institutions devoted to the care and education of children. Article 51 prescribes detailed provisions regarding labor conditions. Article 52 prohibits all measures aiming at creating unemployment or restrictions of job opportunities in the occupied territory for the purpose of inducing local workers to work for the occupying power. Article 55 imposes on the occupant the duty to ensure the food and medical supplies of the population, and Article 56 requires the occupant to ensure and maintain the medical and hospital establishments and services and public health and hygiene. In case of inadequate supply of the abovementioned needs, the occupant is required in Article 59 to agree to relief schemes and to facilitate them by all means at its disposal.

---

to both Hague and Geneva Conventions, the Geneva Convention "shall be supplementary to" the Hague Regulations. But since the Geneva law comprehensively discusses the issues concerning the prescriptive powers of the occupant, it replaces the relevant Hague rules. *See* Pictet, *supra* note 150, 614, stating that "when a State is party to the Fourth Geneva Convention of 1949, it is almost superfluous to enquire whether it is also bound by the Fourth Hague Convention of 1907 or the Second of 1899."

[177] Paragraph 3 of Article 27 states: "Without prejudice to the provisions relating to their state of health, age and sex, all protected persons shall be treated with the same consideration . . . without any adverse distinction based, in particular, on race, religion or political opinion." This duty would empower and oblige the occupant to abolish discriminating laws similar to those enacted by Nazi Germany. However, it is worth noting that a suggestion by the Mexican delegate to prescribe a more detailed definition of human rights was not accepted. That suggestion was to adopt "a wording to the effect that the Occupying Power could only modify the legislation of an occupied territory if the legislation in question violated the principles of the 'Universal Declaration of the Rights of Man'." 2A *Final Record, supra* note 166, at 671.

These "very extensive and complex"[178] prescriptive powers are restricted by some general safeguards. Penal provisions should, before coming into force, be published and brought to the knowledge of the inhabitants in their own language, and they must not be retroactive (Article 65); the military penal law should be enforced only in "properly constituted, non-political military courts" (Article 66); the penal provisions should be "in accordance with general principles of law, in particular the principle that the penalty shall be proportionate to the offence" (Article 67); and the death penalty is prohibited except for certain enumerated exceptions (Article 68).[179]

The Contribution of the Fourth Geneva Convention to the Law of Occupation

The contribution of the Fourth Geneva Convention to the law of occupation is significant in two related matters. First, it delineates a bill of rights for the occupied population, a set of internationally approved guidelines for the lawful administration of occupied territories. Second, it shifts the emphasis from political elites to peoples.

The first element, the bill of rights, is a major improvement over the Hague Regulations and the vague commands of its Article 43. Yet the guarantees inscribed in it are minimal. The commands of the Fourth Geneva Convention do not, for example, direct the occupant to treat the occupied people with standards similar to the ones employed for its own nationals. Moreover, the guidelines of the Fourth Geneva Convention stop short of requiring the occupant to develop (not just maintain) the economic, social, and educational infrastructures. In a protracted occupation, this restriction might lead to stagnation, and consequently to the impoverishment and backwardness of the occupied community. Finally, Article 64 does not provide a clear proposition for balancing the conflicting interests of the parties involved in the occupation: the needs of the population on the one hand and the security of the occupation forces on the other. These two concerns should have equal weight, but realistically, one cannot expect the occupant, who is entrusted with the discretion to balance the conflicting interests, to compromise its security interests in favor of the interests of the population.

The second innovation of the Fourth Geneva Convention is the shift of attention from governments to the population. One could explain this em-

---

[178] This is Pictet's remark. Pictet, *supra* note 150, at 337.

[179] Further limitations regarding the criminal procedure and the treatment of detainees are prescribed in Articles 69–78.

phasis by the general structure of the convention, and its aim of protecting civilian persons in times of war. Thus, one could argue, this should be interpreted as changing the emphasis of the traditional law of occupation by defining the interests of political elites as secondary to the interests of the population. While this reasoning is plausible, it fails to account for the fact that the very decision to dedicate the Fourth Geneva Convention to persons and not to governments signified a growing awareness in international law of the idea that peoples are not merely the resources of states, but rather that they are worthy of being the subjects of international norms. This general awareness was bound to find its way into the law of occupation, and diminish the claim of ousted elites to return to areas that they had controlled before the occupation but in which they did not continue to enjoy the support of the indigenous population. The Fourth Geneva Convention is an important first step in this direction.

Interestingly enough, the provisions of the Fourth Geneva Convention regarding occupation have not been regarded as innovative. Rather, it has been generally held that the Geneva rules were in essence little more than a repetition of the Hague Regulations.[180] Municipal courts that adjudicated matters concerning occupied territories continued to refer only to the Hague Regulations.[181] Probably because of the poor formulation of Article 64, its relevance was lost on international scholars, and Article 43 of the Hague Regulations continued to provide the framework for discussing the occupant's prescriptive powers.[182]

[180] *See, e.g.*, Pictet, *supra* note 150, at 335, 614, 617; Greenspan, *supra* note 135, at 226; A. Gerson, *Israel, the West Bank and International Law* 7 (1977).

[181] *See, e.g., Aboitz and Co. v. Price*, 99 F. Supp. 602 (D. Utah 1951). Similar disregard of Article 64 was shown by scholars who elaborated on the jurisprudence of the courts in these issues. *See, e.g.*, Morgenstern, *supra* note 37. McNair and Watts, *The Legal Effects of War* 369 n.6 (4th ed. 1966), give only scant attention to Article 64.

[182] Some scholars refer to Article 64 as defining the limits of only penal legislation. *See, e.g.*, Greenspan, *supra* note 135, at 226). Others fail to mention the article entirely. G. von Glahn's, *The Occupation of Enemy Territory* (1957), chapter on laws under military occupation refers to the article only in a footnote, without elaborating on it.

5

The Israeli Occupation of the Golan Heights, the West Bank, Gaza, and Sinai

THE LAW of occupation continued to undergo changes in the post–World War II era. The numerous wars that have taken place since have brought about many new instances of occupation. Generally it can be said that the law of occupation has become more complex because of the practice of occupants and the reactions thereto, and because of the new instruments that have been adopted in various international forums, with or without immediate relation to those new situations. The principles of self-determination and self-rule (decolonization) took on a larger significance in the postwar era, and have had an impact on the law of occupation. If the Hague law dealt with the relations between governments, and the Geneva law focused on the welfare of individuals, the modern law of occupation has to consider also the claims of peoples as distinct subjects of international law.

In addition, the issue of enforcing the law of occupation on the recalcitrant occupant has become more problematic than ever before. The constraints embodied in the Hague Regulations and the Fourth Geneva Convention were not respected by the majority of contemporary occupants. Most of the post–World War II occupations were not administered according to the principles of the law of occupation; rather, most occupants asserted claims for exclusive control, through annexations or through the establishment of secessionist states. As a result of these factors, the law of occupation nowadays faces a double challenge: a challenge to the principles that underlie the laws of occupation, and a challenge to their enforceability.

This chapter outlines some aspects of the Israeli administration in the territories occupied during the June 1967 war. This occupation is unique from two important aspects. First, this is the only occupation since World War II in which a military power has established a distinct military government over occupied areas in accordance with the framework of the law of occupation. All other modern occupants who have assumed control over a foreign territory have rejected this body of laws as inapplicable and irrelevant. Second, the Israeli occupation has been prolonged; it has lasted for over two decades as of 1992. This length of time enables us to assess various problems encountered during occupation, and also to appraise whether the law of occupation should be modified to accommodate long-term occupations, and if so, how. After outlining the legal framework of the administration of the Israeli-occupied territories, I shall examine in more detail the ensuing economic integration between Israel and these territories. Lastly, I shall refer to the problem of prolonged occupation, as reflected in the practice of the administration, the jurisprudence of the Israeli Supreme Court, and the writing of commentators.

The Applicability of the Law of Occupation to the Israeli-Occupied Territories: Theory and Practice

Israel gained control over various territorial units in the June 1967 war. They differed from one another in their geographic and demographic conditions, as well as in their legal status. The Golan Heights, previously part of Syria, a high plateau overlooking the Israeli Upper Jordan Valley and the Sea of Galilee, was evacuated by the great majority of its inhabitants during the war. The Sinai peninsula, a vast, sparsely populated desert, was under Egyptian sovereignty. The densely populated Gaza Strip had been under Egyptian military administration from 1948 until 1967. Egypt never claimed any title over Gaza, nor did it express any intention to annex it. Rather, Gaza retained its distinct status as part of the former British Mandate of Palestine.[1] The so-called West Bank (Judea and Samaria, as the region is officially called in Israel, following the region's biblical names) was the only territory whose status had been disputed prior to the Israeli occupation. Since 1948 it had been under Jordanian administration, and Jordan claimed to have annexed it in 1950. This purported annexation was, however, widely regarded as illegal and void, by the Arab League and others, and was recognized only by Britain, Iraq, and Pakistan.[2] Thus, in contrast to the Golan Heights and Sinai, which were under the sovereignty of existing states, neither the West Bank nor Gaza had in 1967 a government that could validly claim to represent its interests as its sovereign.

---

[1] On the legal status of that area until 1967, *see* Farhi, *On the Legal Status of the Gaza Strip, in* 1 *Military Government in the Territories Administered by Israel 1967–1980—The Legal Aspects* 61 (M. Shamgar ed., 1982) [hereinafter Shamgar, *Military Government*].

[2] The Arab League censured Jordan for this act, and decided to treat Jordan's status in the West Bank (including East Jerusalem) as that of a "trustee," pending a future settlement. On this annexation and the reactions thereto *see* Blum, *The Missing Reversioner: Reflections on the Status of Judea and Samaria*, 3 ISLR 279, 289–93 (1968); A. Gerson, *Israel, the West Bank and International Law* 77–78 (1977); Malanczuk, *Israel: Status, Territory and Occupied Territories, in* 12 EPIL 149, 171 (1990).

Theoretical Applicability

THE WEST BANK AND GAZA

Although the framework of the military administration of the West Bank and Gaza (and during the first fifteen years of occupation, also of the Golan Heights and Sinai) followed the dictates of the Hague Regulations, their de jure applicability to the territories was never officially recognized by the Israeli government. Neither was the Fourth Geneva Convention formally recognized as applicable to the territories. It was the unique status of the West Bank and Gaza—territories with no existing sovereign governments—that gave rise to this official attitude.

In 1971, Meir Shamgar, then Israel's attorney general, asserted the Israeli position with respect to the applicability of the Fourth Geneva Convention: Israel would not acknowledge the de jure applicability of the Fourth Geneva Convention, but would observe "its humanitarian provisions."[3] The stated reason was that under the second paragraph of Article 2 (common to all the Geneva conventions of 1949), the conventions apply only to "occupation of the territory *of a High Contracting Party*" (my emphasis); Israel never recognized that the West Bank and Gaza were territories of Jordan and Egypt, respectively; the formal recognition of the applicability of the Fourth Geneva Convention might therefore have implied a recognition of the former administrations' sovereignty.[4]

This position has been severely criticized by the United Nations, the International Commission of the Red Cross, states, and scholars.[5] Accord-

---

[3] Shamgar, *The Observance of International Law in the Administered Territories*, 1 IYHR 262 (1971). Israel never officially enumerated the provisions it regarded as "humanitarian." Shamgar did not refer at that point to the applicability of the Hague Regulations. Nine years later, in *Legal Concepts and Problems of the Israeli Military Government—The Initial Stage*, *in* Shamgar, *supra* note 1, at 13, 48 [hereinafter Shamgar, *Legal Concepts*], he mentioned that the Hague Regulations and customary law were also observed only on a de facto basis. As Professor Bar-Yaacov points out, a reservation as to the applicability of the Hague Regulations, similar to that made with respect to the Fourth Geneva Convention, could have been made by emphasizing the title of Section III, which mentions the territory "of the Hostile State," the reference in Article 43 to the "legitimate power," and other provisions. Bar-Yaacov, *The Applicability of the Laws of War to Judea and Samaria (the West Bank) and the Gaza Strip*, 24 ISLR 485, 492–93 (1990). However, in contrast to the case of the Geneva Convention, such an *explicit* argument was never officially offered.

[4] *See* Shamgar, *Legal Concepts, supra* note 3, at 34. On the internal Israeli politics concerning the status of the territories, *see* Rubinstein, *The Changing Status of the "Territories" (West Bank and Gaza): From Escrow to Legal Mongrel*, 8 Tel-Aviv U. Studies in Law 59 (1988).

[5] *See, e.g.*, Dinstein, *The International Law of Belligerent Occupation and Human Rights*, 8 IYHR 104, 107 (1978) [hereinafter Dinstein, *Human Rights*] (the Israeli government's position "is based on dubious legal grounds, considering that the Fourth Convention does not make its applicability conditional on recognition of titles"). Two recent critical discussions of

ing to these, the Israeli concern for an implied recognition of sovereignty was exaggerated, since the applicability of the Geneva conventions to territories occupied during wars could and should have been explained as mandated by the *first* paragraph of common Article 2, which does not link a territory to a High Contracting Power,[6] and therefore it would have been difficult to infer recognition of sovereignty from the decision to apply the Geneva conventions. This concern was, in any case, irrelevant to the occupations of Sinai, the Golan Heights, and even Gaza (before and after the 1979 peace treaty), since no questions of sovereignty were raised with respect to them (Israel did not challenge Egypt's title to Sinai or Syria's to the Golan Heights, and Egypt never claimed sovereignty over the Gaza Strip).

The Israeli interpretation of the conditions for the applicability of the Fourth Geneva Convention seems curious when compared with the only implicit rejection of the Hague Regulations' applicability (and, as will be explained below, with the Israeli Supreme Court's recognition of the applicability of the Hague law). As noted above, the characteristic difference between these two instruments lies in their different scope: while the Hague Regulations primarily protect governmental interests, the Fourth Geneva Convention caters to the interests of individuals under foreign rule (Article 4). Therefore, if the special status of the West Bank and Gaza should have carried any legal effects, the natural target would have been the Hague Regulations, not the Fourth Geneva Convention. Indeed, as Allan Gerson argues, in view of Jordan's lack of title over the West Bank, Israel was not required to protect Jordanian interests under the Hague Regulations.[7] Similarly, Israel was not required to protect Egyptian interests in the Gaza Strip. But when it comes to the interests of *individuals* under occupation, the application of the Fourth Geneva Convention is warranted, notwithstanding conflicting claims of sovereignty.

As of 1992, the Israeli Supreme Court has long refrained from explicitly declaring the de jure applicability of the law of occupation to the territories. The Israeli government never raised its reservation before the Court, and thus the Court did not find it necessary to resolve the matter,[8] although

---

the Israeli claim and the reactions thereto appear in Bar-Yaacov, *supra* note 3, at 485–94, and Roberts, *Prolonged Military Occupation: The Israeli-Occupied Territories since 1967*, 84 AJIL 44, 62–66 (1990).

[6] According to the first paragraph, the convention "shall apply to all cases of declared war or of any other armed conflict. . . ."

[7] Gerson, *supra* note 2, at 81–82 (Gerson describes Israel's status as that of "trustee-occupant").

[8] For the Court's refusal to adjudicate this issue, *see Ayyub v. Minister of Defence*, 33 (2) PD 113, 127 (1979) (the "Beith-El case"), *translated in Military Government, supra* note 1, at 371; *Douykat v. Government of Israel*, 34 (1) PD 1, 13 (1979) (the "Elon-Moreh case"), *translated in Military Government, supra* note 1, at 404). According to some Justices' comments,

it did recognize the de facto applicability of the Hague Regulations to the West Bank and Gaza.[9] In 1988, however, the question of de jure applicability came squarely before the Court, when a petitioner argued that with the signature of the 1979 Peace Treaty with Egypt, the Israeli military administration in the Gaza Strip had ended, and therefore the local commander lacked powers to order the petitioner's deportation.[10] Now acting as the president of the Court, Justice Meir Shamgar rejected this claim, holding that the law of occupation did apply to the Gaza Strip, simply because Israel continued to control the area.[11] The necessary and sufficient condition for that law's applicability, according to Justice Shamgar, was effective control over the territory. This reasoning, which is indeed supported by many authorities,[12] was not compatible with the government's equivocal stance regarding the applicability of the Hague Regulations to the territories. Moreover, it questioned the government's claim with respect to the applicability of the Fourth Geneva Convention. For if in customary law what matters is effective control, and the legal status of the territory is never relevant, why did it supposedly become so relevant in the eyes of the drafters of the Fourth Geneva Convention, who decided, per the Israeli government's argument, to qualify its applicability? The argument does not offer a satisfactory answer. It seems therefore, that with this case the Israeli Supreme Court came as close as ever to a repudiation of the government's internationally criticized interpretation. The Court stopped short of referring explicitly to the Israeli official position, and did not make the link between its holding and the claim of the nonapplicability of the

---

had the government raised its claim in Court, the Court would have ruled the issue not justiciable. *Douykat, id.* at 29; *Ruweidi v. Military Court in the Hebron District,* 24 (2) PD 419, 423 (1969).

[9] *See Jama'iat Iscan v. Commander of the IDF in Judea and Samaria,* 37 (4) PD 785, 792 (1983) ("Judea and Samaria [the West Bank] are administered by Israel by way of 'belligerent occupation'. . . . The Military Commander's powers and duties stem from the norms of public international law, whose concern is belligerent occupation."). The Court reserved the question of the applicability of the Fourth Geneva Convention. *Id.* at 793.

[10] *Affu v. Commander of the IDF Forces in the West Bank,* 42 (2) PD 4, 49 (1988), *translated in* 29 ILM 139 (1990). According to the 1978 Camp David accords, negotiations were to be held regarding the future status of the Gaza Strip as well as the West Bank.

[11] *Id.* at 49–50 ("As long as the military power effectively controls an area, the laws of war will apply to its actions . . . despite the signature of the Peace Treaty, as long as the military administration did not leave the area of the Gaza region, and as long as the relevant parties have not agreed otherwise, the respondent continues to hold the area under belligerent occupation, and is subject to the customary international laws applicable in times of war").

[12] *See supra* note 5; specifically regarding the Gaza Strip, *see* Roberts, *supra* note 5, at 65. *But cf.* Dinstein, *The Israeli Supreme Court and the Law of Belligerent Occupation: Reunification of Families,* 18 IYHR 173, 174 (1988); *id., Deportations from Administered Territories,* 13 Tel Aviv U. L. Rev. 403, 415 (1988) (in Hebrew), who holds that military occupation is contingent on a continuing state of war, and that on the basis of the Peace Treaty with Egypt, Israel should end the military administration, but retain the Israeli civil administration.

Fourth Convention.[13] In any case, as a practical result of the Israeli Supreme Court's jurisprudence, the official Israeli refusal to recognize the applicability of the law of occupation did not prove a stumbling block to judicial review: The Hague Regulations were applied by the Court without regard to the territories' formal status, whereas the Geneva law cannot be conclusive anyhow. Even if the Fourth Geneva Convention applied to the territories, it would not have been enforceable in Israeli courts, since, as interpreted by the Supreme Court, the Fourth Geneva Convention constitutes treaty law as opposed to customary law, and as such, it is not part of the Israeli internal law and thus is not justiciable in Israeli courts.[14]

As of 1992, the legal status of the West Bank and Gaza has not changed since these areas were first occupied in June 1967. The Peace Treaty with Egypt did not, and indeed could not, produce changes in the status of the Gaza Strip, nor did it effect a change in the structure of the Israeli administration in the Gaza Strip.

On July 31, 1988, Jordan renounced its claim for sovereignty over the West Bank, when King Hussein declared Jordan's acceptance of the wishes of the Palestinian people to secede.[15] However, aside from the political significance of this announcement, its international legal implications were necessarily minimal. Similarly of little legal significance was the proclamation of the State of Palestine by the Palestine National Council on November 15, 1988, because this entity failed to qualify as a state under international law.[16]

EAST JERUSALEM

On June 28, 1967, the Israeli government applied the Israeli "law, jurisdiction and administration" over East Jerusalem, and put it under the existing Israeli municipality of West Jerusalem.[17] To the international community, the act was explained not as an annexation, but rather as an administrative measure aimed at equalizing the municipal services to all the residents of the single municipal area and at the protection of the Holy Places.[18] The

[13] In a previous decision (January 11, 1987), Justice Shamgar reiterated with approval (although in a dictum) the government's interpretation of Article 2 of the Fourth Geneva Convention. *Shaheen et al. v. Commander of the IDF in the Judea and Samaria Region et al.*, 41 PD 197, 207–8 (1987).

[14] *See infra* text accompanying notes 57–58.

[15] N.Y. Times, August 1, 1988, at A1, col. 6; 28 ILM 1637 (1988).

[16] Crawford, *The Creation of the State of Palestine: Too Much too Soon?* 1/2 European J. Int'l L. 307 (1990); Malanczuk, *supra* note 2, at 173; van de Craen, *Palestine, in* 12 EPIL 275, 279 (1990).

[17] Law and Administration Order [no. 1], 5727–1967.

[18] "The term 'annexation' is out of place," wrote the Israeli minister of foreign affairs to the Secretary General of the United Nations. "The measures adopted relate to the integration of Jerusalem in the administrative and municipal spheres, and furnish legal basis for protection of the Holy Places." July 10, 1967, UN Doc. S/8052 (1967).

Israeli Supreme Court stopped short of interpreting the order as effecting annexation. As the court reasoned, "The mere application of an Israeli norm to an area situated outside Israel does not necessarily make that area a part of Israel."[19] The adoption in 1980 of the Basic Law: Jerusalem the Capital of Israel, which asserted that "[u]nified Jerusalem is the capital of Israel," did not create any legal change in the internal legal situation in East Jerusalem, but it did express unequivocally Israel's claim to the right to exercise its sovereignty over the area.

Internationally, both measures were understood as attempts to annex East Jerusalem, and were criticized accordingly. The UN Security Council and General Assembly considered the 1967 act "invalid."[20] The Security Council condemned the 1980 Basic Law as a "violation of international law," in addition to its being "null and void," and decided not to recognize it, and to continue to deem Israel the occupant of the area.[21]

For the purposes of the law of occupation, it is sufficient to note, without getting into the details of the arguments that have been presented concerning the merits of Israel's claim to title over East Jerusalem,[22] that under Article 47 of the Fourth Geneva Convention, the law of occupation continues to apply even if the annexation was legally effective.[23] Even if an occupant asserts a reasonable—albeit contested—claim for sovereignty, it is not allowed to use its effective control to have its claim prevail. A different view would undermine the entire structure that the law of occupation establishes for the protection of occupied communities.[24]

THE GOLAN HEIGHTS

The analysis of the legality of the application of Israeli law to the Golan Heights is similar to the case of East Jerusalem. In December 1981, the

[19] *Kanj Abu Salakh v. Minister of Interior*, 37 (2) PD 718 (1983) (approving Justice Cohen's opinion in *Ruweidi, supra* note 8). *But cf.* Justice Kahan's opinion in *Ruweidi*, holding the 1967 declaration as affecting annexation.

[20] *See* Security Council Resolutions 252 (1967); 267 (1969); 298 (1971); 446 (1979); 445 (1980); General Assembly Resolutions 2253 (ES-V)(1967); 2254 (ES-V)(1967); 31/106A (1976); 33/113 (1978).

[21] Security Council Resolution 478 (1980). *See also* General Assembly Resolutions 36/120E (1981); 37/123C (1982); 39/146C (1984).

[22] For the opinion that Israel has the right to declare its sovereignty over East Jerusalem and other areas in the West Bank and Gaza, *see, e.g.*, Blum, *supra* note 2. For the latest restatement of this claim, *see* Rostow, Letter to the Editor, 84 AJIL 717 (1990). These arguments have been widely contested. *See, e.g.*, Dinstein, *Zion Shall Be Redeemed by International Law*, 27 *Hapraklit* 5 (1971) (in Hebrew); E. Cohen, *Human Rights in the Israeli-Occupied Territories 1967–1982*, at 43 (1985).

[23] Last sentence of the article (the text appears above, in Chapter 4, near note 156).

[24] Carroll, *The Israeli Demolition of Palestinian Houses in the Occupied Territories: An Analysis of Its Legality in International Law*, 11 Michigan J. Int'l L. 1195, 1201–2 (1990) ("The humanitarian protections provided by the drafters of the Fourth Convention cannot be allowed to be negated by a legal dispute involving the sovereign status of the Occupied Territories").

Israeli Knesset adopted a law applying the Israeli "law, jurisdiction and administration" to the Golan Heights.[25] The significance of this law was mainly political, since the Israeli administrative and legal systems had effectively been introduced in the Golan area through military enactments in 1970. As in the case of the 1967 application of the law to East Jerusalem, the text was vague enough to permit the interpretation that the measure did not effect the formal annexation of the area into Israel.[26] Nevertheless, the measure was internationally received as a purported annexation, and consequently was condemned as "null and void,"[27] and even as an "act of aggression."[28]

De Facto Application

Despite the distinctions between the occupied areas, and the legal arguments about their status, the type of governance adopted in all of them was the same: military government according to the principles of the Hague Regulations and the humanitarian provisions of the Fourth Geneva Convention.[29] A separate military administration was established for each region. The military administrations were based on the law in force immediately prior to the occupation. The "Proclamation concerning Law and Administration (no. 2)" of June 7, 1967, issued by the military commander of the West Bank declared:

> The law in existence in the Region on June 7, 1967, shall remain in force, insofar as it does not in any way conflict with the provisions of this Proclamation or any other proclamation or Order which may be issued by me, and subject to modifications resulting from the establishment of government by the Israeli Defence Forces [IDF] in the Region.

Similar proclamations were issued to the other territories. Thus, despite Israel's nonrecognition of the Jordanian annexation of the West Bank, it respected the latter's existing laws in order to maintain public order.[30] Nor were any objections raised regarding the validity of laws passed in the Egyptian-occupied Gaza Strip. During the entire period of occupation,

[25] Section 1 of the Golan Heights Law, 36 L.S.I. (Laws of the State of Israel) 7 (5742–1981/2).

[26] See Kanj Abu Salakh, supra note 19.

[27] Security Council Resolution 497 (1981).

[28] General Assembly Resolutions 36/226A (1981); 39/146A (1984).

[29] On the early stages of the occupation, see Shamgar, Legal Concepts, supra note 3. On the legal system in the West Bank during the first decade, see Drori, The Legal System in Judea and Samaria: A Review of the Previous Decade with a Glance at the Future, 8 IYHR 144 (1978).

[30] Ha'etzni v. State of Israel (Minister of Defence) et al., 34 (3) PD 595 (1980).

this basic principle of retention of preoccupation law, subject to the occupant's power under the Hague Regulations to modify it from time to time, has been adhered to. The only significant exception to this rule was in the Golan Heights, where according to the Israeli military administration, the lack of local executive and judicial personnel, as well as of lawyers and law-books, necessitated the introduction of the Israeli law (subject to security enactments) and judicial system to replace the Syrian legal system.[31]

LEGISLATION

The preoccupation local law formed the second tier of the two-tiered legal system of the territories. It was subordinate to the primary tier, which was the legislation of the military administration, named "security enactments." The system was immune to outside influence: new laws introduced by the enemy government were not respected.[32] The first tier consisted of various types of enactments, all which were organized in an internal hierarchy. This hierarchy was, however, not organized according to the type of enactment (order, regulation, announcement, license, etc.), but according to the rank of the promulgator: the commander of the Israeli Defence Forces in the region was empowered to enact primary legislation; other army commanders, and since 1981 the head of the civil administration,[33] issued secondary enactments.

The Israeli *Manual for the Military Advocate in Military Government* instructed the authorities on how to enact orders.[34] There were issues of form, according to which every enactment must be translated into Arabic, must carry a consecutive number, and must be published in an official series available to the general public. There were also issues of substance, which determined, *inter alia*, that the enactments could not be inconsistent

---

[31] *See* Order Concerning Courts (Ramat Hagolan [the Golan Heights]) (no. 273) (1970), *reproduced and translated in Military Government, supra* note 1, appendix C, no. 3, at 453. Similar situations, with similar solutions, occurred in British-occupied Cyrenaica, *see supra* Chapter 4), and British-occupied Iraq after World War I, *see* G. Bell, *Review of the Civil Administration in Mesopotamia*, 1920, Cmd 1061.

[32] The Order Concerning Interpretation (the West Bank) (no. 130), 5727–1967, paragraph 8, provides that "security enactments supersede any law [that is, any law effective in the region on the eve of the occupation (paragraph 1 (8))] even if the former does not explicitly nullify the latter." Security enactments may modify conflicting local laws even implicitly: *Khassan v. Commander of the IDF in Judea and Samaria*, 39 (3) PD 245 (1985). In the discussion that follows I shall refer to orders that deal primarily with the situation in the West Bank. The situation in the Gaza Strip is essentially similar, and important variances from the situation concerning the West Bank will be indicated.

[33] Order Concerning the Establishment of the Civil Administration (Judea and Samaria) (no. 947), 5742–1981, paragraph 4.

[34] Some of the rules translated into English were reproduced in Shamgar's article, *Legal Concepts, supra* note 3, at 27–31.

with international law (with "special attention being paid to the norms of the Hague Regulations and the Fourth Geneva Convention"),[35] and that they could not be retroactive. In the basic statement that established the military government, the Promulgation Concerning Law and Administration (the West Bank Region) (no. 2), 5727–1967, the military commander announced that the publication of enactments could be made "in any manner I may deem fit."[36] The practice, however, was more or less in line with the manual's instructions. The various instruments were first circulated as stenciled copies to those who appeared on the mailing list of the authorities (anyone could ask to be placed on the list). At a later stage, the instruments were published in pamphlets.[37]

MILITARY, ADMINISTRATIVE, AND LOCAL COURTS

The military administration set up military courts, which had exclusive jurisdiction to adjudicate infringements of security legislation, especially violations of the Security Code which defined offenses against the occupation forces. The military courts sat in panels of three army officers, at least one of them a lawyer, all appointed by the area commander on the recommendation of the IDF's advocate-general.[38] Following the Israeli Supreme Court's recommendation,[39] a military court of appeals was established in April 1989. In addition to the recent appeals procedure, convictions could be contested through petitions.[40]

A 1988 amendment to the Security Code added a provision to the effect that "[t]hose who exercise judicial functions are, in judicial proceedings, subordinate to nothing but the law [the local laws[41]] and the security en-

---

[35] *See* rule no. 3 in *id.* at 30.

[36] Paragraph 6 of the promulgation.

[37] A special order controls the possibility of different versions in the two modes of publication: Order Concerning the Compilation of Promulgations (The West Bank) (no. 111), 5727–1967. Not all the enactments are published in this way. Some enactments, including those concerning the Jewish settlements, which will be described below, do not appear in the pamphlets. In some other cases, maps that had formed an integral part of certain orders were not attached.

[38] There may also be adjudications by a single judge (an officer with legal training). The latter has the same jurisdiction that the panel has, but the punishment is limited to five years maximum imprisonment (paragraph 50).

[39] *Arjub et al. v. Commander of IDF Forces in Judea and Samaria et al.*, 42 (1) PD 353 (1988).

[40] The petition is submitted to the military commander (if the judgment was rendered by a panel) or the area commander (if a single judge gave the decision). These officials may pardon the petitioner, mitigate his or her sentence, order a new trial, or, since 1988, order a retrial (the discretion to order a retrial is not limited).

[41] The "law" is defined in the Order Concerning Interpretation as "an enactment of a legislative body which was effective in the area on the eve of [June 7, 1967], including every rule issued pursuant to such an enactment, and excluding security enactments."

actments."[42] This provision, in addition to formally ensuring the impartiality of the military judges, had another outcome: it blocked in these tribunals the opportunity to invoke international law against the authorities.[43]

In addition to the military courts, other tribunals were set up. Prominent among them was the Appeals Committee. This institution had a modest beginning as a tribunal that handled appeals against decisions regarding abandoned property,[44] and property of the local government.[45] As more and more issues subsequently were allocated to this tribunal, it gradually became the administrative court of the occupation authorities, where many administrative acts could be challenged.[46] It could issue subpoenas,[47] and later was given power to issue injunctions.[48] Once this committee had become an institutionalized tribunal, the administration began to allocate some adjudicatory functions to special committees.[49]

Formally, the members of the committee were independent of the administration.[50] In fact, however, they were appointed by the area commander, and could be dismissed by him.[51] They sat in panels of three. At least one of them was required to have legal training. The outcome of the proceedings was not a judgment that was binding on the authorities, but a recommendation that the area commander could accept or reject. The Israeli Supreme Court strictly enforced principles of due process with regard to the proceedings of these committees,[52] but unless a committee acted *ultra vires* the Court was unlikely to hear a petition against its deci-

[42] Paragraph 7A, February 3, 1988.

[43] In the past, some panels of the military courts did hear arguments that military acts were contrary to international law. On the other hand, other panels were of the opinion that they did not have jurisdiction to entertain such claims. See Sommer, *Eppur si applica—The Geneva Convention (IV) and the Israeli Law*, 11 Tel-Aviv U. L. Rev. 263, 269–70 (1986) (in Hebrew); M. Drori, *The Legislation in the Area of Judea and Samaria* 66–72 (1975). Since there was no military court of appeal, the question remained open until finally resolved by legislative fiat.

[44] Order Concerning Abandoned Property (Private Property) (Judea and Samaria) (no. 58), 5727–1967.

[45] Order Concerning Appeals Committees (the West Bank Region) (no. 172), 5728–1967.

[46] In 1986 the committee published its rules of procedure: Rules Concerning Procedure in Appeals Committees (Judea and Samaria), 5746–1986.

[47] *Id.* at paragraph 8(c).

[48] *Id.* at paragraph 9A, November 1987.

[49] See Order Concerning Supervision over Building (Provisional Rules) (Judea and Samaria) (no. 1153), 5746–1985. Another special appeals committee hears claims against the cancellation, suspension, or nonrenewal of driver or vehicle licenses. Order Concerning the Transportation on Roads (the West Bank) (no. 56), 5727–1967, paragraph 8.

[50] Order Concerning Appeals Committees, *supra* note 45, at paragraph 7.

[51] *Id.* at paragraph 2.

[52] *Shmalawi v. Appeals Committee*, 39 (4) PD 598 (1985); *Al Nazer v. Commander of Judea and Samaria*, 36 (1) PD 701, 707 (1982).

sion: under principles of the Israeli administrative law, the Court could not replace the committee's discretion with its own. As a result, the existence of the Appeals Committee, and the subsequent enlargement of its jurisdiction, had the effect of limiting the scope of affairs brought to review before the Israeli Supreme Court.

The local courts continued to operate. The occupant did not restrict their jurisdiction except for claims against its own forces.[53] The major change, in the West Bank, was the abolition of resort to the Court of Cassation, which sat in Amman, Jordan, outside the occupied territory.[54]

THE ISRAELI SUPREME COURT

The Israeli Supreme Court in its capacity as the High Court of Justice adjudicates complaints against the Israeli public administration. At the outset, the Court was hesitant to extend its jurisdiction to the acts of the military authorities in the occupied territories, and emphasized the government's acquiescence to having its measures scrutinized by the Court. In subsequent decisions, the Court made it clear that its jurisdiction over occupation measures was mandated by law, and independent of the government's consent.[55]

The Court has declared its competence, under Israeli law, to review the measures of the military administration in the territories in light of the Hague Regulations, as customary international law, and in light of Israeli administrative law.[56] On the other hand, the Court does not view itself as empowered to examine the administration's conduct under the Fourth Geneva Convention. This is not due to doubt as to whether or not the convention applies to the West Bank and Gaza, but because the Court views the convention as constitutive treaty law, and under Israeli law, only customary international law is automatically incorporated into the internal Israeli law.[57] Under the assumption that the Fourth Geneva Convention

[53] The Appeals Claims Committee handles claims for damages done by the military. Order Concerning Claims (Judea and Samaria) (no. 271) (1968).

[54] This measure follows similar acts by the British in Cyrenaica, *see supra* Chapter 4, note 73, and by the Allies in Venezia Giulia in northeastern Italy, *see supra* Chapter 4, note 118.

[55] *Jama'iat Iscan, supra* note 9, at 809–10 ("Now there is no doubt that . . . this court has the right to review [administrative acts in the territories]. It stems from the fact that the military commander and his subordinates are public servants, who perform public duties according to law. . . . Every Israeli soldier carries with him in his knapsack the rules of customary international law and the principles of Israeli administrative law"). *See also Abu-Aita et al. v. Commander of Judea and Samaria et al.*, 37 (2) PD 197 (1983); 7 Selected Judgments of the Supreme Court of Israel, 1, 30 (1983–1987). The court also asserted its jurisdiction with regard to activities in Lebanon during the war there. *Al-Nawar v. Minister of Defence*, 39 (3) PD 449, 461 (1985).

[56] *Abu-Aita, supra* note 55, at 230–31; *Jama'iat Iscan, supra* note 55, at 809–10.

[57] *Ayyub, supra* note 8, at 128; *Douykat, supra* note 8, at 29; and lately, *Affu, supra* note 10,

does not embody customary norms, and the lack of legislation incorporating the convention into Israeli law, the Court is barred from referring to it.[58]

The jurisdiction exercised by the Israeli Supreme Court is unique.[59] Although the legality of occupation measures has been examined by courts on various occasions, in no prior occupation were such measures scrutinized by a home court of the occupant that was competent to prevent them from taking effect.[60] The government's readiness to have its measures adjudicated was explained as being motivated both by humanitarian concerns[61] and by the wish to intensify ties between the local residents and the Israeli system, encouraging them to have faith in the Israeli legal system.[62] The Court was also concerned with humanitarian considerations when it decided to allow petitions of inhabitants of the territories.[63] This was no doubt motivated by a desire on the part of Israel to prove to the occupied population that it was an enlightened occupant, better than their former rulers. This desire is also apparent in other prescriptions, for example, the abolition of capital punishment and the extension of suffrage in municipal elections to women and to men who were not landowners, who had been disenfranchised before. In extending its jurisdiction to the territories, the Supreme Court clearly stated that it would pursue humanitarian concerns, even giving them precedence over traditional international norms that called for the conservation of the *status quo ante*.[64]

Unfortunately, this ideal vision did not persist. Faced with unbridgeable

---

at 67. However, these rulings notwithstanding, the Court has continued to examine acts of the authorities in light of the convention in long dicta. *See, e.g.*, in the case of deportations: *Kawassme v. Minister of Defence*, 35 PD (1) 617, 626–7 (1980), and *Affu*. Two Justices have suggested treating the Geneva Convention as applicable to the extent that the government officially views it as such, that is, as internal self-imposed rules of conduct, or as a unilateral pledge that is binding on the Executive until revoked by it. *Jama'iat Iscan, supra* note 9, at 794 (Barak, J.); *Affu, supra* note 10, at 78 (Bach, J.) (under Israeli administrative law, officials must give reasons for deviating from internal self-imposed rules of conduct).

[58] On the incorporation of international law, and especially the Fourth Geneva Convention, into Israeli law, *see* Lapidoth, *International Law within the Israeli Legal System*, 24 ISLR 451 (1990); Bar-Yaacov, *supra* note 3.

[59] Another way to challenge administrative measures in the territories, under specific security enactments, is through an appeal to the Appeals Committee. See *supra* text accompanying notes 44–48.

[60] One rare exception was a U.S. Supreme Court judgment in 1913 against the U.S. administration of Puerto Rico. *Ochoa v. Hernandez y Morales*, 230 U.S. 139 (1913). This precedent, however, was not followed in subsequent occupations.

[61] This reason was put forward by Shamgar, *Legal Concepts, supra* note 3, at 42.

[62] *See* M. Negbi, *Justice under Occupation* 16–17 (1981) (in Hebrew). The author interviewed Justice Shamgar and others for the purpose of his book.

[63] *Id.* at 21. The author details the recollections of (by then retired) Justice Vitkon.

[64] *See Al-Tali'ah v. Minister of Defence*, 33 (3) PD 505, 512–13 (1979); *Jama'iat Iscan, supra* note 9, at 799–800.

conflicts between Arab and Israeli interests, especially in matters of security and Jewish settlement in the Territories, the Court's decisions were not always conceived as giving equal weight to interests of the occupied community. Indeed, the fact that the Court almost always upheld the administration's security considerations led some to conclude that the Court's principal function was to bestow an aura of legitimacy, in Israeli public opinion, upon the occupation.[65]

One important trait in the Supreme Court's jurisprudence was its stated policy of deference to the discretion of the military authorities whenever the latter invoked security considerations. In such cases, the court's scrutiny was usually confined to an examination of whether the act was *ultra vires*, and whether the reasons cited did not simply hide irrelevant or illegal considerations that were the true or dominant motives.[66] This policy was not unique to matters concerning the occupied territories. It was consistent with the Court's decisions regarding internal Israeli matters that involved claims to security considerations cited by authorities within Israel.[67] But because of the continuing state of war in the region, terrorist activities, and since late 1987, frequent clashes between soldiers and demonstrators, security reasons were much more frequently invoked with respect to measures taken in the territories. Only in two cases—the *Elon Moreh* case and *Electricity Company of East Jerusalem Case (no. 2)*[68]—did the Court declare that security concerns were not the real motives behind the administrative acts and therefore nullify the acts. In both cases, the court learned the real underlying motive from the authority itself. Since the fact-finding procedure in the Israeli Supreme Court when it sits as the High Court of Justice is usually based only on affidavits, it is generally difficult to challenge the motives put forward by the authorities.[69]

---

[65] Shamir, *"Landmark Cases" and the Reproduction of Legitimacy: The Case of Israel's High Court of Justice*, 24 Law and Society Rev. 781 (1990); *id., Legal Discourse, Media Discourse, and Speech Rights: The Shift from Content to Identity—the Case of Israel*, 19 Int'l J. of the Sociology of Law 45 (1991).

[66] *Ayyub, supra* note 8, at 126; *Douykat, supra* note 8, at 20, 21.

[67] *See, e.g., Abu-Gosh v. Military Commander of the Corridor to Jerusalem*, 7 PD 941, 943 (1953).

[68] *Electricity Co. for the District of Jerusalem v. Minister of Energy*, 35 (2) PD 673 (1981).

In *Samara v. the Commander of Judea and Samaria*, 34 (4) PD 1 (1980), the refusal to issue permission for the petitioner's husband to reside in the West Bank was rejected by the Court since the authorities did not claim to have had security reasons for the act. *See id.* at p. 5.

[69] This supervision of the High Court can be further curtailed when the minister of defense issues a Certificate of Privileged Evidence declaring the evidence that formed the basis of the administrative decision privileged for security reasons. In such a case a Justice of the Supreme Court may decide to reveal the evidence, despite the minister's declaration, in cases where the former finds that the interests of justice override the concern that led to the declaration. Evidence Ordinance [new version], paragraph 44A. The tendency to defer to the authority's judgment in security matters would imply that the decision to reveal the evidence despite the

While the Court definitely gave precedence to security considerations, a significant positive outcome of the Court's role should nevertheless be acknowledged. While most of the decisions turned petitions down, some, on crucial issues, were accepted,[70] and in a few others the Court issued recommendations that the administration found hard to resist.[71] In other cases the government reversed its acts in view of a petition.[72] One may assume that the prospects of adjudication by the Court did loom large among the considerations taken by the authorities. During the intifada the Court stood guard to prevent abuses of power by individual members of the security forces,[73] although it did not question the legality of the harsh security measures themselves, such as deportations or the demolition of homes.

With regard to procedural due process in military tribunals in the territories, the Court was strict in insisting that the procedural rights of individuals be respected, whether the tribunal was a military court,[74] the Appeals Committee,[75] or the advisory committee established under the Emergency Regulations of 1945.[76]

When security reasons were not invoked, the Court was able to apply the general criteria of Israeli administrative law, such as the relevance of considerations, impartiality, nondiscrimination, and reasonableness.[77] Ac-

---

stated security interests would take place only where no real security concerns existed and the minister had misused his or her powers. In order to review the merits of a case despite the Certificate, a practice has developed in which the panel reviewing the case examines the privileged evidence ex parte. Zamir, *The Rule of Law and Control of Terrorism*, 8 Tel-Aviv Studies in Law 81, 88–90 (1988).

[70] The most famous case is the Elon Moreh case, *Douykat, supra* note 8, where the Court declared an order seizing private land to establish a settlement illegal. During the intifada, the Court ordered the government to give prior hearing before making decisions about the demolition of houses, a procedure that did not exist under the local emergency regulations. *Civil Rights Association in Israel v. Commander General of the Central Area*, 43 (2) PD 529 (1989).

[71] *See* the recommendation to erect a military court of appeal in *Arjub, supra* note 39.

[72] In July 1991 the authorities decided to abandon a plan to build a cemetery for Israelis on "state lands" in the West Bank near Jerusalem; the Attorney General's office decided that the plan was in violation of international law and therefore there was no prospect of refuting a petition to the Supreme Court. Kol Ha'ir (weekly local newspaper), July 12, 1991.

[73] *See, e.g., Khamdan v. Minister of Defence*, 42 (3) PD 337 (1987); *Nasman v. IDF Commander in the Gaza Strip*, 44 (2) PD 601 (1989). The Court was especially critical of the IDF's Attorney General's decision not to prosecute a high-ranking officer for ordering the brutal beating of Palestinian detainees, and demanded that criminal proceedings take place. *Tsufan v. IDF Attorney General*, 43 (4) PD 718 (1989).

[74] *Al-Gazawi v. Panel of the Military Court in Gaza*, 34 (4) PD 411 (1980).

[75] *Shmalawi v. Appeals Committee*, 39 (4) PD 598 (1985)

[76] *Kawassme v. Minister of Defence*, 35 (3) PD 113 (1980).

[77] On the applicability of the regular tests for lawfulness of administrative acts to the acts of the occupation administration, *see Jama'iat Iscan, supra* note 9, at 810. The principle of equal treatment of the residents of the territories was upheld by the Court, which ordered the

cording to the Court, the occupation authorities were entitled to include in their considerations the interests of the Jewish settlers in the territories, since these settlers were part of the population under their jurisdiction.[78] The occupation administration was precluded from considering the interests of Israel or of Israelis who reside outside the territories,[79] unless an administrative act in question could also benefit the indigenous population.[80] Furthermore, the occupation administration was authorized, according to the Court, to cooperate with the Israeli government on matters that were of interest both to Israel and to the territories, as two sovereign governments would do.[81]

The settlement of Jews in the territories was perhaps the single most controversial issue within the Israeli body-politic in connection with the administration of the territories. Therefore, petitions against the expropriation of lands (for the purpose of erecting settlements) put the Court in a politically difficult position. In decisions concerning land expropriation for the purposes of erecting settlements or building highways, the Court openly acknowledged its concerns with the adverse political implications of its rulings. In the only case where a settlement project was declared illegal, the *Elon Moreh* case, Justice Landau, D.P., observed:

> It is . . . greatly to be feared that the Court will appear to be abandoning its proper place and descending into the arena of public debate, and that its decision will be received by one part of the public with acclamation and by another part with utter emotional rejection. In this sense I regard myself here as bound by the obligation to decide in accordance with the law in every matter duly brought before the Court, knowing well from the outset that the public at large will not pay attention to the legal reasoning but only to the final conclusion, and the proper status of the Court as an institution, beyond the disputes which divide the public, is likely to be prejudiced. But what can we do, this is our task and duty as judges.[82]

The decision in the *Elon Moreh* case did not challenge the legality of expropriations in general. Rather, the reason for the ruling was the lack of military necessity for that particular taking. The Court never criticized set-

---

distribution of gas masks to all the residents of the West Bank on the eve of the 1991 Gulf War: *Morcous v. Minister of Defence*, 45 (1) PD 467 (1991).

[78] *Electricity Co. for the District of Jerusalem v. Minister of Defence*, 27 PD (1) 124, 138 (1972); *Zalum v. Military Commander of Judea and Samaria*, 41 (1) PD 528, 532 (1987).

[79] *Jama'iat Iscan, supra* note 9, at 794–95.

[80] *Id.*; *Ayyub, supra* note 8 (Vitkon, J.).

[81] *Jama'iat Iscan, supra* note 9, at 811. This emphasis on the thin veil that separates the occupation administration from the Israeli government seems incompatible with an earlier decision, in another matter, that actually pierced that veil. *See infra* text accompanying notes 128–29.

[82] *Douykat, supra* note 8, at 4.

tlement plans after the *Elon Moreh* case,[83] nor did it otherwise impede the integration of the territories with Israel. Since the issues of settlements and economic integration were so contentious within Israeli public opinion, the Court's stance would seem warranted: the parliament is the proper place to sort out issues that divide the public, not the court. The problem, in this unique situation, was that only part of the concerned public enjoyed access to the parliament, the Israeli Knesset. The Court did not—indeed, for the same political reasons, could not—balance the inherent political inferiority of the Arab population by requiring the government to refer to the Knesset to receive a clearer mandate for its policies. In addition, since the relevant criterion for adjudication would have been international law, any ruling against the government under the law of occupation (and any consequential clearer mandate from the Knesset) might have depicted Israel as a violator of international law, tainting the government's general claim of legitimacy under this law. In light of these considerations, and facing a government that was committed to expanding the settlements, the Court carefully avoided a ruling on their legality.

The jurisprudence that the Israeli Supreme Court developed over the years of occupation is perhaps the most elaborate and consistent effort by a domestic court to apply the law of occupation. The Court's approach to specific policies involving the occupation will be outlined in the following pages, in connection with the description of those policies.[84]

Integration of the Territories with Israel

With the commencement of occupation in 1967, the Israeli government resolved to create a "common market," which would consist of Israel and the territories. An official publication explained the new economic reality: "The Six Day War abolished to all intents and purposes the 'green line' that in the past demarcated the Israeli sector from the administered territories. Naturally and unavoidably, these areas are becoming dependent upon Israel for all their economic and service needs."[85] This policy was described

[83] After the Elon Moreh decision, *id.*, the method for acquiring land for settlements was changed. The new method utilized what the authorities claimed to be state lands and not private lands. The Supreme Court noted that this method precluded its review: *Al Nazer v. Commander of Judea and Samaria*, 36 (1) PD 701 (1982); *Araieb v. Appeals Committee*, 40 (2) PD 57 (1986).

[84] Specific reference is given to the Court's view on the economic ties between Israel and the occupied territories. *Infra* notes 179–80. In addition, the Court, sitting in its capacity as the Supreme Court (hearing appeals from Israeli district courts), fashioned the legal status with respect to the extraterritorial application of Israeli laws in the occupied territories. *See infra* text accompanying notes 129, 139.

[85] Coordinator of Government Operations in the Administered Territories, Ministry of

and approved by the Israeli Supreme Court, as being consistent with—indeed, imperative under—the law of occupation:

> In view of the economic realities created by the conjunction of political facts (military government) and geography (territorial contiguity) directly bound up with the relative sizes of the economies and the sectors comprising them (agriculture, industry, employment), the economy of the territories is umbilically tied to the economy of Israel. For this reason, it was decided at the time of the establishment of the military government that the two economies would not be separated . . . along the lines, as it were, of the Armed Truce before 1967. To separate them as aforesaid would impede the possibility of return to orderly life and prevent the effective observance of the duty regarding the assurance of "la vie publique."[86]

The integration of the economies was motivated not only by the desire to maintain and promote public order and civil life in the territories, as mandated under Article 43 of the Hague Regulations. Another consideration was that the economic prosperity and the higher standard of living that this integration would bring to the local population would create incentives for them to interact peacefully with the Israeli authorities.[87]

The policy of economic integration was implemented through various modifications in all the local legal systems involved. These modifications included, *inter alia*, the abolishment of "internal" customs barriers and the erection of a single "external" barrier for international trade, the unification of indirect taxation, and the enabling of free passage of people between Israel and the territories. The measures taken for these purposes are outlined below.

Measures Creating a Single Economy

IMPORT AND EXPORT

Imports and exports between Israel and the territories were exempt from import duties. Imports from abroad (including Jordan) directly to the territories were subjected to the same duties as goods imported through Israeli ports.[88] There were no restrictions on the export of Israeli goods into

---

Defence, *The Administered Territories 1967/1971—Data on Civilian Activities in Judea and Samaria; the Gaza Strip and Northern Sinai*, cited in Abu-Aita, *supra* note 55, at 99.

[86] *Abu-Aita, supra* note 55, at 104.

[87] *Id.* at 98.

[88] Order Concerning Duty Tariffs (Judea and Samaria) (no. 1093), 5744–1984. This order delegates the authority to impose duties from the military government to the Israeli legislature and Executive. It provides that any change in the Israeli law will apply automatically to imports that pass through Jordan. *See* the similar provision in the law of occupied Venezia Giulia, *supra* Chapter 4, note 127.

the territories.[89] With regard to movement in the other direction, a general permit was issued according to which exports from the West Bank and Gaza to Israel were not restricted. Specific permits were needed to export certain specific goods, such as agricultural produce, from the territories to Israel or abroad.[90] This permit system enabled the authorities to control the flow of these commodities to Israel, to prevent the saturation of the Israeli market, and to control supply and pricing. Direct trade between the territories and Jordan or Egypt was generally permitted, but trade in some goods required special permits.[91]

INDIRECT TAXATION

In 1976 the Value Added Tax (VAT) was the first indirect tax to be introduced in the territories, simultaneously with its introduction in Israel.[92] In 1983 a levy of 1 percent was imposed on any purchase of foreign currency in the territories.[93] A 15 percent tax was imposed in 1986 on the transfer of foreign currency abroad for the purchase of foreign goods and services.[94] The two last orders also followed identical Israeli laws from the same period.[95] The levy on vehicles was introduced in 1985, to coincide with the Israeli levy on vehicles, one of the measures of the Israeli austerity plan.[96] This order imposed a levy on the owner of each vehicle according to year of manufacture and engine size. A levy on credit in foreign currency was introduced in late 1987, following its introduction in Israel.[97] It imposed a 3 percent tax on credit in foreign currency extended by banks to local importers, mainly through letters of credit.[98]

[89] Order Concerning Transport of Goods (Judea and Samaria) (no. 1252), 5748–1988. This order replaced the order in force since 1967.

[90] Order Concerning the Transfer of Agricultural Produce (Judea and Samaria) (no. 47), 5727–1967.

[91] General Permit to Import Goods (Judea and Samaria), 5748–1988; General Permit to Export Goods (Judea and Samaria) 5748–1988.

[92] The legality of the VAT was discussed in the *Abu-Aita* case, *supra* note 55.

[93] Order Concerning Levy on the Purchase of Foreign Currency (Judea and Samaria) (no. 1055), 5743–1983.

[94] Order Concerning Levy on the Purchase of Imported Services and Foreign Assets (Provisional Order) (Judea and Samaria) (no. 1183A), 5746–1986.

[95] The comparable Israeli laws are Levy on Purchase of Foreign Currency, 5743–1983; Levy on the Purchase of Imported Services and Foreign Assets (Provisional Order) Law, 5745–1984.

[96] Order Concerning Levy on Vehicles (Provisional Order) (Judea and Samaria) (no. 1150), 5746–1985. In Israel the law is Levy on Property Law (Provisional Order), 5745–1985, part C. The Israeli version also included levies on other properties.

[97] Order Concerning Levy on Loans in Foreign Currency (Judea and Samaria) (no. 1228), 5748–1987.

[98] For the Supreme's Court evaluation of the legality of the new taxes under international law, *see infra* text accompanying notes 179–80.

LEGAL TENDER AND FOREIGN CURRENCY REGULATION

Israeli currency was introduced as legal tender in the territories. In Gaza it was the only currency, while in the West Bank the Jordanian dinar was also legal, and the exchange rate between the two currencies was adjusted by the authorities according to fluctuations in world markets.[99] For Israelis, however, including those who lived or did business in the West Bank, the dinar was a foreign currency, and the same restrictions that applied to transactions in foreign currency applied to the dinar as well.[100] The same restrictions on trade in foreign currency, foreign stocks and bonds, and gold that were imposed in Israel applied in the territories.[101] The only exception was that local residents of the West Bank were allowed to transfer dinars out of the area.

BANKS

The banks that operated before the 1967 war were ordered immediately afterwards to freeze all transactions. Subsequently, the Palestine Bank in Gaza and the Cairo-Amman Bank in Nablus were reopened. Israeli banks opened branches in the territories, which conducted business according to Israeli law and were controlled by the Israeli supervisor of banks. Before the reopening of the locally owned Cairo-Amman Bank, the local Banks Law was amended to reflect Israeli banking practices, and to provide full control over the bank's activities. The bank was placed under the supervision of the military authorities, with accounts in the Bank of Israel.[102]

ANTIINFLATIONARY MEASURES

The inflation that affected the Israeli economy had similar effects in the territories, and the measures taken to reduce it were similar. Thus, for example, the Israeli law that established an indexing clause in all pecuniary judgments was also introduced in the territories.[103]

Under the 1985 austerity plan, all prices of goods and services were fro-

[99] Order Concerning the Establishment of the Israeli Currency as Legal Tender (Judea and Samaria) (no. 76), 5727–1967.

[100] Order Concerning the Israeli Currency as Legal Tender (Further Provisions) (Judea and Samaria) (no. 83), 5727–1967, paragraph 3. There is a criminal sanction for refusal to accept shekels at their face value.

[101] *See* Order Concerning Currency Control (Judea and Samaria) (no. 952), 5742–1981, and the General Permit issued under the order.

[102] Order Concerning the Amendment of the Banks Law (Judea and Samaria) (no. 1180), 5746–1986, and the directions issued pursuant to this order.

[103] Order Concerning Awarding Interest and Indexing (Judea and Samaria) (no. 980), 5742–1982.

zen in Israel. No one was allowed to raise prices without the prior approval of both the minister of finance and the minister of industry and trade. The same price freeze was imposed in the territories.[104] Subsequent changes in the Israeli law regarding the price freeze were simultaneously implemented in the territories. An amendment to the Order from 1988 stipulated that price hikes decreed by the Israeli authorities would also apply in the territories.

EMPLOYMENT

A substantial component in the economic integration was employment of residents of the West Bank and Gaza in Israel. Employment in Israel, with comparatively higher wages, was a major reason for the significant rise in the standard of living in the territories. Given no comparable alternatives in the territories, the occupied population was dependent on employment in Israel. The fact that most of the workers from the territories were employed in unskilled or semiskilled jobs made certain sectors of the Israeli economy dependent on them, at least in the short run.[105] The flow of workers to Israel was regulated by a general permit, which specified the conditions under which residents of the territories were allowed to enter Israel. Among other conditions, the residents were not allowed to stay in Israel overnight and were required to work only where they were sent by the labor exchanges operating in the territories.[106] Those employers who hired through the labor exchanges were required to deduct from their employees' wages percentages equal to those deducted from comparable wages of Israeli workers for social benefits provided under the Israeli National Insurance Law, even though the non-Israeli workers were not entitled to the same National Insurance benefits as were Israelis. The requirement for equal deductions was necessary to ensure equal net wages for Israelis and non-Israelis in comparable jobs so that employers would not prefer non-Israeli employees. The surplus created from the excess deductions from the non-Israeli workers' wages was transferred to the Israeli treasury. Part of it was transferred to the civil administration in the territories and was used for improving local social services, and the rest was

[104] Order Concerning Stability of Prices of Goods and Services (Temporary Provisions) (Judea and Samaria) (no. 1125), 5745–1984.

[105] According to *State Comptroller Report no. 40*, at 487 (1989), about two-thirds of the workers coming from the West Bank and Gaza, that is, about 70,000 out of 109,400 (in 1988), were employed in unskilled jobs. They comprised 42 percent to 45 percent of the total employees in building, sanitation, and agriculture. In 1987 those who worked in Israel comprised 39.8 percent of the entire work force in the territories.

[106] General Exit Permit (no. 5) (Judea and Samaria), 5732–1972. Most workers—more than 60 percent in 1988—found employment illegally, that is, not through the labor exchanges. *Id.* at 489.

apparently placed in a special fund to be disposed of when the status of the territories was determined.[107]

TRAFFIC LAWS AND INSURANCE

In order to facilitate traffic within the entire area of Israel and the territories, the Israeli traffic code replaced the local codes.[108] The Order Concerning Compensation to Victims of Road Accidents[109] introduced in the territories the Israeli law that provided for strict tort liability for bodily injuries caused by the use of motor vehicles. The Order Concerning Insurance of Motor Vehicles[110] prescribed mandatory insurance for motor vehicles, similar to that in Israel. Insurance policies for motor vehicles generally covered accidents both in Israel and in the territories. Thus, anyone driving from one region to the other[111] did not have to adjust to different rules.

UTILIZATION OF COMMON NATURAL RESOURCES

The water resources in Israel and the territories are limited. Their careful management is necessary to ensure their continuing availability and good quality. A substantial portion of Israel's water potential, about one-third, originates in the West Bank. A portion of the Gaza Strip's water potential originates in Israel.[112] Most of these waters are groundwater located in undergound aquifers. The scarcity of water has been an important restriction on the development of irrigated agriculture.[113]

Israeli institutions control the utilization of these water resources. One

[107] Ruth Ben-Israel, an Israeli expert in labor law, maintains that this arrangement does not conform to the Israeli law or to the standards set by the ILO. Ben-Israel, *On Social Rights for Workers of the Administered Areas*, 12 IYHR 141, 150 (1982). An Israeli weekly has reported that the officials in charge avoid giving information regarding the whereabouts of these funds. Kol Ha'ir, July 26, 1991. This paper claims that in 1990 the total deduction amounted to about forty-five million U.S. dollars, of which three million went to the National Insurance fund, and seventeen million were received by the Civil Administration; according to the report, the remaining sum was unaccounted for. *Id.*

[108] Order Concerning the Traffic Law (Judea and Samaria) (no. 56), 5727–1967, and other orders enacted thereafter. The Israeli requirements with regard to safety belts are also imposed in the territories. Order Concerning Safety Belts in Vehicles (Judea and Samaria) (no. 600), 5735–1975.

[109] (Judea and Samaria) (no. 677), 5736–1976.

[110] (Judea and Samaria) (no. 215), 5728–1968.

[111] A driver's license from one region is valid in the other regions. *See* paragraph 9A of the Order Concerning the Traffic Law, *supra* note 108.

[112] D. Kahan, *Agriculture and Water Resources in the West Bank and Gaza (1967–1987)* 20–22 (1987).

[113] *Id.* at 114.

of the earliest security enactments consolidated the powers regarding the regulation of water resources under the military commander.[114] The military administration regulated the use of water within the territories, and the planting of crops, whereas the total availability of water in the territories was determined by the Israeli institutions in charge of distributing the waters drawn from the common groundwater aquifers. According to both the law of occupation and the international law regarding the utilization of international groundwaters, it seems that the occupant, in administering the use of common groundwater aquifers, must strive to ensure equitable utilization of groundwaters by all parties concerned.[115] While the Palestinian water consumption increased after 1967, it did not match the Israeli consumption either in agriculture or domestically.[116]

Extension of Jurisdiction of the Israeli Civil Courts

The Israeli civil courts assumed jurisdiction over people and property in the territories and over events occurring there. In effect, the courts exercised this jurisdiction in all cases except those in which all the parties to the litigation were non-Israeli residents of the territories. From the point of view of the Israelis, this situation ensured that they would not have to sue in courts in the territories even when the litigant was a local resident. From the point of view of the Arab population, the consequence was that they had the option of suing Israelis in Israel, and were liable to be sued by Israelis in Israeli courts.

This jurisdiction was formally concurrent with the jurisdiction of the local courts of the territories (with regard, of course, to issues that were under the jurisdiction of these courts). But these local courts suffered from poor conditions.[117] Moreover, summoning Israeli witnesses (including members of the military administration) to testify was difficult to achieve, and the prospects of enforcing judgments on Israeli defendants were

[114] Order Concerning Powers with Regard to Water Laws (the West Bank) (no. 92), 5727–1967.

[115] On the international law of groundwater utilization, *see* Caponera and Althéritiere, *Principles for International Groundwater Law*, 18 Natural Resources J. 589 (1978). The viewpoint of the law of occupation on this matter is discussed in El-Hindi, *The West Bank Aquifer and Conventions Regarding the Laws of Belligerent Occupation*, 11 Mich. J. Int'l L. 1400 (1990).

[116] Kahan, *supra* note 112, at 23–24, 110–13.

[117] The poor conditions have motivated local residents to sue other local residents in the Israeli courts. Thus, the plaintiff in *Gabour v. Hanitan*, [1983] (A) PSM 499, a Palestinian, requested that the court not decline its jurisdiction, because of the poor quality of the local judicial system. *See also infra* cases cited in note 135.

slim.[118] In addition, it became physically dangerous for Israelis to travel to the Arab town centers where the local courts are situated.

The decision to extend the jurisdiction of Israeli courts to the territories was not taken in the Knesset. It came about as the result of measures taken by both the Justice Ministry and the Israeli Supreme Court. The minister of justice, pursuant to his/her general power under the Courts Law to regulate procedure in the civil courts, prescribed that service of "documents"[119] from an Israeli civil court be effected in the territories in the same manner as in Israel.[120] This technical provision was interpreted by the Israeli Supreme Court in *Alkir v. Van der Hurst Rotterdam*[121] as exempting the plaintiffs in the Israeli court from the otherwise applicable requirement of obtaining the court's permission to service the process abroad,[122] and as a result wiped out, for the purposes of personal jurisdiction, the pre-1967 borders, extending the jurisdiction of Israeli courts to all the residents of the territories, even in matters that had no contact points with Israel.[123]

---

[118] *See* Association for Civil Rights in Israel, *Reflections on the Civil Rights in the Administered Territories: The Judicial and Administrative System* 17 (1985) (in Hebrew) ("We have heard complaints that civil suits against Jews [in the local courts] face obstacles since they resist the local police force and the clerks of the local court and execution offices. . . . Thus it seems that the local court system continues to apply mainly to disputes between local [that is, Arab] residents.").

[119] "Documents" include also subpoenas and court interim and final decisions. *See Bank Leumi Le-Israel B.M. v. Hirschberg*, 32 (1) PD 617 (1978) ("document" includes any legal act that can be effected through a document issued by a court, including an order freezing bank accounts). An attachment of property, an act that entails registration in official registers, or any other act required under Israeli law in addition to the document must be done by the Execution Bureau of the Territories. *Po'alim Bank v. Daks*, 44 (1) PD 201 (1989).

[120] Regulation of Procedure (Service of Documents in the Administered Territories), 5729–1969. A similar regulation was enacted by the minister with regard to documents of the labor courts.

[121] 25 (2) PD 13 (1971).

[122] The extraterritorial jurisdiction of Israeli courts is fashioned according to the common law principle of the service of the summons on the defendant. By the act of service itself, the court's extraterritorial jurisdiction is established. The service of process is conceived as an act of sovereignty, in fact, the only relevant act of sovereignty; thus no additional contact points of the defendant with the forum are formally required (although the courts have discretion not to establish jurisdiction where there is no connection between the claim and the forum). Therefore, when the defendant is in Israel, even as a tourist, there is no obstacle to serving the summons on him or her, thereby granting the court jurisdiction to adjudicate the claim. When the defendant is abroad, the crucial act of service is not controlled by the local sovereign, but rather is contingent upon the cooperation of the country where that person is found. Thus, the Israeli rules regarding international jurisdiction in civil matters are defined through regulations of civil procedure that prescribe the conditions on which the courts shall grant leave to serve documents abroad.

[123] Another interpretation of the regulation was possible, and, indeed, more appropriate: Bracha, *Service of Documents to the Administered Territories*, 4 Mishpatim 119 (1972–1973) (in Hebrew), suggests that the regulation be interpreted as regulating the means by which

Usually the service was effected through the mail or personally by the plaintiff. No special procedure was required. The military commander issued an order respecting the methods of service prescribed by the Israeli regulation.[124]

Once a judgment had been rendered, its execution was effected by its submission to special Execution Bureaus, one for each territory.[125] Initially, these bureaus executed only judgments rendered against Israeli residents of the territories, but because of difficulties in enforcement during the intifada, their powers were extended to cover judgments against Palestinians.[126] There was no need to submit the judgment to the prior scrutiny of a local court.[127] The fact that the Israeli court orders would be enforced in the territories, with the local authorities' having no discretion not to respect them, was decisive in an Israeli court's decision to adjudicate a claim concerning title to real estate located in the territories.[128]

The validity of the regulation that extended the courts' jurisdiction has not been attacked directly in the Israeli courts. Nevertheless the Israeli Supreme Court did refer to this issue. In a series of decisions by the president of the Court, Justice Sussman, the Court approved the validity of that extension of the courts' jurisdiction under international law. The Court ex-

---

such a service may be effected *after* the court has granted a service of process to the territories. This interpretation would also have been compatible with international law. *See infra* text accompanying notes 130–32.

[124] Paragraph 2 of the Order Concerning Legal Aid (Judea and Samaria) (no. 348), 5730–1969, states: "A document issued by [an Israeli civil court or execution office] shall be served in the region in the manner prescribed in the Israeli civil procedure regulations." This order was criticized as being in violation of the law of occupation. Nathan, *Israel Civil Jurisdiction in the Administered Territories*, 13 IYHR 90, 115 (1983) ("The powers of the military government [or of the Israeli government] over the administered territories under the laws of belligerent occupation would not appear to include the power to extend the civil jurisdiction of the Israeli courts over the residents of the Administered Territories in such a manner. . . .").

[125] Paragraph 4 of the Order Concerning Legal Aid, *supra* note 124. Registrations of court orders concerning immovables that are registered in the military-run Registry of Land (which registers the land held by the authorities) can be effected directly by the military registrar if the court has so ordered: Paragraph 16 of the Regulations Concerning Registration of Transactions in Certain Immovables (Management and Registration) (Judea and Samaria), 5735–1975. A parallel order for the Gaza Strip is Order Concerning Legal Aid (The Gaza Strip and Northern Sinai) (no. 318), 5730–1969.

[126] Order Concerning Legal Aid (Amendment) (Judea and Samaria) (no. 1294), 5750–1989; *id.* (the Gaza Strip) (no. 997), 5749–1989.

[127] Judgments rendered in the territories can be enforced in Israel as if they were Israeli judgments, provided that the military commander of the relevant area confirms the document's authenticity and the Israeli attorney general does not oppose that execution as one that is "likely . . . to harm Israel's sovereignty, its security, or its public policy." Paragraph 5 of the Order Concerning Legal Aid, *supra* note 124, and the parallel Israeli Emergency Order (Judea, Samaria, and Gaza—Legal Aid) (no. 2), 5736–1976, paragraphs 3 and 4.

[128] *Levi v. Barouch*, [1984] (3) PSM 45, at 55.

amined it in view of the general international norm regarding states' right to establish extraterritorial jurisdiction, and not with regard to the law of occupation, apparently since it viewed the latter law as delimiting only the powers of the military government and not those of the national legislature. The general international norm, the Court reasoned, did not apply in this case since the Israeli jurisdiction did not interfere with the sovereignty of any other state:

> Israel is exercising [the sovereign's suspended powers in the territories] in fact, by virtue of the law of occupation under the rules of international law . . . [the Israeli court] acts only in theory in the territory of another sovereign. In fact, as long as the territory is held by the IDF, the authority is in the hands of Israel, and there is no fear of violation of any other authority. . . .[129]

In other words, in a situation of occupation, there are no limits imposed by customary international law on the exercise of extraterritorial adjudicative jurisdiction by the occupant's country over the residents of the occupied areas, provided that this jurisdiction is prescribed by the laws of the occupying country and not by military orders issued by the commander of the occupying force. This reasoning takes what is advantageous to Israeli interests from both worlds. It pierces the veil of the separate authority of the military administration of the territories by saying that it is Israel that controls the territories and in fact exercises sovereign powers there.[130] At the same time, however, it does not impose on the Israeli government the same limits that international law imposes on the military administration as an occupant. By this reasoning, the opinion purports to avoid all the limits recognized in international law on the extraterritorial exercise of adjudicative powers. This decision is contrary to a prior Israeli precedent, which held that the powers of the occupant rest a fortiori in its home government.[131] Indeed, the occupant's government, as well as its national courts, are obliged under the law of occupation to respect the same duties that are imposed on the occupation administration. The legality of the extension of the Israeli civil courts' jurisdiction to the territories should have been examined under the law of occupation.[132]

---

[129] *Shurpa v. Wechsler*, 28 (1) PD 512, 517 (1973). *See also Bank Leumi v. Hirschberg, supra* note 119, at 620, holding that "even though the administered territory does not form a part of the [Israeli] territory, and from the procedural point of view it is *prima facie* outside the jurisdiction of an Israeli court, an act of an Israeli court performed in the administered territory does not infringe in fact upon the sovereignty of any other power."

[130] In later cases, the Court would emphasize the opposite claim, namely, that the occupation administration is quite distinct from the Israeli government. *See* discussion of the *Jama'iat Iscan* case, *supra* text accompanying note 81.

[131] *Attorney General for Israel v. Sylvester*, [1948] AD Case no. 190 (February 8, 1949).

[132] On this point, *see also infra*, text accompanying note 181.

DISCRETION NOT TO ENTERTAIN CLAIMS AGAINST RESIDENTS
OF THE TERRITORIES

According to Israeli law, the civil courts may use their discretion to decline
to exercise their jurisdiction. Faced with actions against non-Israeli residents of the territories, the Israeli Supreme Court adopted a flexible criterion, the notion of the "natural forum,"[133] for the use of the discretion to
decline jurisdiction.[134] Despite the flexibility of the criterion, its application in a number of claims concerning residents of the territories has been
fairly steady, to such an extent that one can restate the rules as follows:
When all the parties to the litigation are non-Israeli residents of the territories, and the cause of action arose in the territories, the Israeli courts will
not entertain the case.[135] When either the plaintiff or the defendant is an
Israeli citizen or resident, the court will adjudicate the claim.[136]

APPLICATION OF ISRAELI LAWS IN THE TERRITORIES THROUGH
ISRAELI COURTS

Using their extended jurisdiction, the Israeli courts contributed to the application of Israeli norms to the territories. Thus, the application of the
Israeli tort and contract laws to transactions in the territories was the outcome not of enactments by the military administration but rather of the
Israeli civil courts' implementation of judicially developed unique conflict-
of-laws rules. In view of the intense interregional economic interaction, it
is surprising that only a few cases regarding the proper law that applies to
transactions between Israelis and Arab residents of the territories were ad-

---

[133] *Abu-Atiya v. Arabtisi*, 39 (1) PD 365, 385 (1985) (examination of the reasonable expectations of the parties to the litigation).

[134] The older rule, which would have narrowed significantly the prospect of rejecting such
claims, permitted the court to decline jurisdiction only on condition that the defendant
showed that (1) the continuation of the trial would be unfair to him or her, and (2) that the
dismissal of the case would not jeopardize the plaintiff's claim. This was the test laid down in
the English case of *St. Pierre v. South American Stores Ltd.*, [1936] 1 K.B. 382, and adopted
in Israel in *Hachamov v. Schmidt*, 12 PD 59 (1957). *See* Goldstein, *International Jurisdiction
Based on Service on the Defendant*, 10 Mishpatim (Hebrew U. L. Rev.) 409 (1980) (in Hebrew).

[135] *Abu-Atiya v. Arabtisi, supra* note 133, at 372, 385; *Elraias v. Arab Insurance Co. Ltd.*, 38
(3) PD 495, 496 (1984). *See also* the Jerusalem District Court decisions: *Gabour v. Hanitan,
supra* note 117; *Arab Insurance Co. Ltd. v. Khader*, [1984] (2) PSM 172.

[136] *Abu-Ita v. Ya'akobi*, C.A. 425/81, unpublished decision (1981); *Abu-Atiya v. Arabtisi,
supra* note 133, at 386. Some questions are still left open. For instance, what will the case be
when the only contact to Israel is the place of the act or omission that gives rise to action (a
variation on the first rule)? Will it make any difference if all but one of the litigants in a
multiparty litigation were non-Israelis (a variation on the second rule)?

judicated.[137] Nevertheless, the few relevant court decisions set forth a clear rule, applicable generally to almost all such transactions.

An Israeli claimant was injured in a fire that had broken out in the Palestinian defendant's factory in the West Bank. The district court judge decided to apply Israeli law to determine the parties' rights and duties. After reviewing the relevant Israeli conflict-of-laws rules, the judge decided to adopt a unique rule, which she deemed more proper in light of the economic union between Israel and the territories:

> Many Israelis live, work, travel in Judea and Samaria, and have commercial relations with the local residents. This state of affairs creates an anticipation that not only the legal proceedings concerning a tort in Judea and Samaria which involves both Israeli residents and local residents shall be held in a competent court in Israel, but also that the Israeli law shall be applied.
>
> The Israelis, even if present in Judea and Samaria, do not conceive themselves as under Jordanian law, and do not anticipate that the norms practiced in Jordan will be applied to their case. They are linked to Israel and to Israeli law.
>
> These facts influence also the anticipation of the other side—in this case the tortfeasor who is a local resident.[138]

This decision relied on an opinion of the Supreme Court, which emphasized the *sui generis* status of the territories. Since the territories were not foreign countries, but in fact formed an integral part of Israel, the courts were obliged to recognize the legal ramifications of the situation:

> The routines of daily life linking the State of Israel, and its residents, with the Administered Territories, and their residents, converge into an economic system that is unified in fact. There are multiple commercial and economic ties. Transportation lines are open; in the area of employment there is a convergence; and in fact in all these areas, there are usually no barriers or restrictions.[139]

These reasonings, in general, could be applied to most tort claims involving Israelis and Palestinian residents of the territories. Moreover, the attitude of the courts seemed to indicate a general preference for Israeli over local law, which affected almost all private transactions between Israelis and Palestinian residents of the territories. One exception to this rule was labor contracts between Israeli employers and Palestinian employees, which were treated as governed by the local law of the territories, rather than the Israeli law.[140]

---

[137] All reported decisions, without exception, ruled that the Israeli law applied to transactions among Israelis even if they took place in the territories. *See infra* notes 138, 163.

[138] *National Insurance Institution v. Abu-Ita*, [1988] (2) PSM 133, 143.

[139] *Abu-Ita v. Ya'akobi*, C.A. 425/81, unpublished decision at 6–7 (1981).

[140] This proposition is supported by the case law. According to a National Labor Court decision, a Palestinian policeman employed by the Israeli police in Gaza was not entitled to the benefits of the Israeli Pensions Law and Discharge Indemnifying Law. According to the

The Integration of the Jewish Settlements into Israel

The measures described above enabled the creation of a single market encompassing Israel and the territories. This single market allowed almost entirely free movement of people, goods, and services across the "green line." It stopped short, however, of providing similar economic conditions within the different regions. An important line still divided the economy of the territories from that of Israel. Yet this line was not the "green line." Rather, the Israeli economy encompassed the areas of the Israeli settlements in the territories. The economic conditions in the settlements were almost identical to those within Israel. These settlements were enclaves where Israeli law applied exclusively, connecting them legally, economically, and socially to Israel. In November 1991, 112,000 Israelis were registered in the settlements as residents.[141]

The extension of Israeli law and administration to the settlements took effect mainly through two parallel systems: the extraterritorial application of Israeli laws by the Israeli Knesset and government to the Israeli residents of the settlements, and the adoption of Israeli laws by the military administration to be applied exclusively in the settlements.

The laws extraterritorially extended to Israelis[142] in the territories included the criminal law,[143] fiscal laws,[144] the Elections to the Knesset

---

court, there was "no fault in the fact that the working conditions of a policeman who is a resident and citizen of Israel who serves in the Territories were different from those of a local policeman who was not a citizen of Israel." *Abu-Tir v. Israeli Police*, Case 7-4/1985, unpublished decision at 7 (1989). This seems to be also the approach of the military authorities. *See* Order Concerning Employment of Workers in Certain Places (Judea and Samaria) (no. 967), 5742–1982. The "certain places" are the Israeli settlements, and the implicit assumption of the order is that the local law applies to labor contracts in those places.

[141] Ha'Aretz (Israeli daily newspaper), January 23, 1992, part A, at 2. Of these, about 108,000 resided in the West Bank, and about 4,000 resided in the Gaza Strip. Since the outbreak of the intifada, 12,000 Israelis have moved into the territories.

[142] "Israelis" are defined for the purpose of the extension of Israeli laws. Paragraph 6B (enacted in 1984) of the Israeli Emergency Regulations (Judea, Samaria, and Gaza—Adjudication of Offenses and Legal Aid), 5727–1967, provides that the term "Israeli" shall include "also a person whose place of residence is the area [that is, the West Bank and Gaza] and who is an Israeli citizen, or who is entitled to immigrate to Israel under the Law of Return, 5710–1950, and had his residence been in Israel that person would have been included under the same expression [that is, a non-Israeli Jew who settled in the area]."

[143] *Id.* at paragraph 2(a), as amended in 1988, provides that the courts in Israel "have jurisdiction to adjudicate according to the Israeli law a person who is present in Israel, with regard to that person's act or omission that has occurred in the area [that is, the territories] and that would have constituted an offence had it occurred within the area under the jurisdiction of the Israeli courts." For the purposes of this regulation, "a person who is present in Israel" includes those registered in the Israeli Population Register and corporations registered in Israel or conducting business there or controlled by one of the above.

[144] Paragraph 3A (enacted in 1978 and amended in 1990) of the Income Tax Ordinance

Law,[145] and the National Insurance Law.[146] The duty to serve in the IDF was also imposed on settlers, as was the requirement to register in the Israeli Population Register.[147] Secondary legislation by government Ministers was very effective in equalizing economic conditions in the settlements with those in Israel: ministers were empowered to extend to the territories Israeli regulations concerning the qualities of goods and services;[148] state insurance was extended to cover loss to property in the territories incurred because of its "Israeli character" and loss of agricultural investments of Israelis in the territories due to drought;[149] Israelis who quit their jobs in Israel in order to settle in the territories had a right to severance payments from their former employers as if they had been dismissed from work;[150] an administrative decision declared the settlements to be "development areas" under the Israeli Encouraging Capital Investments Law, 5719-1959, thereby creating economic incentives to reside or invest in the settlements. In one case the Israeli Supreme Court held that this method of extraterritorial extension of laws was perfectly legitimate under international law. In its answer to settlers' claim that the extraterritorial extension of the Income Tax Ordinance was incompatible with the powers of the occupant, the court rejected the link between these issues, maintaining that the law of

provides that income of Israeli persons and corporations, including corporations that reside in the territories but are controlled by Israelis, procured in the territories is deemed to have been procured inside Israel, and that the tax is to be paid to the Israeli treasury, with a deduction of the amount of income tax paid to the military authorities in the territories. Paragraph 144A of the Value Added Tax Law, as amended in 1979, provides that transactions between Israelis in the territories will be deemed to have occurred in Israel. The Land Appreciation Tax Law, Amendment 15, 5744–1984, extends the land appreciation tax, which serves in Israel as a capital gains tax with regard to the sale of immovables, and also taxes the buyer of immovables, to immovable property in the territories.

[145] The Elections to the Knesset Law provides that only Israelis registered in the Israeli Population Register as residents of Israel can vote, and then only by voting in the ballot of the registered Israeli residence. The settlers are the only nonresidents who are given the right to vote, and this right to vote abroad is given to them, the diplomatic corps, and sailors only.

[146] See schedule to the Emergency Regulations, *supra* note 142. In the National Insurance Regulations (Application on Special Categories of Insured), 5747–1987, and in the National Insurance Order (Categories of Volunteers Outside Israel), 5747–1987, the minister of labor and social affairs extended the National Insurance Law to cover also Jews who work in the territories, and those who volunteer in the Jewish settlements.

[147] Therefore, any law that would apply to those who are required to register in the Population Registry would automatically also apply to the Israeli residents of the territories. See the amendment to the Land Appreciation Tax Law, which defined "Israeli citizens" simply as those who are registered or must be registered in the Population Register.

[148] The Supervision of Goods and Services Law (Amendment no. 12), 5742–1982.

[149] Paragraph 38A of Property Tax and Compensation Fund Law, 5721–1961, and Property Tax and Compensation Fund (Payment of Compensation for Damages) (Israeli External Property) Regulations, 5742–1982.

[150] Regulation 12(d) of the Dismissal Compensation Regulations (Computation of Compensation and Resignation That is Seen as Dismissal), 5742–1964.

occupation does not control the extension of laws by the occupant's government to its citizens in the occupied territory.[151]

The second method used for extending Israeli laws relied on the basic communal arrangement of Israeli life in the territories, namely, the settlements as municipal units. The enactments of the military authorities created a special legal system in the settlements, a system that adopted Israeli law, administration, and jurisdiction while at the same time excluding them from otherwise applicable local laws. The system was based on by-laws (one set for Regional Councils, which are rural settlements, and another set for Local Councils, which include urban settlements), which were enacted by the two military commanders of the territories. The municipal regime of the settlements enacted by the by-laws was fashioned according to the Israeli municipal system. Many provisions in the by-laws explicitly incorporated Israeli primary and secondary legislation, including provisions relating to planning and building and to licensing of businesses. Changes in these Israeli laws were to automatically take effect within the local municipalities.[152] In short, the by-laws created in the settlements a legal environment very similar to that found within Israel. Since the by-laws were signed by the military commanders, they enjoyed a status of primary legislation in the territories, immunizing the settlements from the local laws, which would otherwise be applicable.[153]

A 1983 amendment to the by-laws expanded the scope of Israeli laws that applied in the settlements and also enabled the application of Israeli administration and jurisdiction to the settlements. In an unusual method of drafting, this was achieved through the extension of the jurisdiction of the Court of Domestic Affairs. Originally these courts were empowered to

---

[151] *K.P.A. Co. v. State of Israel*, 38 (1) PD 813, 819 (1984). The Court did not discuss its prior conflicting holding in *Sylvester, supra* note 131, where it did see a connection between such legislation and the law of occupation. In that case the Court ruled that the law of occupation may vest the power to legislate in occupied territories in the occupant's home government.

[152] Thus, for example, the rules that regulate the process of accepting personnel to the Israeli local administration are incorporated as a living body of rules in the by-laws. As this process includes examination and approval of nominees by Israeli authorities, the local authorities are also subject to the rules. So are the rights of the local and regional councils to allow their taxpayers to pay the annual municipal tax in installments, to collect interest on outstanding debts, to exempt from taxation, and to determine the fines for violations of local regulations.

[153] *See* Order Concerning Interpretation, paragraph 8, *supra* note 32. Even the regulations issued by the municipalities under the by-laws are elevated, for the purposes of the Order Concerning Interpretation, to the level of a security enactment of the military commander of the region (and therefore considered primary legislation in the territories): Paragraph 76 of the regional by-laws and paragraph 93 of the local by-laws provide that: "For the purpose of paragraph 8 of the Order Concerning Interpretation . . . the regulations made in pursuance of these bye-laws shall be deemed security enactments issued by the area Commander."

adjudicate claims between the residents of the settlements and their municipalities. Under the amendment, the courts' jurisdiction was enlarged. Not
only were they empowered to adjudicate issues arising under the by-laws
and the regulations enacted by the municipalities; they were also granted
jurisdiction over violations of certain security enactments, such as traffic
violations and infringements of building restrictions. But the most important grant of jurisdiction refered six to schedules that were attached to the
by-laws in this 1983 amendment. These six schedules represented six general fields of law ("welfare law," "statistics law," "personal status law," "education law," "health law," and "labor law"). Each schedule contained laws
that were incorporated into the by-laws in their entirety, including every
piece of secondary legislation, announcement, license, and other administrative instrument, and including any changes that would take effect in
Israel from time to time. The Court of Domestic Affairs had jurisdiction
to adjudicate any matter arising under these laws and to apply their substantive provisions. In this way, twenty-nine Israeli laws were incorporated
to cover the residents of the settlements, among them the Israeli laws that
determine the personal status of the inhabitants, interfamily rights, and
succession.[154] The domestic courts were also empowered to assume the
functions of the Israeli small claims court, thereby adjudicating small-scale
claims regarding private transactions.[155]

The domestic court system was two-tiered: a "domestic court of appeals" would hear appeals from the courts of first instance.[156] The judges
of the courts were nominated by the military commander from among the
acting judges of the Israeli courts.[157] The domestic court of Kiryat Arba,

[154] Schedule 3 applies to the settlers the Israeli laws of personal status that regulate, among
other things, adoption, marriage (including the age of marriage, the ownership and administration of communal property, and the duty to financially support members of the family),
and questions of legal competence, guardianship, and inheritance. The domicile of the settlers
for the purpose of these laws is also determined. The schedule creates a nonrebuttable presumption that these people are domiciled in Israel. See paragraphs 4(e)(2), 4(g)(6)(b),
4(k)(7). In other schedules, the Israeli requirements with regard to education and the practice
of medical, psychological, and related occupations are imposed. In the "labor law" schedule,
the Israeli order concerning minimum wages is extended to employees who are settlers. Rabbinical courts, erected by military orders, handle marriage and divorce matters.

[155] By-Law no. 138.

[156] Until now, the commander has established in the West Bank two courts of first instance:
one in Kiryat Arba, and the other in Ariel. An interesting question concerns the jurisdiction
of the Supreme Court of Israel sitting as a High Court of Justice over decisions of that domestic court system. It seems that such a jurisdiction exists, certainly in habeas corpus petitions (as jail orders of the domestic courts are to be executed by the Israeli authorities), but
also in other cases, since the High Court has already decided that it has jurisdiction over the
military personnel and other Israeli officials who exercise public executive functions in the
territories in the name of the military government. See, e.g., *Harpaz v. Head of the Civil Administration of Judea and Samaria*, 37 (4) PD 159 (1983).

[157] Judges of the Israeli magistrates' courts can be appointed to courts of first instance;
judges of the Israeli district courts, to the court of appeals.

for example, consisted of judges of the magistrates' court of Jerusalem; the domestic court of appeals consisted of judges of the district court of Jerusalem, which was also its place of meeting. Indeed, this appointment system assimilated the domestic courts as much as possible into the Israeli civil courts.

The 1983 schedules also gave Israeli administrative officials direct powers over the settlements with regard to the laws mentioned in the schedules.[158] Following this authorization, the director general of the Israeli Ministry of Education and Culture integrated the educational institutions of the settlements into the ministry,[159] and the director of the Employment Agency established a labor exchange to handle employment of Palestinians in the settlements.[160]

Finally, two other methods for extending Israeli laws should be mentioned: enactments of the military commander other than those in connection with the municipal by-laws, and the jurisprudence of the Israeli civil courts. The military orders relevant to economic conditions in the territories extended the Israeli minimum wage and the adjustment of wages to the cost-of-living index to all those who work in the settlements.[161] Another order established a special execution bureau to deal only with judgments rendered in Israel against Israelis (natural or legal entities).[162] The jurisprudence of the Israeli courts in choice-of-laws issues also contributed to the extension of Israeli law to the settlements, as torts committed in the territories between Israelis were held to be governed by Israeli law.[163] Probably the same rule applied to contracts between Israelis.[164]

---

[158] Paragraph 140A of the by-laws.

[159] The director general decided on the division of districts on February 20, 1984.

[160] *See* Order of the Employment Services (The Establishment of an Office for Employment and its Jurisdiction) of May 29, 1985.

[161] Order Concerning the Employment of Workers in Certain Places (Judea and Samaria) (no. 967), 5742–1982, paragraph 3 (as amended on November 19, 1987). There are no minimum wage or index adjustments in other workplaces in the territories.

[162] Paragraph 4A of the Order Concerning Legal Aid, *supra* note 124. In this bureau there is no need to append an Arabic translation of the document.

[163] *Kaplan v. Gabai*, [1982] (2) PSM 290; *Katz v. Segal*, [1986] (2) PSM 119. These cases followed a line of reasoning that is accepted in many jurisdictions. In the United States, the first such case was *Babcock v. Jackson*, 12 N.Y.2d 473 (1963); in England, it was *Chaplin v. Boys*, [1969] 2 All E.R. 1085. The same rule is accepted in many European countries. 2 H. Batiffol and P. Lagarde, *Droit international privé*, paragraph 558, at 239–42 (7th ed. 1983). In fact, the first use of this rule was made by Germany during World War II, through an ordinance of December 7, 1942, which applied German tort law to torts committed abroad by German nationals or German institutions against other Germans. This wartime ordinance has not been invalidated since, and seems to be still in effect. G. Kegel, *Internationales Privatrecht* 465–66 (6th ed. 1987).

[164] Contracts between Israeli employers and employees for labor to be performed in the territories are governed by Israeli law. *Kiryat Arba Administrative Board v. National Labor Court*, 34 (2) PD 398, 403 (1979) ("To Israeli workers who are employed by the Com-

Applicable International Law

THE SETTLEMENTS

Aside from the economic, social, and political effects of the creation of Israeli enclaves in the territories, the question of the intrinsic legality of such enclaves under the law of occupation arises. The conventional debate regarding the legality of Israeli settlement in the territories revolves around Article 49(6) of the Fourth Geneva Convention, which provides that the "Occupying Power shall not deport or transfer parts of its own civilian population into the territory it occupies." The settlement policy has been criticized by the United Nations, the ICRC, and various countries and commentators.[165] On the other hand, an Israeli interpretation of this article[166] asserted that the settlements did not contravene the Fourth Geneva Convention since "Arab inhabitants have not been displaced by Israeli settlements," and that the article "refers to State actions by which the government in control transfers parts of its population to the territory concerned. This cannot be construed to cover the voluntary movement of individuals . . . not as a result of State transfer but of their own volition and as an expression of their personal choice."[167] This interpretation is doubtful, since it seems that the purpose of the article is to protect the interests of the occupied population, rather than the population of the occupant.[168] But assuming it were correct, this interpretation does not explain from where the occupant derives the legal power to undertake a massive settlement project such as that which the Israeli government planned and nurtured, as described above.[169] It is also questionable whether the settlement policy is in line with the Article 43 of the Hague Regulations, since this

---

mander of the Area . . . apply the Israeli labor law, including the right to litigate in Israel's labor courts.").

[165] The International Committee of the Red Cross viewed the settlement issue as being controlled by Article 49 in *The Middle East Activities of the ICRC*, 10 Int'l Rev. Red Cross 424 (1970). It states that the ICRC has intervened against settlement efforts when such were "immediately detrimental to the Arab residents." *Id.* at 459. On the reactions of the UN General Assembly and Security Council, *see Roberts, supra* note 5, at 85–86.

[166] The Israeli section of the International Commission of Jurists, *The Rule of Law in the Areas Administered by Israel* 54–55 (1981).

[167] *See also* Dinstein, *Human Rights, supra* note 5, at 124; Rostow, *Palestinian Self-Determination: Possible Futures for the Unallocated Territories of the Palestine Mandate*, 5 Yale Studies in World Public Order 147, 160 (1979).

[168] J. Pictet, ed., *Commentary: The Fourth Geneva Convention* 283 (1958); H. Lauterpacht, ed., *Oppenheim's International Law* 452 (7th. ed. 1948). The general theme of the Fourth Geneva Convention is to protect people from acts of a government that is not their own. Under Article 4 of the convention, the persons protected under the convention are those who find themselves in the hand of the occupant "of which they are not nationals."

[169] *See* Roberts, *supra* note 5, at 85.

policy cannot be deemed a matter of security of the occupation forces, and it is even more difficult to demonstrate its contribution to "public order and civil life."

Aside from this debate, another claim can be made on another level. The cumulative effect of the methods described here regarding the application of Israeli law, administration, and jurisdiction to the settlements and their residents was in fact the extension of Israeli jurisdiction, which was in many respects similar to the extension of Israeli rule to East Jerusalem and the Golan Heights.[170] The same criticism of these two explicit acts can be directed toward the much more complicated process of de facto annexation of the settlements. Indeed, only if one subscribes to the opinion that Israel had a better title over the territories and therefore was entitled to assume sovereignty over them, would one be able to argue that this practice was legal.[171] However, Israel refrained from asserting sovereignty, and relied instead on the occupant's powers under the law of occupation. It seems that the law of occupation does not sanction such acts.

THE ECONOMIC UNION

The Israeli Supreme Court justified the establishment of the economic union as being in line with—indeed, required by—Article 43 of the Hague Regulations.[172] In view of the relative strength of the different economies, the geographic proximity, and, in the case of Gaza, the lack of trade with Egypt, the economic convergence was inevitable. Maintaining an economic, pre-1967 "green line" would have meant stagnation, unemployment, and social unrest in the territories. The creation of a single market, on the other hand, boosted the standard of living in the territories.[173] Theoretically, two options were possible at the beginning of the occupation, in view of the poor condition of the occupied economies: their integration with the Israeli economy or their massive development as self-sustaining economies. The first option was more realistic, as it relied on the existing infrastructure of the much larger and more developed Israeli economy. That option was also preferred by the military administration because it was deemed to be in line with Israeli economic interests. The intifada and the resulting attempt to restrict the flow of workers from the territories into Israel seem to have led to a reappraisal of this policy, and measures

[170] On the status of East Jerusalem *see supra* text accompanying notes 17–24; on the Golan Heights, *see supra* text accompanying notes 25–28.

[171] On this claim, with respect to Jerusalem, *see supra* note 22.

[172] *Abu-Aita, supra* note 55.

[173] *See, e.g.,* Kahan, *supra* note 112, at 68–70.

were taken to encourage private initiatives to develop the economic infra-structure of the territories.[174]

While the economic integration was conducive to maintaining "public order and civil life" in the territories, it was also beneficial to the Israeli economy. The territories were an unfailing source of cheap labor, and a sizable market for consumer goods.[175] Whenever Israeli interests could have been jeopardized by the free flow of goods, services, and people, mea-sures were taken to counter the risks. Thus the flow of workers to Israel was restricted in time (no overnight stay), and their wages reduced to en-sure equality with the net wages of Israeli workers after deductions for social benefits.[176] The flow of fresh produce from the territories into Israel and abroad, which could at times compete with Israeli produce, was con-trolled by granting individual permits.[177] Transactions between Israelis and residents of the territories were governed by Israeli law and adjudi-cated in Israeli courts.

The unification of the economies was in fact an economic annexation. Although the territories retained their separate legal status, and were gov-erned by military administrations based on international law and indepen-dent of Israeli law, the regulation of the economies in the territories was directed by the Israeli legislature and government. Given the necessity of maintaining the economic union, the military authorities had to follow closely the changes introduced in the Israeli economy and to adopt them in the territories.

The decision of the Israeli Supreme Court regarding the adoption of the VAT in the territories[178] may serve as a confirmation that economic unifi-cation came to mean economic annexation. The imposition of the VAT in the territories coincided with a similar one that was introduced in Israel. The military authorities claimed that the new tax was necessary to protect the local residents from a situation in which the VAT was imposed only in Israel. In such a case, they reasoned, Israel would have had to resurrect the economic borders and impose restrictions on the free flow of goods and services. This alternative, so they claimed, would have worked to the det-riment first and foremost of the local population. In other words, the main reason for the tax was not to increase revenues, but to retain the interde-

---

[174] *A Change of Policy in the Territories: The Inhabitants Will Be Permitted to Build Factories in Order to Develop an Independent Economy*, Ha'Aretz, December 23, 1990, at 1, col. 2. The *State Comptroller Report, no. 41*, at 850 (1990), noted that between 1986 and early 1990, about eighty requests for permits were presented to the authorities, of which only seven were approved. Later, in August of 1990, thirty-six requests were granted.

[175] By extending the import duties to the territories, the highly protected Israeli industry enjoyed a larger consumer market for its products.

[176] *See supra* text accompanying note 107.

[177] *See supra* text accompanying note 90.

[178] *Abu-Aita, supra* note 55.

pendency of the economies.[179] The Israeli Supreme Court, holding that under international law occupants could introduce new taxes, upheld the new tax, affirming the authorities' concern:

> As a result [of the economic integration], the military government at its outset took action to equalize rates of indirect taxes. . . . Having seen that a Value Added Tax *must* be introduced in Israel, the wheel could not be turned back without affecting the proper fulfillment of the duties deriving from Article 43.[180]

In other words, the decision to impose the VAT in the territories was in reaction to the introduction of the VAT in Israel, which was a "must." This reasoning authorized the military authorities, indeed, obliged them, to follow the changes that took effect within Israel and implement them in the territories so that the Israeli government would not resurrect the pre-1967 borders. Given the necessity of maintaining integration, the military authorities were left without any real discretion regarding economic policies. Rather, they served as proxies for the implementation of economic policies decided upon by the Israeli body-politic. The fiction of an independent military administration immunized decisions of the Israeli government from their scrutiny under international law by the Court, and at the same time provided a justification for the military "reactions." The fiction attempted to conceal the fact that the interests of the local population had become secondary to the occupant's interests and policies, which were taken for granted. This concept of occupation permitted the democratic processes within Israel to continue without sharing of political power with the indigenous population of the territories.

It is arguable that the law of occupation would object to such an outcome: if economic integration is necessary to maintain "public order and civil life," then the decisions taken by the national institutions of the occupant concerning economic policies that also affect the occupied territory should also be subject to the requirements of the law of occupation. In other words, the government must foresee the eventual adoption of its policies in the occupied territory, and therefore is required under the law of occupation to give ample consideration at the outset to the interests of that area's inhabitants. However, it is highly unlikely that a legislature and government would recognize a duty to balance the interests of their national economy with those of the occupied territory, whether in economic matters or in any other matter. Realistically there is little hope that the law of occupation will loom large among the considerations influencing policymaking in such an integrated economy. It seems, therefore, that removal of trade barriers between the occupied and occupant regions and further

---

[179] *Id.* at 105–6 (references are to the English translation).
[180] *Id.* at 104 (my emphasis).

economic integration would sooner or later evolve into an actual economic annexation.[181] Moreover, this economic integration is a measure that is likely to create unwarranted incentives for the occupant to carry on with the occupation. Thus, economic integration is not necessarily a proper avenue for the occupant to take. For the occupied community, there is much to be lost from such an embrace. It is therefore suggested that measures aimed at economic integration are justified only as long as the economic situation in the occupied region is severe and separation is not likely to improve the situation. Thus, it would probably be illegal to integrate an affluent occupied region into an occupant's impoverished economy. If upon occupation, the occupied region suffers economic hardship, then integration might be a proper step. But even if integration is justified, this does not mean that it continues to be justified for the entire period of occupation: ideally, the justification for economic integration should be reevaluated from time to time, in light of new data on the current strength of the occupied economy and its potential to sustain itself. The problem is that the occupant's policies may easily shape the predicament of the occupied economy, according to its interests. This is especially true of long-term occupations, an issue dealt with more closely in the following pages.

Long-Term Occupations and the Law of Occupation

The protraction of the Israeli occupation provides an opportunity to discuss some general issues concerning long-term occupations. The Hague Regulations did not envision that a peace treaty between the rival powers would take long to reach. In the nineteenth century, military defeats were soon followed by peace treaties and border modifications, and thus occupations were short lived. The Fourth Geneva Convention did envision the possibility of protracted occupation, providing in Article 6, *inter alia*, that "[i]n the case of occupied territory, the application of the present Convention shall cease one year after the general close of military operations," except for specific enumerated provisions, which were to continue in force for the duration of the occupation. Most of the articles dealing with occupation, including the important Article 64, which deals with the occupant's prescriptive powers, are enumerated as the exceptions that are retained as long as the occupation lasts. Therefore the two major instruments regarding the law of occupation do not provide meaningful guidelines for

---

[181] Feilchenfeld observed that "it would seem less clear that a mere occupant is free to abolish all the customs lines between his own country and the occupied region; for this almost invariably would be an intrinsic measure of complete annexation which a mere occupant has no right to effect." E. Feilchenfeld, *The International Economic Law of Belligerent Occupation* 83 (1942).

lawful deviations from the regular rules of occupation in cases of protracted occupations.

Is There a Time Limit to Occupation?

Does the occupant have the right to retain control over the occupied territory until its conditions for a peaceful arrangement are met? Does it have a duty to relinquish control under certain circumstances? Ultimately, the question is, upon whom does the burden of breaking political stalemate lie when negotiations for peace fail?

The basic principles of traditional occupation law call for the occupant to assume control over the affairs of the occupied territory for the duration of the occupation. Neither the Hague Regulations nor the Fourth Geneva Convention limits the duration of the occupation or requires the occupant to restore the territories to the sovereign before a peace treaty is signed. As Oppenheim succinctly described this principle,

> If a belligerent succeeds in occupying the whole, or even a part, of enemy territory, he has realized a very important aim of warfare. He can now not only use the resources of the enemy country for military purposes, *but can also keep it for the time being as a pledge of his military success, and thereby impress upon the enemy the necessity of submitting to terms of peace.*[182]

Some of the UN resolutions regarding the Israeli occupation can be seen as an effort to revise that position. At first, Security Council Resolution 242 (1967) was widely accepted as being in line with the abovementioned proposition, as it linked the withdrawal from occupied territories with the establishment of a just and lasting peace.[183] However, later resolutions of the General Assembly voiced another message. In large part because of the Israeli occupation, a 1973 General Assembly resolution "resolutely supported" the efforts of peoples under "foreign occupation in their struggle to regain control over their natural resources."[184] This time the message was that occupation in itself is unlawful, or at the very least, that the occupant is not entitled to delay with respect to a peaceful solution of the conflict.[185]

[182] 2 Lauterpacht, *supra* note 168, at 432 (my emphasis). Shamgar, *Legal Concepts, supra* note 3, at 43, adds that "pending an alternative political or military solution [occupation] . . . could, from a legal point of view, continue indefinitely."

[183] 22 UN SCOR (1382d mtg.) at 8–9 (1967).

[184] General Assembly Resolution 3171 (XXVIII), of December 17, 1973.

[185] The occupant's powers were further curtailed by Resolutions 3175 (XXVIII) (1973) and 3336 (XXIX) (1974), which would render unlawful, and subject to full compensation, the exploitation of natural and human resources in occupied territories.

It is suggested that an occupation regime that refuses to earnestly contribute to efforts to reach a peaceful solution should be considered illegal. Indeed, such a refusal should be considered outright annexation. The occupant has a duty under international law to conduct negotiations in good faith for a peaceful solution. It would seem that an occupant who proposes unreasonable conditions, or otherwise obstructs negotiations for peace for the purpose of retaining control over the occupied territory, could be considered a violator of international law. There is a fine but definite line between the permitted use of the occupation as a bargaining chip, and the illegal use of the occupied population as hostages.[186] The problem is to determine when the inflexible occupant crosses that fine line of legal bargaining. It is suggested that no such claim of illegality would be proper as long as the occupant's conditions for peaceful settlement of the conflict are motivated by reasonable security interests.

Changes in the Occupant's Powers during Long-Term Occupations

Does the mere fact that the occupation lingers on confer upon the occupant more powers than in a short-term occupation, or is it, rather, the other way round? The answer given by the Israeli Supreme Court accords with the first proposition. Four years into the occupation, the Court held that as the occupation period gets longer, the occupant's powers to prescribe widen:

> Life does not stand still, and no administration, whether an occupation administration or another, can fulfil its duties with respect to the population if it refrains from legislating and from adapting the legal situation to the exigencies of modern times.[187]

A 1983 decision went even further. Not only was the occupant entitled and obliged to react to changing conditions; it was empowered to undertake major investments and long-term planning that would anticipate the future demands of the local community.[188] In contrast to this view, Adam

---

[186] This position might be criticized by the following proposition: since the occupant's rivals would probably claim that the occupant is not a bona fide occupant, they would similarly treat its prescriptions as illegal and void. These conflicting positions would inject political considerations into the law of occupation, destroy its promise of an impartial and apolitical administrative mechanism, and undermine any prospects of certainty and stability of expectations in this field. I doubt if such repercussions will be significant, given the fact that rivals' reactions to occupants' measures have usually been negative even without the claim I make now. For the reactions of ousted and returning governments, *see, e.g., Supra* Chapter 2.

[187] *The Christian Society for the Sacred Places v. Minister of Defence*, 26 (1) PD 574, 582 (1971).

[188] *Jama'iat Iscan, supra* note 9, at 811.

Roberts maintains that "it could be argued that in a prolonged occupation, as in a pacific one, the rights of the occupants are vastly curtailed."[189]

Both approaches are based on the assumption that in a prolonged occupation the maintenance of the *status quo ante* could prove insupportable to the local population. Indeed, it would be wrong, and even at times illegal, to freeze the legal situation and prevent adaptations when an occupation is extended. But this does not mean that it is the occupant who is entitled to assume the duty to update the law. In prolonged occupations conditions change quite regularly, partly because of the occupant's own policies; to recognize the occupant's widening powers to react to these changes or even to initiate new ones would effectively grant the occupant almost all the powers a modern sovereign government would wield. In modern times, the occupant's interests encompass not only the safety of its troops but also a wide variety of economic concerns, and not only temporary benefits but also long-term advantages. Politicians and soldiers are not saints, and one must expect the occupant to be prejudiced in favor of its own country's interests at the expense of the indigenous community. Therefore, instead of allowing the occupant to extend its powers as new circumstances require, the aim of the law of occupation should be to encourage the participation of the indigenous community and of the ousted government, all subject to the occupant's safety concerns.

Indeed, the law of occupation allows for indigenous input in the affairs of the occupied territory, in fact, mandates it. The prevailing scholarly opinion is that the ousted government is entitled to have its prescriptions respected by the occupant (as long as they do not impinge on the latter's powers and duties).[190] Thus, changes in the legal system introduced by the ousted government to meet novel circumstances not involving the occupant's security concerns would, according to the theory, also be automatically applicable in the occupied territory. If the occupant wanted to prevent these changes from taking effect, it would have to abolish the new act and justify the measure under the law of occupation. In the same vein, decisions relating to administrative matters that do not impinge on the occupant's security interests may be entrusted to the local administrations, the municipalities for example.

This solution is plausible in theory, but it has been never applied. No occupant has ever allowed the prescriptions of the ousted government to take effect in the territory under its control. Upon assuming control, occupants would seal the legal system from outside intervention.[191] There-

---

[189] Roberts, *supra* note 5, at 52. He does, however, recognize the occupant's power to make drastic and permanent changes in the economy or system of government if such are needed. *Id*. at 53.

[190] *Supra* Chapter 2, text accompanying notes 45–49.

[191] *See supra* note 54; *supra* Chapter 2, text accompanying note 45.

fore it is important to emphasize that by law, in severing the legal ties between the occupied area and the indigenous government, the occupant is not relieved, at the very least, from the duty to *consult* the latter's prescriptions. Whenever there is a need to update the existing law, the occupant must weigh whether a solution introduced by the ousted government in the unoccupied part is not also suitable to the occupied area; whenever the ousted government introduces changes, the occupant should inquire whether a similar change is warranted in the area under its control.[192] Any deviation from the enactments of the ousted government must be justified under the law of occupation.

This suggestion would not be helpful if the ousted government failed to undertake the necessary modifications in the area under its control, or if for any reason its prescriptions were not suitable for the occupied area. In such a situation it is suggested that the occupant's expanded powers be recognized, but at the same time that it be recognized that the occupant is required to delegate powers as much as possible to locally elected officials, such as mayors or heads of economic associations, and consult with them on major initiatives prior to their implementation.

[192] In case of conflict of interests between the population under occupation and the ousted government, the Fourth Geneva Convention, if not the Hague Regulations, would seem to prefer the interests of the local population. *See supra* Chapter 2, text accompanying notes 79, 81). The long-term occupant is therefore required under the law of occupation to pay ample attention to the input of the occupied community regarding the management of the latter's country.

6

Occupations since the 1970s and Recent International Prescriptions

WITH THE exception of the Israeli occupation after the 1967 war, all other occupants after World War II refrained from resorting to the Hague Regulations or the Fourth Geneva Convention as the source of their authority or as a guide to their actions. The propensity to avoid the regime of occupation is particularly noticeable in the various occupations of the 1970s and early 1980s. These occupations, the international reactions to them, and other international developments during this era, have greatly complicated the law of occupation. In this chapter I shall try to extract from the factual account of these occupations the salient principles that emerge to qualify the traditional conception of occupation and help assess the promise of future compliance with the law of occupation.

It is not a coincidence that modern occupants fail to recognize the applicability of the law of occupation to their actions in foreign countries under their control. In many cases this denial is an indirect outcome of their purported justification for using force. Thus, to take a recurring example, a state that explains its use of force as being in support of another state whose government had purportedly requested its intervention would treat that local government as the only source of authority within that state, although actual control would be in the occupant's hands. The occupations in Afghanistan, Grenada, and Panama would seem to follow this pattern. In other cases, the occupants would not acknowledge the applicability of the law of occupation because they were interested in permanent and exclusive control over coveted foreign territories, which is, of course, incompatible with the basic tenets of the law of occupation. Clear examples of such a policy are the occupations of Kuwait, Western Sahara, and East Timor. Thirdly, the applicability of the law of occupation is likely to be ignored when title to territory is disputed between the warring factions, as with respect to the Israeli-occupied territories, or in cases where the principle of self-determination is invoked against the conflicting idea of territorial integrity, as in the cases of Bangladesh and Cyprus. Lastly, occupants conducting limited-scale operations inside another state's territory tend not to recognize formally the applicablity of the law of occupation, in order not to create the impression that they plan to stay in the occupied region for a long time. This was the case in the occupations of southern and northern Iraq during the 1991 Persian Gulf War and the Israeli 1982 invasion of Lebanon. Since these four types of conflict comprise the bulk of contemporary conflicts, the prospects that future occupants will voluntarily recognize the applicability of the law of occupation and respect its provisions are rather slim.

The international community regarded most, but not all, of those recent instances as occupations. Why were not all instances regarded as occupations? And in what circumstances will the international community recognize cases in which force is used to gain control over areas as occupations? The goal of this section is to provide an answer to these questions by analyzing the claims and conduct of recent occupants, and the international reactions to them.

Attempts to Annex Adjacent Regions: Kuwait, Western Sahara, and East Timor

In the last two decades, three occupants attempted to annex territorial units adjacent to the occupant's country, attempts that were widely regarded as illegal. The overall strong international condemnation of those acts, and the successful military operation to force one of these actors, Iraq, to end its occupation of Kuwait, reinforced the basic premise of the law of occupation, namely that the use of force does not confer sovereignty over a territory. However, in contrast to the solid reaction to Iraq's proclaimed annexation of Kuwait, the international community's half-hearted reaction to another case, the Indonesian "annexation" of East Timor, is sorry evidence of the persistent shortcomings of international enforcement mechanisms.

The Iraqi Occupation of Kuwait

The Iraqi invasion of Kuwait on August 2, 1990, was purportedly undertaken at the behest of Kuwaiti revolutionaries who had launched a coup against the emir.[1] On the same day a Provisional Free Kuwaiti Government (PFKG) claimed to have replaced the al-Sabah regime. Apparently, the Iraqis failed to enlist Kuwaiti dissidents in this government, and according to Kuwaiti officials, the membership list of the PFKG released on August 5 included only Iraqi nationals. After staging an Iraqi "withdrawal" and the establishment of a so-called Republic of Kuwait by the PFKG, Iraq annexed Kuwait on August 8, following the PFKG's request. On August 28, Iraq incorporated Kuwait as its nineteenth province, after having renamed the Kuwaiti towns and other locations.

[1] The facts are drawn from 36 Keesing's Record of World Events 37632–35 (1990).

The international response was firm. A series of UN Security Council resolutions condemned the Iraqi invasion and demanded Iraq's immediate and unconditional withdrawal;[2] decided that "annexation of Kuwait by Iraq under any form and whatever pretext has no legal validity, and is considered null and void"; and "call[ed] upon all states, international organizations and specialized agencies not to recognize the annexation, and to refrain from any action or dealing that might be interpreted as an indirect recognition of the annexation."[3] The Security Council further demanded that Iraq rescind its actions purporting to annex Kuwait and its orders for the closure of the diplomatic and consular missions in Kuwait,[4] and reaffirmed Iraq's responsibility under international humanitarian law, including the Fourth Geneva Convention.[5] The demands of the Security Council were backed by an effective blockade, implemented under Resolution 661 of August 6, and later the authorization of the states cooperating with the government of Kuwait to use all necessary means to uphold and implement the resolutions regarding the crisis (Resolution 678 of November 29). In line with this resolution, a twenty-nine-nation coalition, led by U.S. forces, attacked Iraqi forces in Kuwait and Iraq on January 16, 1991, and defeated them on February 25.

I chose to begin the survey of recent occupations with this incident because it was a simple case from the vantage point of the law of occupation, as the illegality of the purported annexation and the applicability of the law of occupation were obvious, and, indeed, were recognized as such by the international community. It was also the first instance since World War II where concerted international reaction forcefully undid the illegal measures. Thus this incident reaffirmed the basic tenet of the law of occupation, the inalienability of sovereignty through the use of force. This seems to be a good starting point for a discussion of other instances of occupations in the last two decades, where a less than firm reaction met similar illegal acts.

The Moroccan Occupation of Western Sahara

This is also a tale of illegal annexation internationally recognized as such.[6] Contrary to the case of Kuwait, however, in this case the international reaction proved less effective.

[2] Resolution 660 of August 2, Articles 1 and 2. The Arab League reached a similar decision on August 10, although nine of the twenty-one members did not vote in favor of the decision.

[3] Resolution 662 of August 9, paragraphs 1 and 2.

[4] Resolution 664 of August 18, paragraph 3.

[5] Resolution 666 of September 13, 1990, Preamble and Article 2; Resolution 674 of October 29, Preamble and Articles 1 and 3.

[6] On the Moroccan seizure of power in Western Sahara, *see* 22 Keesing's Record of World's Events 27575–77 (1976). Factual account of later developments in the region is provided in

As Spain was about to relinquish control over Western Sahara, then a colony named Spanish Sahara, King Hassan of Morocco was determined to prevent the Saharawi people's opportunity to exercise their right to self-determination,[7] reaffirmed in an advisory opinion by the International Court of Justice.[8] After the International Court of Justice rejected Morocco's claims regarding Western Sahara, Morocco nevertheless reiterated its claim to historical title over the territory and announced its plan to stage the "Green March," a march of about 350,000 unarmed Moroccans across the international border. The four days' march (November 6 through 9, 1975) precipitated a tripartite agreement among Spain, Morocco, and Mauritania, signed in Madrid on November 14, and approved by the Spanish Cortes on November 21.[9] Under the Madrid Agreement, a provisional administration would assume Spain's powers and responsibilities over Western Sahara. Moroccan and Mauritanian representatives would participate in this administration. In fact the Madrid Agreement was nothing less than the transfer of authority over that area to Morocco and Mauritania. Soon thereafter, the Moroccan and Mauritanian governments agreed on the partition of the area between themselves and the joint utilization of the area's rich phosphate deposits, and proceeded to occupy their respective parts. Morocco claimed to have annexed the areas under its control. In 1979 Mauritania signed a peace agreement with the Polisario (Popular Front for the Liberation of Saguia el Hamra and Rio de Oro) as the exiled government of the self-proclaimed Saharan Arab Democratic Republic (SADR), and withdrew from Western Sahara. Thereupon, Moroccan forces occupied the areas evacuated by Mauritania. Since 1979 Western Sahara has been internally divided into four provinces, each having assigned seats in the Moroccan Parliament. In 1992 it was estimated that about one hundred thousand permanent troops were stationed in Western Sahara, costing Morocco at least $100 million a year.

The occupation of Western Sahara met with strong criticism. Despite the Madrid Agreement, the General Assembly "deeply deplore[d]" the situation resulting from the "continued occupation of Western Sahara by Morocco,"[10] and reaffirmed the right of Western Sahara to freely exercise

---

A. Day, ed., *Keesing's Border and Territorial Disputes* 172–83 (2d ed. 1987). For legal analyses of the Western Sahara problem, *see* Franck, *The Stealing of the Sahara*, 70 AJIL 694 (1976); Vance, *Recognition as an Affirmative Step in the Decolonization Process: The Case of Western Sahara*, 7 Yale J. World Public Order 45 (1980–1981).

[7] Under the UN General Assembly's *Declaration on the Granting of Independence to Colonial Countries and Peoples*, Resolution 1514 (XV) of December 14, 1960.

[8] *Western Sahara (Advisory Opinion)*, [1975] ICJ Rep. 12.

[9] 30 UN SCOR, Supp. for October–December 1975, at 41, UN Doc. S/11880, Annex (1975) III.

[10] *See* Resolution 34/37 of November 21, 1979. The colonial power has no power to transfer title with regard to a colony or to recognize the right of another state to claim the territory.

its right to self-determination under the 1960 decolonization declaration in an internationally monitored referendum. Otherwise, international pressure on Morocco was limited, generally consisting of recognition extended to the SADR. The Organization of African Unity added the SADR to its list of members only in 1984, yet failed to induce Morocco to comply with its duties under the 1960 decolonization declaration. It is believed that the continuing guerilla warfare of the Polisario forces against Morocco was the cause of the Moroccan acceptance in 1991 of the UN-sponsored plan to hold a referendum early in 1992 on the future of the region. For that purpose, a UN Mission for the Referendum in Western Sahara was established by the Security Council in April 1991.[11]

The Indonesian Occupation of East Timor

As in the case of Western Sahara, the case of East Timor also involves the intervention of a neighboring state that prevented the indigenous community from exercising its internationally recognized right to self-determination to end a colonial rule.[12] The account of the occupation and purported annexation of East Timor is of special significance for international lawyers and politicians since, in sharp contrast to other similar incidents, in this case the world has by and large acquiesced to Indonesia's measures.

The Island of Timor is located at the eastern tip of the Indonesian archipelago, to the northwest of Australia. Its western part, which had been a Dutch colony, became part of Indonesia with the latter's independence. Its eastern part, East Timor, had been a Portuguese colony since the sixteenth

---

See separate opinion of Judge De Castro in *Western Sahara (Advisory Opinion)*, *supra* note 8, at 145. This principle is implicit in Article 73 of the UN Charter, which delimits the powers of the colonial power with respect to the inhabitants of the "non-self-governing territories."

[11] International Herald Tribune, June 26, 1991, at 2.

[12] The history of the Indonesian annexation of East Timor is well documented. Invaluable and credible information is found in J. Dunn, *Timor: A People Betrayed* (1983). Its author, who has been the Australian consul in Dili, the East Timorese Capital, draws on innumerable sources, including interviews of Timorese refugees and "a number of well placed Indonesian sources." *Id.* at x. Other accounts, which generally support Dunn's findings, although less rich with confidential sources, are B. Nicol, *Timor: The Stillborn Nation* (1978); J. Jolliffe, *East Timor: Nationalism and Colonialism* (1978); Clark, *The "Decolonization" of East Timor and the United Nations Norms on Self-Determination and Aggression*, 7 Yale J. World Public Order 2 (1980). Two comprehensive accounts of the practices of the occupation authorities after the "annexation" are C. Budardjo and L. Soei Liong, *The War Against East Timor* (1984); F. Hiorth, *Timor: Past and Present* (South East Asian Monograph no. 17, 1985).

For legal analyses of the East Timor question, *see* Clark, *supra* note 12; Elliott, *The East Timor Dispute*, 27 ICLQ 238 (1978); Franck and Hoffman, *The Right of Self-Determination in Very Small Places*, 8 N.Y.U. J. Int'l L. and Politics 331 (1976); Lawrence, *East Timor*, in 12 EPIL 94 (1990).

century. In 1974, the new Portuguese regime, which had just overthrown the Salazar government, recognized its duty to enable the Portuguese colonies to exercise their rights to self-determination and independence. At that time, the population of East Timor was estimated at over 688,000 people, 97 percent of them indigenous East Timorese.

The process of decolonization of East Timor, which began in July 1974 with the amendment of the Portuguese constitution, ended two years afterwards, with Indonesia's formal annexation of the country as its twenty-seventh province. The annexation was the culmination of a gradual Indonesian process to gain control over the territory. At first, when Portuguese forces were still present in East Timor, Indonesia supported local East Timorese elements, who on August 11, 1975, started an armed struggle against the popular Fretilin movement (Frente Revolutionaria de Timor Leste Independente). This attempt failed: Fretilin gained the upper hand within less than three weeks. After the Portuguese pullout, by the end of August, Fretilin consolidated its control over the entire territory, and forced the pro-Indonesian leaders out of the country. The Indonesian plan to intervene as "peacemakers" in the internal fighting failed after Fretilin's swift victory brought almost all fighting to an immediate halt. Therefore the Indonesian army organized those pro-Indonesian leaders on Indonesian soil as a "movement," which requested their host country to intervene on their behalf. In October units of the Indonesian army seized three towns just across the border from West Timor, and finally the major offensive came on December 7. This offensive, which caused an estimated loss of between one hundred thousand and two hundred thousand lives among the East Timorese (15–30 percent of the population), brought East Timor under Indonesian control.

Indonesia invaded a territory under the indigenous effective control of Fretilin. During its three-month rule, the Fretilin administration enjoyed wide popularity among the people. Yet its Central Committee, seeking Portuguese aid, stated as late as September its continued recognition of Portugal's sovereignty. The unilateral declaration of independence was made only on November 28, 1975, in a desperate move aimed at gaining international support.

Immediately after the invasion, the Indonesians established a "Provisional Government of East Timor" consisting of the same pro-Indonesian figures. In February 1976, all the political parties in East Timor were unified, and a "People's Assembly" was convened. On May 31, this body unanimously approved a petition to President Suharto for integration with Indonesia. On July 16, 1976, the Indonesian Parliament passed a bill incorporating East Timor as Indonesia's twenty-seventh province. The bill took effect the following day, upon the signature of President Suharto.

OCCUPATION POLICIES

The first appointed governor of the new province was the leader of the former provisional government. Ostensibly the province was to have a large measure of autonomy, through the "Regional People's Representative Council." In fact, East Timor was under the administration of the Indonesian army since its incorporation. While the military commander was in charge of military operations, the regional area secretary, called the sekwilda, was in charge of the political, social, and economic integration of the province with Indonesia.[13] The sekwilda has always been an army officer. In 1982, general elections were held in Indonesia, and also in the "twenty-seventh province." The official returns for East Timor indicated a turnout of more than all the registered voters, 99 percent of whom voted for Golkar, the army's party.

The policy of *integrasi* (integration) entailed both acculturation of the East Timorese and resettlement plans. The Timorese population was subject to indoctrination by Indonesian teachers according to the curriculum effective in Indonesia.[14] The only language spoken in schools was the official Indonesian language, Bahasa Indonesia. Since the Indonesian functionaries did not speak Tetum, the East Timorese lingua franca, everyone had to master Bahasa Indonesia in order to communicate with the authorities. The resettlement effort was two-pronged. One prong was an internal resettling of East Timorese in highly populated centers, with limited access to land. The large centers facilitated the occupant's control over the indigenous population, and the further isolation of the Fretilin. The policy also had the secondary advantage of gaining control over the arable lands, made inaccessible to the locals.[15] The other resettlement policy concerned the migration of families from densely populated areas in other parts of Indonesia to the East Timorese countryside. Concurrently, despite the high death toll of the recent past, the government was running a birth control program, which provided contraceptives to all residents. The utilization of

[13] A detailed account of the integration policies is found in C. Budiarjo and L. Soei Liong, *supra* note 12.

[14] *See* Department of Foreign Affairs, Republic of Indonesia, *Decolonization in East Timor* 49 (undated pamphlet), stating: "Recognizing that education will play a very important role in the province's efforts to make progress, the provincial government has requested a large quantity of text books in the Indonesian language. In response to this plea, substantial quantities of educational materials have already been sent to East Timor and hundreds of qualified teacher-volunteers have also begun to instruct the East Timorese people in a number of fields."

[15] The Indonesians claim that the concentration of communities is required to bring them education, public health, and other services of a modernized society. D. Weatherbee, *The Situation in East Timor* 20–23 (Occasional Paper, University of South Carolina, Institute of International Studies, 1980). The author gives a grim account of deliberate malnutrition and poor health conditions in those concentration camps.

economic resources was allotted to a single firm, P.T. Denok Hernandez International, an Indonesian company controlled by military personnel. P.T. Denok established a monopoly over the important coffee and sandalwood industries.[16]

Despite all these measures, it seems that the Indonesian *integrasi* plan did not diminish the East Timorese desire for self-determination. Despite Indonesia's claims to the contrary, it was generally recognized (and was affirmed by UN resolutions until 1982) that the East Timorese people were historically, culturally, and religiously distinct from the other peoples of Indonesia. In the summer of 1992, there were still reports of several hundred Fretilin fighters, who continued to stage sporadic guerilla attacks against the Indonesian army. When Pope John Paul II visited Dili in October 1989, there was a demonstration, which indicated that the East Timorese were not ready to abandon their fight.[17]

THE INTERNATIONAL REACTION

In contrast to the continuing East Timorese resistance to the occupation, the interest of the international community in the situation there waned over the years. In 1986, the Indonesian foreign minister, Mochtar Kusumaatmadja, said that the emphasis in the international debate over the fate of East Timor "has shifted from the political issue, of its integration into Indonesia, to the question of human rights."[18] This observation has been strengthened since. Portugal, the nation still recognized by the United Nations and many other nations as the "administering power" of East Timor, and one of the few nations that did not abandon the East Timorese people, retreated on September 1987 from its demand for self-determination for the half-island, calling for a "worthy solution" to the issue.[19] This move, which was received in Jakarta as a breakthrough, paved the way for reopening of bilateral talks regarding East Timor.[20] These have been low-level talks, between the two countries' ambassadors to the United Nations, under the auspices of the UN Secretary General.[21] After 1989 Australia signed the Timor Gap Treaty with Indonesia, which implicitly recognized Indonesia's annexation of East Timor. Portugal brought a claim against Australia in the International Court of Justice, challenging this treaty's validity.[22]

---

[16] *See, e.g.,* Hiorth, *supra* note 12, at 70–72.

[17] *Visiting a Forgotten War,* Newsweek, October 23, 1989.

[18] *Indonesia to Launch Information Campaign on East Timor,* Reuters, March 29, 1986.

[19] On the legal status of Portugal in East Timor, in light of the case of Western Sahara, *see infra* text accompanying note 34.

[20] *Indonesia and Portugal Reopen Talks on East Timor,* Reuters, September 7, 1987.

[21] *Indonesia Optimistic over Talks with Lisbon on East Timor,* Reuters, May 11, 1989.

[22] For the text of the treaty *see* 29 ILM 469 (1990).

The key to the muffled international reaction to the annexation of East Timor lies in the strategic importance of Indonesia. With a population of about 180 million, Indonesia is the fifth-largest nation in the world, with the largest Moslem population in the world. Its archipelago commands the waterways between the Pacific and Indian oceans, between Southeast Asia and Australia. It has had a stable regime, and in terms of world politics, a moderate one. It has been one of the key members of the Non-Aligned Movement and of the Organization of Petroleum Exporting Countries (OPEC). In the mid-1970s, against the background of the U.S. pullout from South Vietnam and the North Vietnamese moves in Indochina, as well as the oil crisis, Indonesia's strategic importance to the West was substantially enhanced. In contrast, East Timor was a tiny colony. Indonesia described its people as backward, unable to manage self-rule, and thus prone to be exploited by the Communists, who allegedly supported the Fretilin movement.

The odds were therefore against the East Timorese. The United Nations proved utterly ineffective. The initial General Assembly resolutions were strongly worded against Indonesia, and were backed by large majorities, but as time passed, the terminology was watered down, and the majority dwindled. The first General Assembly resolution, Resolution no. 3485(XXX) of December 12, 1975, "[s]trongly deplore[d] the military intervention of the armed forces of Indonesia in Portuguese Timor," called for their withdrawal "without delay," and recommended that the Security Council "take urgent action to protect the territorial integrity of Portuguese Timor and the inalienable right of its people to self-determination." This resolution was adopted with seventy-two votes in favor, ten against (including the Association of South East Asian Nations [ASEAN] countries, Iran and Japan), and forty-three abstentions (including the United States, other North Atlantic Treaty Organization [NATO] countries, and Moslem countries). Resolution 34/40 of November 21, 1979, no longer mentioned the call for Indonesia's withdrawal or reaffirmed the prior resolutions. Despite its moderate tone, there were only sixty-two favorable votes, against thirty-one nays (including the United States) and forty-four abstentions. On November 23, 1982, an even milder resolution was adopted (Resolution no. 37/50), which failed even to reaffirm the right of the East Timorese people to self-determination. Even so, those in favor outnumbered those against by only four votes (50–46–50). Since the 1983 session the question of East Timor has been consistently deferred to the following year's meeting.

The Security Council, to which the General Assembly recommended "urgent action to protect the territorial integrity of Portuguese Timor and the inalienable right of its people to self-determination," requested the Secretary General on December 22, 1975, to send a special representative to assess the situation there.[23] The second and last session of the Security Council dealing with this issue, reviewed this envoy's report, which indicated the need to consult the people of East Timor on the future status of the territory,[24] and requested the Secretary General to continue the envoy's assignment.[25] The United States and Japan abstained in the vote, complaining that the resolution did not mention the fact that Indonesia had begun pulling out its troops.[26]

The greatest political defeat of the Indonesian government in the international arena came from the Non-Aligned Movement, urged by some African states. Jakarta's bid for the chair of the summit of the Non-Aligned Heads of States has been unsuccessful ever since the invasion.[27] Yet even in this forum, the protest against the Indonesian move has been dwindling. Starting with the 1983 summit in New Delhi, the reaffirmation of the right of the people of East Timor to self-determination has been dropped from the final declaration.

Although the annexation of East Timor was not formally recognized by the majority of states, many were considering it as a plausible outcome in the immediate future.[28] The United States recognized Indonesia at least as an administrative power in East Timor. A State Department briefing indicated that "[t]he United States accepts Indonesia's incorporation of East Timor without maintaining that a valid act of self-determination has taken place."[29]

The position of the Roman Catholic church provided crucial moral support for the East Timorese community, which is entirely Christian. The Vatican has not recognized the annexation of East Timor, and has administered the local church not through the Indonesian Church but directly from Rome.[30] The Church's position has proven a major stumbling block for the implementation of Indonesia's policy of integrasi.[31] During the

---

[23] Resolution 384 of December 22, 1975.

[24] Dunn claims that this envoy's mission was obstructed by the Indonesians and the Australians. *See* Dunn, *supra* note 12, at 359–61.

[25] Resolution 389 of April 22, 1976.

[26] 31 UN SCOR, at 5, UN Doc. S/PV.1915 (1976).

[27] *Conciliatory Tone at Non-Aligned Summit Marks Turning Point*, Reuters, September 8, 1989. *See also Cyprus Says Non-Aligned States Should Exploit Opportunities*, Reuters, September 2, 1988, reporting that "the forcible take-over of East Timor remained the main stumbling block in Indonesia's candidacy."

[28] A West German MP, on a visit to East Timor, was quoted as saying that living conditions have dramatically improved there and this could lead to broader international recognition of Indonesia's claim to the troubled territory. *West Germans See Improvements in East Timor*, Reuters, July 8, 1989.

[29] This quote is taken from the State Department Regular Briefing by Charles Redman, Federal News Service, November 1, 1988.

[30] *See* C. Bodiardjo and L. Soei Liong, *supra* note 12, at 119–24.

[31] The local church has been defiant in its resistance against integration and in monitoring

pope's visit to the area in 1989, everybody was waiting to see whether or not he would kiss the ground upon his arrival in East Timor (his traditional rite upon entering any country for the first time). He did not kiss the ground on landing at the airport, but during Mass he kissed a crucifix that had been placed on a cushion laid upon the ground. What the cheering crowd saw was the pope kissing the ground.[32]

APPRAISAL

The largely conciliatory international reaction to Indonesia's actions in East Timor should not be viewed as impinging upon entrenched international norms. The worldwide acquiescence to the annexation was the result of international politics. It serves as a reminder of the limits of international law as a system that constraint states' behavior. It should not be used as precedent for justifying other violations of the law of occupation.

Does Portugal hold the key to the future of the East Timorese people's claim for self-determination? Some have suggest that Portugal's continuing protests have stood in the way of consolidation of Indonesia's title over East Timor by prescription.[33] In view of possible shifts in Portugal's position, it should be emphasized that Portugal could not in any way compromise the rights of the East Timorese under the 1960 decolonization declaration: the case of Western Sahara establishes that no future agreement between the colonial ruler (there Spain, here Portugal) and the neocolonial ruler (Morocco or Indonesia) can legally affect the rights of the local people, who are entitled to exercise the right to self-determination.

Assisting an Indigenous Government: Afghanistan, Kampuchea (Cambodia), Grenada, and Panama

Many occupants of the last two decades have claimed that they were invited by the territory's lawful government to assist it in quelling illegal opposition forces. Some occupants, such as Iraq and Indonesia, went further by "granting" the local government's purported request for incorporation into the occupying state. Others assisted in the establishment of new entities, for example, Bangladesh and Northern Cyprus. The third avenue was to install the inviting government in power, and to operate in the oc-

---

and reporting on the violation of human rights and the plight of the population. A recent news report suggests that this is still the case. *West Germans See Improvement in East Timor, supra* note 28 (the East Timorese bishop called for a referendum but was doubtful that such a vote would take place).

[32] *Mêlée Erupts as Pope Speaks in East Timor,* N.Y. Times, October 13, 1989.

[33] Lawrence, *supra* note 12, at 95.

cupied territory under the formal authority of that government. Often privileges to the occupant would be secured in bilateral treaties with the local government. This section describes the latter practice. It is important to recall that under the law of occupation, specifically under Article 2 of the Fourth Geneva Convention, this law also applies to territories under the actual control of a foreign power that are administered through indigenous institutions or governments. No arrangement with the local institutions would affect the occupant's duties under that law (Article 47 of the Fourth Geneva Convention).[34]

The Soviet Intervention in Afghanistan

On April 27, 1978, a coup raised to power a communist government in Afghanistan.[35] Its ties with Moscow were formally delineated by a Treaty of Friendship, Good Neighborliness and Cooperation, signed on December 5, 1978.[36] In early 1979 opposition to the new Afghan government mounted, and various rebel groups began to stage attacks against loyal army units and their Soviet military assistants. On December 27, 1979, after a failed attempt to remove the Afghan strongman, Hafizullah Amin, Soviet forces entered the country to defend it "from the imperialist enemies of the Afghan people," and from Mr. Amin, who, according to a *Pravda* report[37] had "teamed up with the enemies of the April revolution."[38] Moscow also invoked a request made by the "Afghan government" to intervene, but in fact the only request at that time came from Babrak Karmal, who held no position in the Afghan government, and in fact stayed in the Soviet Union at the relevant time. One day after the major airlift into Kabul, on December 28, 1979, Karmal was unanimously elected general secretary of the Central Committee of the Afghan Communist Party, chairman of the Revolutionary Council, and prime minister of the cabinet,

[34] On these two articles *see supra* Chapter 4, text accompanying notes 156–61.

[35] For background on the Soviet invasion into Afghanistan, *see* A. Arnold, *Afghanistan: The Soviet Invasion in Perspective* (rev. ed. 1985); H. Bradsher, *Afghanistan and the Soviet Union* (1983); A. Hyman, *Afghanistan under Soviet Domination 1964–83* (1984); B. Sen Gupta, *Afghanistan: Politics, Economics and Society* (1986); Noorani, *Afghanistan and the Rule of Law*, 24 Int'l Comm. of Jurists Rev. 37 (1980).

[36] 30 Current Digest of Soviet Press [CDSP], No. 49, at 10–11.

[37] Petrov, *On Events in Afghanistan*, December 31, 1979, *translated in* 31 CDSP, no. 52, at 5, 6.

[38] Petrov, *id*. at 6–7, refers to the right to self-defense embodied in Article 51 of the UN Charter to explain that "the Afghan leadership's request and the Soviet Union's positive reaction to it also stem from the provisions of [Article 51], which provides for the inherent right of a state to individual or collective self-defence to repel aggression and restore peace."

whose formation was also announced on the same date.[39] The new government issued a statement that it had "asked the USSR for urgent political, moral and economic assistance, including military assistance, which the government of the Democratic Republic of Afghanistan had earlier repeatedly requested from the government of the Soviet Union" and that "[t]he government of the Soviet Union ha[d] satisfied the Afghan side's request."[40]

Later it was announced that the Soviet and the Afghan governments signed and thereafter ratified (on April 4, 1980) a treaty "on the terms of the temporary stay on Afghan territory of the limited Soviet military contingent."[41] The text of the treaty has not been published, and apparently was not submitted to the United Nations. The Soviet Union claimed that it did not interfere in the internal affairs of Afghanistan. A Soviet official, B. N. Ponomarev, declared on February 5:

> The Soviet Union is not interfering in Afghanistan's internal affairs in any way whatsoever. That country is living according to its own laws and norms, and its government alone is determining national policies. Only Afghan citizens are working throughout the structure of state and administrative agencies, which are operating in an entirely sovereign fashion from top to bottom.[42]

[39] *Report from Kabul*, Pravda, December 29, 1979, *translated in* 31 CDSP, no. 52, at 2. The same communique announced Amin's "sentencing" to death for "crimes against the noble people of Afghanistan, crimes as a result of which many compatriots were killed" and the execution of that "sentence."

[40] *Appeal by the Government of Afghanistan*, Pravda, December 29, 1979 (citing Radio Kabul), *translated in* 31 CDSP, no. 52, at 2.

[41] *See* Noorani, *supra* note 35, at 49. Noorani's source is Foreign Broadcast Information Service, Middle East, April 7, 1980. The Soviet media referred to an "agreement reached between the two countries on practical questions relating to the conditions of the temporary stay in [Afghanistan] of [the Soviet troops]." *Translated in* 32 CDSP, no. 11, at 10 (1980).

[42] *Tass* report, Pravda, February 5, 1980, *translated in* 32 CDSP, no. 5, at 5. In the past Soviet occupations of Hungary in 1956 and of Czechoslovakia in 1968, treaties concerning the terms of the stay of the Soviet forces were signed in the wake of the invasion. However, the texts of those treaties were not concealed. For the Soviet-Hungarian treaty, see 407 UNTS 170 (1961); the Soviet-Czech treaty was reproduced in 7 ILM 1334 (1968). If the Soviet-Afghan treaty is based on the same principles as the former treaties, then *formally* Pomarev's claim is true. In the Soviet-Czech Treaty on the Conditions for the Temporary Stationing of Soviet Troops on C.S.R. Territory, Article 2 provided, *inter alia*, that "Soviet troops are not interfering in the internal affairs of the Czechoslovak Socialist Republic . . . Soviet troops, persons serving with them and members of the families of such persons who are in the C.S.R. will observe the legislation in effect in the C.S.R." The treaty stipulated that Czech laws would apply to crimes and misdemeanors committed by persons serving with the Soviet troops or by members of their families on Czechoslovak territory and that the adjudication would take place in Czechoslovak courts. The fact that the Soviet-Afghan treaty has not been published may imply more Afghan concessions to the Soviets.

The Afghan government has also held the appearance of unfettered sovereignty. On April 21 a constitution was adopted by the Revolutionary Council, outlining the basic political rights, as well as the organs of government and their competencies. In May, Radio Kabul announced that antigovernment demonstrators arrested earlier that month would be tried by the Afghan Revolutionary Courts, yet the statute setting up these courts had not been published at that time.[43]

Despite the formal Soviet policy of nonintervention in Afghanistan's internal affairs, the Soviet Union, with its massive support and immense investments and with its army of advisors, had the leverage to implement measures at all levels that were conceived as conducive to the success of the socialist transformation of Afghan society and to overcome armed resistance. Under the authority of the responsive Afghan government, long-term Soviet domination was sought through measures that included not only financial investments in the infrastructure, but also acculturation projects, such as indoctrination by Soviet personnel in Afghanistan or in the USSR, and a divide-and-rule strategy regarding Afghanistan's many tribes. Among other means to achieve these goals were instruction in Russian and in unique tribal languages (instead of the language that had been used before for intertribal communications) in the public schooling system and the encouragement of the use of these languages by the media.[44] These were measures similar to those successfully used before in the Soviet effort to colonize its Central Asian Republics. In addition, a strategic area, the Wakhan Corridor, was ceded to the Soviet Union in a treaty signed by Karmal's regime.[45]

THE INTERNATIONAL REACTION

The Soviet intervention in Afghanistan was widely denounced. The UN General Assembly condemned the intervention in an emergency session;[46] 104 nations voted for a resolution in which the General Assembly

> [r]eaffirm[ed] that respect for the sovereignty, territorial integrity and political independence of every State is a fundamental principle of the Charter of the United Nations, any violation of which is contrary to its aims and purposes;
>
> [s]trongly deplore[d] the recent armed intervention in Afghanistan which is inconsistent with that principle; [and]

[43] Noorani, *supra* note 35, at 51.
[44] *See* Arnold, *supra* note 35, at 109.
[45] The Economist, August 9, 1980; *id.*, July 4, 1981.
[46] A draft resolution of the Security Council was vetoed by the Soviet Union on January 7, 1980. Thereafter, the Security Council called for an emergency session of the General Assembly on the basis of the *Uniting for Peace* resolution of November 3, 1950. Resolution 462 of January 9, 1980.

[c]all[ed] for the immediate, unconditional and total withdrawal of foreign troops from Afghanistan in order to enable its people to determine their own form of government and choose their economic, political, and social systems free from outside intervention, subversion, coercion or constraint of any kind whatsoever.[47]

It is noteworthy that the draft resolution was sponsored by twenty-four third world countries and many others were in favor of it.[48] This resolution was reaffirmed annually until the Soviet withdrawal in 1988, with the same substantial majority.

Many third world countries denounced the Soviet occupations in other forums as well. An extraordinary meeting of the Islamic Conference in Islamabad in January 1980 "strongly condemned" the Soviet "military aggression" and called for the "immediate and unconditional withdrawal" of the Soviet forces. In the meantime, it suspended Afghanistan from participating in its meetings, and denied recognition to the new regime.[49] The 1983 New Delhi summit of the Non-Aligned Heads of States reiterated in its Political Declaration the position expressed in a 1981 conference of the Non-Aligned foreign ministers, which called for a political solution based on withdrawal of foreign troops from Afghanistan and respect for the sovereignty and independence of that country.[50]

APPRAISAL

The crucial factors in the evaluation of an occupant's claim regarding an invitation by the local government are the internal lawfulness of the government and the genuineness of the invitation it extends to the foreign state. The Soviet intervention in Afghanistan was a clear-cut case in this respect because there was little doubt that the Afghan government which retroactively affirmed the intervention was a mere fabrication. Without the pretext of a friendly invitee, the Soviet Union was an occupant of a foreign territory, obliged to respect the laws of international war,[51] including the law of occupation. The strong international condemnation of the intervention, which supports this observation, was another reaffirmation of the basic principle of the law of occupation: the inviolability of sovereignty, territorial integrity, and political independence through the use of force.

[47] General Assembly Resolution ES-6/2 of January 14, 1980.

[48] The General Assembly resolution was "the worst defeat suffered by the USSR in that forum since the Korean War." Arnold, *supra* note 35, at 115.

[49] *Islamic Conference's Resolution on Soviet Military Intervention in Afghanistan*, Xinhua General Overseas News Service, January 30, 1980.

[50] This position was further reiterated at the 1986 summit in Harare. *Non-Aligned Countries Call for Withdrawal of Foreign Troops from Afghanistan*, Xinhua, September 7, 1986.

[51] Reisman and Silk, *Which Law Applies to the Afghan Conflict?* 82 AJIL 459, 481 (1988).

The Vietnamese Occupation of Kampuchea (Cambodia)

On December 25, 1978, Vietnam invaded Kampuchea, ostensibly at the request of the Cambodian people, who suffered under the murderous Khmer Rouge regime.[52] It claimed to have been assisted by Cambodians from the Vietnamese-backed Kampuchean United Front for National Salvation, though no doubt the bulk of the force was Vietnamese. The invasion ousted the Kampuchean dictator, Pol Pot, and his notorious Khmer Rouge regime. On January 9, 1979, in the capital, Phnom Penh, the leader of that Kampuchean Front, Heng Samrin, declared himself the head of the new People's Republic of Kampuchea.[53] On February 18, 1979, Vietnam and the People's Republic of Kampuchea signed a treaty of peace, friendship, and cooperation.[54] In this treaty, the two governments recognized each other as sovereign and independent nations, pledged to assist each other in various enterprises, and agreed to sign a further agreement on the delineation of the common border "on the basis of the present border."[55]

The UN General Assembly "regretted" the Vietnamese armed intervention, and called for the immediate withdrawal of the Vietnamese forces.[56] On the other hand, the new entity was immediately recognized by the Soviet bloc and later by several third world countries.

In 1981 the Kampuchean constitution was amended, fashioned according to the Communist prototype. According to the constitution, Kampuchea was "moving step by step towards socialism," with the Kampuchean People's Republican party as the sole legitimate political party in the country. During the eleven years of the Vietnamese presence in Kampuchea, it could not be disputed that the indigenous government was highly dependent on the military arm of the Vietnamese troops. Ample evidence was also given of the implementation of Vietnamese Communist policies in Kampuchea, including the indoctrination of young and old according to

[52] Objective background on the invasion of Kampuchea can be found in E. Becker, *When the War Was Over* (1986); C. Pao-Min, *Kampuchea between China and Vietnam* (1985); M. Vickery, *Cambodia 1975–82* (1984). A description of the Vietnamese pullout and aftermath is found in 36 Keesing's Record of World Events 37289–91 (1990); 37 *id.* at 38194–95 (1991). An account of the genocide committed by the Khmer Rouge appears in Hannum, *International Law and the Cambodian Genocide: The Sounds of Silence*, 11 Human Rights Q. 82–138 (1989).

[53] The title of the state under the Khmer Rouge government was Democratic Kampuchea.

[54] *Reproduced in* 18 ILM 394 (1979).

[55] The animosity between Vietnam and Kampuchea is several centuries old, and it was reflected, *inter alia*, in territorial disputes.

[56] Resolution 34/22, adopted on November 14, 1979, by a majority of ninety-one to twenty-one, with twenty-nine abstentions. Resolution 37/6 of October 28, 1982, referred to the situation as occupation.

traditional Communist practice, and even the settlement of Vietnamese on Kampuchean lands.

In fact, the Vietnamese-backed government was, by and large, a blessing to beleaguered Kampuchea, which had suffered from 1975 until the invasion from a self-inflicted genocide, perpetrated by the Khmer Rouge. The new government not only ended that reign of terror, but also instituted important economic reforms. Elizabeth Becker, a historian of the new regime, referred to the humanitarian and economic reforms that took place under the Vietnamese-backed government as "Vietnam's gift to Cambodia."[57] Indeed, many reports indicated that the Hun Sen government was supported by the majority of the Cambodians, who dreaded the return of Pol Pot's forces.

THE INTERNATIONAL REACTION

Only toward the end of the Vietnamese occupation did Western public opinion come to realize that the occupation had saved the Kampuchean people from a murderous government. During the entire period of occupation, the Hun Sen government was denied the right to represent Kampuchea in the United Nations and in other international forums. Instead, in spite of the ample evidence on the Khmer Rouge's atrocities, the latter continued to occupy the Kampuchean seat in the General Assembly. The reason for this attitude was the fact that the new government was dependent on the Vietnamese occupation forces.[58] Indeed, only after the September 1989 withdrawal of the Vietnamese troops, did Western governments begin to show some willingness to acknowledge the fact that the Hun Sen government enjoyed the strong support of the local population, and was not a mere Vietnamese puppet.[59]

International reaction to the Vietnamese occupation was not confined

[57] N.Y. Times, April 11, 1989, Section 1.

[58] The French ambassador to the United Nations maintained: "The notion that because a regime is detestable, foreign intervention is justified and forcible overthrow is legitimate is extremely dangerous. That could ultimately jeopardize the very maintenance of international law and order and make the continued existence of various regimes dependent on the judgment of the neighbors. It is important for the Council to confirm, without any ambiguity, that it cannot condone the occupation of a sovereign country by a foreign country." S/PV.2109, at 17. See also Warbrick, *Kampuchea: Representation and Recognition*, 30 ICLQ 234 (1981). Among the states which felt that, despite what they considered the deplorable record of Democratic Kampuchea, there was no justification for the acceptance of the credentials of a regime installed through external intervention were Australia, Malaysia, New Zealand, Pakistan, Singapore, Somalia, and the United States: 33 United Nations Yearbook 1979, at 292 (1982).

[59] *Phnom Penh, Eye on West, Tries to Shed Image as Hanoi Puppet*, N.Y. Times, January 8, 1990, at A1. See also *Back to the Killing Fields*, Newsweek, September 11, 1989; *Don't Help Pol Pot. Try Him*, N.Y. Times, September 27, 1989.

to words alone. The Kampuchean opposition forces, the Khmer Rouge, backed by China, and Prince Sihanouk, aided by the United States, continued their guerilla warfare against the Vietnamese from bases on the Thai border. The Vietnamese forces were the only barrier the Kampuchean people had against the return of their former tormentors. Indeed, after the Vietnamese pulled out, the Khmer Rouge began to acquire control over Kampuchean territory through the use of force. Only then did the international community begin to put pressure on the warring factions to solve their differences peacefully.[60]

APPRAISAL: THE CONDITIONS FOR "HUMANITARIAN OCCUPATION"

The case of Kampuchea brings to the fore the problem of external intervention from humanitarian concerns. As much as the legality of the claim for "humanitarian intervention" as a justification of the use of force is debated, so is the claim for what might be termed "humanitarian occupation," namely, foreign control over a territory intended to protect a community from its own government. In such a situation, any measures taken by the occupant necessary for securing the well-being of that community would be justified. If the situation warrants the replacement of the government and central institutions, such acts would be deemed legal. The main difficulty with such reasoning, in justifying the use of force as well as occupation, is that it could be too easily abused. If such a justification were recognized, it might be used as a guise for occupants to pursue their own interests. Indeed, the fear of such abuse is the logic behind the view that rejects this justification.[61]

If one overlooks the plight of the indigenous community in the occupied territory, and refers only to the measures of the occupying power, then both the Kampuchean and the Afghan occupations were similarly unlawful. As in the Afghan case, the invasion of Kampuchea was a violation of the prohibition against the use of force; similarly to the Soviet measures in Afghanistan, the Vietnamese occupation policies were in violation of the Hague Regulations and the Fourth Geneva Convention (specifically with respect to the duty to maintain as much as possible the *status quo ante bellum*). But the impact of the two occupations on the life of the population of the occupied country was significantly different, and so was the reaction of the local population toward the occupant. By now, it has been internationally recognized that the Vietnamese occupation has considerably improved living conditions in Kampuchea, and protected the population

---

[60] On May 1, 1991, the warring factions accepted a cease-fire and agreed to discuss a peace plan suggested by the United Nations. 37 Keesing's Record of World Events 38194–95 (1991); *Cambodian Talks Make Headway*, International Herald Tribune, June 27, 1991, at 2.

[61] *See, e.g.*, the classic statement of the French ambassador to the United Nations, *supra* note 58.

against the return of Pol Pot's regime. The fact that the Vietnamese-backed government enjoyed popular support has also been established. Should the law of occupation reflect the difference in outcomes and in the people's attitude toward the occupant, or should the fear of abuse warrant the complete disregard of the wishes of the local community?

It is my opinion that the law of occupation can and should reflect the positive reaction of the occupied population by legitimizing changes in local laws and institutions that go beyond the otherwise applicable limits imposed by the Hague Regulations and Fourth Geneva Convention. I would suggest that the Kampuchean case might be interpreted as an affirmation of this proposition, since shortly after the Vietnamese pullout, the international community was ready to accept the legality of the Hun Sen government, without referring to its origins as a Vietnamese creation.[62] This proposition is further bolstered by the spring 1991 coalition occupation of northern Iraq and the establishment of an exclusion zone for the Kurds.[63] Therefore, when there is unequivocal evidence that a community is under imminent threat to life at the hands of its own government, humanitarian intervention and humanitarian occupation are then justified.[64] Indeed, in extreme cases, there would even be a duty to intervene and occupy.

The belated international acceptance of the legality of the Kampuchean government took place only after the Kampuchean government survived without the Vietnamese, and thereby showed its popular support. This would seem to have been too harsh a test for indigenous support. The fact that foreign troops remain in the territory should not be regarded as conclusive evidence of the local regime's unpopularity. One might say that in the case of Kampuchea the insistence on Vietnamese withdrawal before acceptance of the local government's legality (and, meanwhile, extension of foreign aid to the guerrillas) only prolonged what came to be a bloody civil war orchestrated by the notorious Khmer Rouge. Generally, the burden of proving popular support rests upon the regime that claims to enjoy it. The availability of reliable information regarding occupation measures and indigenous reactions thereto can assist significantly in determining this issue. Thus, a strong indication of the regime's unpopularity would be its denial of access to international fact-finding missions or international media, whose efforts may provide the necessary information.

[62] On November 24, 1989, the European Parliament voted that its twelve member states give de facto recognition to that government. The UN-sponsored peace plan includes that government in the discussion. This should be compared with the regime established by the Soviet Union in Kabul, which did not enjoy international recognition.

[63] *That Slippery Slope*, The Economist, April 13, 1991, at 53–54. *See also* text to n. 106.

[64] The French foreign minister, Roland Dumas, said that because of the mistreatment of the Iraqi Kurds by Saddam Hussein, there was a "duty to intervene" to prevent gross violations of human rights. *Id.*.

The U.S. Occupation of Grenada

On October 25, 1983, some eight thousand U.S. troops, reinforced by three hundred soldiers from six neighboring Caribbean islands, landed in Grenada.[65] In three days the force gained control over the tiny island of about one hundred thousand people. Subsequently, a new government was appointed to replace the existing institutions, which had broken down prior to the invasion. By mid-December, after the appointment of that government, the bulk of the U.S. forces left Grenada, leaving behind about 240 U.S. military personnel, as well as Jamaican and Barbadian forces, to serve as the interim police force of the country.[66]

The replacement of the local political institutions was one of the important aims of "Operation Urgent Fury." As President Reagan stated on the date of the invasion, one of the reasons for the invasion was "to assist in the restoration of conditions of law and order and of governmental institutions to the island of Grenada."[67] The emphasis on establishing democratic institutions was mentioned both by President Reagan[68] and by Ambassador Kirkpatrick in the United Nations.[69] A similar concern was expressed in the formal request of the Organization of Eastern Caribbean States (OECS) for U.S. assistance. The letter of request stated very clearly the aim "to invite the Governor-General of Grenada to assume executive authority of the country under provisions of the Grenada Constitution of

[65] For background on the U.S. invasion of Grenada and legal analyses, *see* U.S. Dep'ts of State and Defense, *Grenada, A Preliminary Report* (December 16, 1983); Romig, *The Legal Basis for United States Military Action in Grenada*, Army Lawyer, April 1985, at 1 (legal analysis by a person in the U.S. military Judge Advocate); Riggs, *Grenada: A Legal Analysis*, 109 Military L. Rev. 1–81 (1985) (another outlook of a U.S. serviceperson). Other U.S. sources are W. Gilmore, *The Grenada Intervention* (1984); Gordon, Bilder, Rovine, and Wallace, *Report of the American Bar Association Committee on Grenada* (1984); Hardt, *Grenada Reconsidered*, 11 Fletcher Forum 277 (1987); J. Moore, *Law and the Grenada Mission* (1984); Joyner, *Reflections on the Lawfulness of Invasion*, 78 AJIL 131 (1984); Vagts, *International Law under Time Pressure: Grading the Grenada Take-Home Examination*, 78 AJIL 169 (1984). Other perspectives are provided by Fraser, *Grenada: Sovereignty of a People*, 7 West Indian L.J. 205–91 (1983); H. O'Shaughnessy, *Grenada: Revolution, Invasion and Aftermath* (1984); Weiler, *Armed Intervention in a Dichotomized World: The Case of Grenada* in A. Cassese (ed.), *The Current Legal Regulation of the Use of Force*, 240 (1986).

[66] L. Garber, *Elections in Grenada: Return to Parliamentary Democracy* 27 (1985).

[67] The first two stated reasons were the protection of up to a thousand U.S. citizens staying there, and to "forestall further chaos." Later, other speakers emphasized the requests for intervention made by the local governor-general and by the Organization of Eastern Caribbean States. Romig, *supra* note 65, at 8. Some scholars have subsequently advanced yet another justification: humanitarian intervention. *See, e.g.*, Riggs, *supra* note 65, at 36–43; F. Teson, *Humanitarian Intervention* 188–200 (1988). Professor Rostow suggested another justification: a broad right of self-defense against the "impending deployment of a hostile force on a large scale on Grenada." *Law Is Not a Suicide Pact*, N.Y. Times, November 15, 1983, at A35.

[68] N.Y. Times, October 26, 1983, at A16, A18.

[69] 83 U.S. Dep't of State Bull., no. 2081, at 76–77 (1983).

1973 and to appoint a broad-based interim government to administer the country pending the holding of general elections."[70] In other words, one of the important aims of the intervention was to revive the democratic regime under the 1973 constitution.

The 1973 constitution was suspended in 1979 by Maurice Bishop, who had led his Marxist New Jewel Movement to a successful coup. Under Bishop's rule the island was gradually drawn into Communist influence, and Cuban troops were engaged in training the small but growing local army.[71] The events that precipitated the invasion of the island, namely, the internal power struggle within the ruling party and the execution of Bishop and other leaders, suggested that the new regime would be even more inclined to adopt Communist-oriented policies.[72] The restoration of the 1973 constitution and thereby of the democratic process were probably viewed by the United States and the OECS neighbors as a guarantee against future Soviet influence.

This aim was fully and quickly accomplished. The Grenadan governor-general was invited to form an interim government, and on December 5 he announced his cabinet, which consisted of nine Grenadan technocrats who had lived outside Grenada. The governor-general pledged elections within a year, and indeed such elections were held towards the end of that period, on December 3, 1984,[73] the constitution of 1973 having been reinstated in November 1984. No other major initiatives were introduced during the life of this interim government.

THE INTERNATIONAL REACTION

The newly elected prime minister, on the day of his appointment, sent a letter to President Reagan and the other foreign governments involved,

[70] *Reproduced in* Romig, *supra* note 65, at 13.

[71] It should be mentioned that the democratic regime under the 1973 constitution failed to ensure freedom of expression to Bishop's party in the 1976 elections, in which it nevertheless received wide support from the voters. The regime that Bishop ousted has been described in a report of the British House of Commons Select Committee on Foreign Affairs as "corrupt, repressive and sustained only by rigged elections." Foreign Affairs Committee, Caribbean and Central America, House of Commons Paper 47, paragraph 113 (1981–1982). The Bishop regime, with its initiatives in welfare legislation, especially with regard to education and health care, enjoyed popularity in Grenada. Garber, *supra* note 66, at 11, 30.

[72] After the dissident faction gained control over the party institutions, it formed the Revolutionary Military Council. Apparently no other institutional or legal change accompanied this act.

[73] On the election process and results, see Garber, *supra* note 66. Mr. Garber was an observer and reporter of the election process on behalf of the International Human Rights Law Group. Generally he found that this process "served to permit Grenadans to select the government of their choice." *Id.* at 36. His account, however, exposes some factors that helped one of the parties to gain a "tremendous advantage" during the campaign, and consequently led to its clear victory (these factors included massive foreign financing of the campaign and the detention of the leaders of the leftist party).

urging them to keep their units in Grenada at least until the coming spring.[74] If this move was intended to show the world the Grenadan support of the foreign intervention, and thereby to legitimize it, there was little need for it. The Grenadan government was not denied international recognition, and in fact, the world's attention was quickly diverted from it. One year after the invasion and the initial rebuke by the UN General Assembly, which "deeply deplored" the military intervention,[75] the only UN forum that showed some interest in the Grenada affair was the Human Rights Commission, which called for respecting the Grenadans' right of self-determination.[76]

APPRAISAL

Was Grenada occupied by the invading forces? The answer would be positive, unless one subscribes to the opinion that those forces had been invited by the island's legal governing authority, the governor-general. Like the Soviet claim in Afghanistan and the Vietnamese claim with respect to Kampuchea, the claim made here for exemption from the applicability of the law of occupation relied on the existence of a lawful local government. Only this time, the Americans argued, the local government was truly lawful.

What powers did the governor-general have? Like the constitutions of some other British Commonwealth countries, Grenada's 1973 constitution vested "the executive authority of Grenada" in Her Majesty (Article 57). The same article conferred upon an appointed governor-general the power to exercise that authority "on behalf of Her Majesty." As the constitution granted executive functions to the prime minister, the governor-general's powers were limited; however, in times of emergency, when the prime minister was absent or ill, the governor-general was given the discretion to use some of the prime minister's powers, acting "in his own deliberate judgment."[77] In any case, after the 1979 revolution and the suspension of the 1973 constitution, the governor-general retained the position of a titular "Head of State," but without any executive functions. John Norton Moore argues that following Bishop's death in October 1983, and

---

[74] Garber, *id.* at 35.

[75] Resolution 38/7 of November 2, 1983. In that resolution, the General Assembly also requested that "free elections be organized as rapidly as possible to enable the people of Grenada to choose its government democratically." This was, of course, compatible with the U.S. intentions.

[76] United Nations Yearbook 1984, at 228.

[77] Article 61 of the 1973 constitution. For a discussion about the governor-general's powers under the constitution, *see* Moore, *supra* note 65, at 51–54; Joyner, *supra* note 65, at 138–39; Vagts, *supra* note 65, at 170–71.

the inability of the dissident faction to form an effective government, "the constitutional Head of State would seem the principal constitutional authority in Grenada."[78] Therefore, the governor-general's letter of invitation to the OECS of October 24, 1983, in which he requested foreign military intervention, was a valid request that the U.S. forces could rely upon. However, even if the governor-general had the capacity to issue such an invitation, one may wonder if his authority was not overshadowed by the position taken by the British government, a representative of Her Majesty, to whom the 1973 Grenadan constitution granted original "executive authority." The British government was not informed of the U.S. plan until one day prior to the invasion. In fact, upon learning of the plan, Prime Minister Thatcher urged President Reagan to reconsider it.[79] Moreover, it seems that the authority of the governor-general did not in any case survive the Bishop regime and its suspension of the constitution. Therefore it is highly questionable whether the foreign invading forces could invoke the governor-general's authority to justify the restoration of the 1973 constitution and the democratic process. The law of occupation was arguably applicable to Grenada, and the significant legal and institutional changes were therefore subject to international scrutiny under the rules of the law of occupation.

In any case, infringements of the law of occupation, if such existed, were healed by the institution of a democratic process through which the general public expressed its endorsment of the new political system. This shows that the law of occupation can be superseded by arrangements that receive the endorsement of the indigenous population, at least as long as the territorial integrity of the occupied state is maintained. Such a conclusion would be in line with the similar international acceptance of the Vietnamese-backed Kampuchean government, and later, the acceptance of the Endara government in Panama. It is also in line with the international approval of the creation of Bangladesh during the Indian occupation of East Pakistan, which is discussed later.[80]

The U.S. Occupation of Panama

In the early morning hours of December 20, 1989, the United States dispatched some 24,000 troops into Panama to overthrow the government of General Manuel Antonio Noriega.[81] Although the Panamanian Defence

---

[78] Moore, *supra* note 65, at 53.

[79] *Invasion of Grenada*, N.Y. Times, October 26, 1983, at A1.

[80] *See infra* text accompanying notes 85–95.

[81] The facts on the invasion of Panama are based on 35 Keesing's Record of World Events 37112–113 (1989); 49 Facts on File 941–61 (1989); 50 *id.* 1–2 (1990).

Forces resisted the U.S. invasion, the U.S. forces quickly managed to secure control over Panama. No military occupation administration was established. Less than an hour before the launch of the assault, at a U.S.
military base in Panama, an alternative Panamanian government, headed
by Guillermo Endara, was sworn into office by a Panamanian judge. The
United States immediately recognized this government as the legal government of Panama, assisted it to gain authority over Panamanian institutions,
and regarded it as the local authority responsible for maintaining public
order in Panama. By deferring to this government, the U.S. troops rejected
the applicability of the law of occupation to their presence in Panama.[82]

Endara was widely believed to have won the presidential elections in
May 1989, but General Noriega effected the annulment of the vote. The
annulment of the elections was revoked by the electoral tribunal on December 27, which announced that of the 64 percent recoverable votes,
62.5 percent supported Endara. The tribunal also confirmed the appointments of President Endara and his two vice presidents. The Endara government seemed to enjoy wide public support as crowds took to the streets
of Panama City to cheer Noriega's downfall and surrender to U.S. officials.
After the capture of General Noriega, the U.S. troops began to pull out
and return to their bases in Panama. In December of 1989, after lifting the
sanctions imposed in 1988, the U.S. government sent fifty million dollars
in cash to bolster the Panamanian economy. The Pentagon said it planned
to send 220 special civil affairs specialists to assist the newly formed government. The State Department appointed a new ambassador to Panama,
saying that this ambassador had the expertise necessary to help Panama in
its transition to democracy.

THE INTERNATIONAL REACTION

The U.S. invasion was internationally criticized. Southern and Central
American governments condemned the invasion, while the Organization
of American States and the UN General Assembly "strongly deplored" the
action and called for the immediate withdrawal of invasion forces. It is
noticeable, however, that during the vote of the General Assembly on December 29, the Latin American states agreed not to challenge the right of
Endara's representative to represent Panama, and the latter voted together

---

[82] In *Industria Panificadora, S.A., et al. v. United States*, 763 F. Supp. 1154 (D.D.C. 1991),
the court dismissed a claim of Panamanian companies to recover damages for property losses
as a result of the invasion. The plaintiffs asserted that the Hague Regulations were applicable
since Panama was an occupied territory. The U.S. government responded by saying that "the
increase in U.S. military forces in Panama did not displace the authority of the legitimate
government in Panama." The court did not find it necessary to address this issue since it
rejected the claim on other grounds.

with the United States and other Western nations against the resolution.[83] To sum up, while the invasion drew criticism, there was very little international challenge to the legality of the Endara government.[84]

APPRAISAL

As in other cases of this type, the answer to the question of whether Panama was occupied by U.S. forces depends on the legality of the new indigenous government. Formally, the Endara government was not the legal government of Panama at the time of the invasion. Thus, the U.S. forces were formally occupying Panama, and as such were subject to the law of occupation. Could they, as occupants, legally change a system of government, when the change was to democracy? This question seemed moot when confronted with the undeniably wide popular support the Panamanians expressed toward these measures. Indeed, these signs of public support could have been clearer had the new government called immediately for elections or a referendum. The ultimate test for the legality of a regime installed by an occupant, is its approval in internationally monitored general elections, carried out without undue delay.

Self-Determination for Occupied Regions versus the Territorial Integrity of the Occupied State: Bangladesh and Northern Cyprus

The cases of Bangladesh and Northern Cyprus represent a major challenge to the law of occupation: in these cases the armed intervention of a foreign state brought about the establishment of a secessionist regime that claimed to exercise its people's right to self-determination. In the case of the Indian invasion and occupation of East Pakistan, the international community accepted that claim and recognized the state of Bangladesh, while the Turkish occupation of Northern Cyprus was denounced, and the claim of the Republic of Northern Cyprus for international recognition was rejected. This section outlines the two cases and discusses the possible reasons for the different outcomes.

---

[83] General Assembly Resolution 44/240 of December 29, 1989 (seventy-five to twenty, with thirty-nine abstentions).

[84] One noticeable exception was Peru's President Alan Garcia, who demanded new elections in Panama and the replacement of U.S. troops with troops of the Organization of American States as an inter-American peacekeeping force. *Peruvian Still Outraged by Invasion of Panama*, N.Y. Times, January 16, 1990, at A16.

Indian Involvement in the Creation of Bangladesh

The events that led to the establishment of the People's Republic of Bangladesh seem at first glance to follow the typical scenario, in which a foreign power invades a neighboring territory, claiming to act on behalf of the indigenous population, and establishes a sham of a local government.[85] In this case, it was the Indian invasion of December 1971 into East Pakistan, then under the internationally recognized sovereignty of Pakistan, and the aid India granted to indigenous elements that enabled the establishment of the Bangladeshi republic.

The Awami League had won the general elections for the Pakistani National Assembly that were held in December 1970. In these elections the Awami League had called for an autonomous East Pakistan. Its overwhelming success in the elections, which reflected the general discontent of the population of East Pakistan, about 55 percent of the entire Pakistani population, with West Pakistani domination. The election results were the precursor of the developments that followed. The first (West) Pakistani reaction was to postpone the convening of the National Assembly, which had been scheduled to discuss a draft constitution for Pakistan. Ultimately, the Pakistani military regime embarked on a large-scale assault on the civilian population of the East Pakistani city Dacca on March 25, 1971. As a result of the Pakistani army's condemnable policies, millions of frightened refugees began to cross the border to India.

The Awami League reestablished itself in India, and on April 10, 1971, declared the independence of Bangladesh.[86] Although India portrayed itself at that time as neutral, the Indian government in fact nurtured the Bangladeshi Mukti Bahini guerrillas and the Awami League. India supplied them with arms, ammunition, and logistic support, and permitted them to recruit and train volunteers, most of them refugees, on Indian soil.[87] There is no doubt that armed incursions by these guerilla forces

[85] For background material on the events that led to the establishment of Bangladesh, *see East Pakistan Staff Study*, 8 Int'l Comm. of Jurists Rev. 23 (1972); Nawaz, *Bangladesh and International Law*, 11 Indian J. Int'l L. 459 (1971); Franck and Rodley, *The Law, The United Nations and Bangladesh*, 2 IYHR 142 (1972). Nanda, *The Tragic Tale of Two Cities—Islamabad (West Pakistan) and Dacca (East Pakistan)*, 66 AJIL 321 (1972), gives an account of the situation prior to the Indian invasion and discusses the social, economic, and other differences between East and West Pakistan. Some documents are reproduced in *Civil War in East Pakistan*, 4 N.Y.U. Int'l L. and Pol. 524 (1971).

[86] The "Proclamation of Independence Order" of April 10, 1971, is reproduced in 4 N.Y.U. Int'l L. and Pol., *supra* note 85, at 557.

[87] On the Indian aid to the Mukti Bahini, *see, e.g., East Pakistan Staff Study, supra* note 85, at 54–55.

throughout November 1971 escalated the military conflict into a full-scale war.

The Indian armed invasion of East Pakistan began on December 6, 1971, after a series of Indian-Pakistani border clashes. Immediately preceding the invasion came India's recognition of the People's Republic of Bangladesh. India's foreign minister in his speech before the UN Security Council, stated that this recognition was made to "provide a proper juridical and political basis for the presence of the [Indian] army in support of the Mukti Bahini [the Bangladeshi liberation army] and the Bangladesh Government in the country."[88] After only ten days, the Pakistani army surrendered, and Indian forces occupied the entire area of East Pakistan, enabling the establishment of the new state of Bangladesh.

THE INTERNATIONAL REACTION

The genuine and widely recognized claim for Bangladeshi self-determination as an entity independent of West Pakistan, coupled with the repulsion caused by the Pakistani measures to suppress that claim, overcame the traditional concern for the sovereignty and territorial integrity of the occupied Pakistani territory. These factors facilitated the swift, worldwide recognition of Bangladesh as a sovereign state. Shortly after its declaration of independence, Bangladesh was recognized by several nations. By the time its admission for membership in the United Nations came before the Security Council, in August 1972, Bangladesh had been already recognized by eighty-six countries.[89]

In the United Nations, the initial reaction to the Indian invasion followed the usual course. The resolutions of the General Assembly and the Security Council expressed the duty of the states involved to respect the territorial integrity of the parties to the conflict,[90] and called for the withdrawal of foreign troops from East Pakistan territory. The Soviet draft resolution, which called upon Pakistan to give immediate recognition to the will of the East Pakistani population as expressed in the elections of December 1970, was not put to the vote.[91] This attitude changed eight months later, when the overwhelming majority in the Security Council voted to admit Bangladesh as a member of the United Nations. However, China vetoed the resolution. Thereupon, the issue was raised in the General Assembly, which, without a debate, adopted a resolution asserting that

[88] 26 UN SCOR, UN Doc. S/PV.1611, at 10 (1971).

[89] United Nations Yearbook 1972, at 218 (1975).

[90] See General Assembly Resolution 2793 (XXVI), 26 UN GAOR, UN Doc. A/C.647/Rev.1 (December 7, 1971); Security Council Resolution 307, UN SCOR, UN Doc. S/10465 (December 21, 1971).

[91] United Nations Yearbook 1971, at 151, 156 (1974).

the People's Republic of Bangladesh was eligible for membership in the United Nations, and expressed the desire that it be admitted to membership "at an early date."[92] That date came in September 1974.[93]

APPRAISAL

In retrospect it appears that the international community was very much relieved by the unilateral Indian act, which solved, in this case satisfactorily, the inherent conflict between the principles of self-determination and territorial integrity. Indeed, India gained important strategic advantages from these developments, which significantly weakened its longtime rival. India acted out of concern for the suffering of another community, but also, and most probably mainly, in view of the benefits it would get out of the weakening of Pakistan. In this sense, the Indian acts were no different than those of other occupants. But the crucial elements in this case were the undisputed genuineness of the Bangladeshis' claim of self-determination and the hopelessness of their situation under Pakistani rule. In this situation, the traditional laws of occupation were deemed beside the point.

The creation of Bangladesh confirms the existence of a major qualification to the concept of territorial integrity that forms the basis of the law of occupation. That concept was superseded in this case by the principle of self-determination. Indeed, the Bangladeshi people had an undisputed claim of self-determination: they were distinct, linguistically, culturally, and ethnically, from the population of West Pakistan; their agenda for political separation had been endorsed by popular vote (in the 1970 Pakistani elections); they were oppressed by West Pakistan; and they were concentrated in one region, which was separated from West Pakistan. The geographic segregation of the two former parts of Pakistan ensured that the creation of Bangladesh would not impinge upon the interests of the (West) Pakistani population. This was a clear-cut case for justifying the supremacy of the principle of self-determination over the notion of territorial integrity.

The Bangladeshi account could be also explained as an example of a lawful humanitarian intervention and humanitarian occupation.[94] As I mentioned while discussing the Vietnamese occupation of Kampuchea and the exclusion zone established for the Kurdish population of Iraq, in cases where the existing political system cannot guarantee protection against

[92] Resolution 2937 (XXVII), 27 UN GAOR (November 29, 1972) (adopted without debate or vote).

[93] General Assembly Resolution 3203 (XXIX) of September 17, 1974. The Security Council's recommendation came on June 10, 1974 (Resolution 351).

[94] *See, e.g.*, Teson, *supra* note 67, at 179–88; *East Pakistan Staff Study*, *supra* note 85, at 57–62.

governmental prosecution and harsh abuses of human rights, the occupant may modify existing laws and institutions for humanitarian goals. The idea that under certain circumstances a genuine humanitarian intervention could effect, if necessary, institutional or even territorial changes in the occupied territory is consistent with that claim, and can be interpreted as having been accepted as such by the international community in the case of Bangladesh.[95]

The Turkish Invasion of Cyprus and the Establishment of the Republic of Northern Cyprus

The Turkish invasion of Cyprus on July 20, 1974, was precipitated by the overthrow of Archbishop Makarios, the Greek Cypriot president of Cyprus, by pro-*Enosis* (unification with Greece) supporters.[96] That overthrow was the last development in the bitter experience of the bicommunal island, independent since 1960. Turkey claimed to have intervened on behalf of the Turkish Cypriot minority on this island, protecting them against a forced unification with Greece.

The Turkish Cypriot minority had never lost its ties with Turkey or the aspiration to be unified with it. This community, which comprised roughly 20 percent of the entire Cypriot population, differed from the Greek Cypriot community in religion, language, culture, and political aspirations, and intercommunal relations were laden with animosity and suspicion. The forced marriage between the two communities did not last long: only three years after the 1960 attainment of independence, an initiative of President Makarios to amend the constitution put an end to the common government. The Turkish community was subsequently effectively prevented from sharing a common government with the Greek Cypriot majority, despite the fact that such a government had been pledged in the 1960 constitution. Disillusioned by the unfulfilled promise of fair representation in

[95] Other recent examples of humanitarian armed interventions that brought about a change of local leadership and were accepted as lawful by the international community are the Tanzanian military intervention in Uganda, which ousted Idi Amin's regime (in 1979), and the French action against Emperor Bokassa of the Central African Republic (also in 1979). On these incidents, *see, e.g.,* Teson, *supra* note 67, at 159 *et seq.* and 175 *et seq.*, respectively.

[96] For general background on the 1974 invasion of Cyprus and its aftermath, *see Keesing's Border and Territorial Disputes, supra* note 6, at 15–26; 36 Keesing's Record of World Events 37514–17 (1990); J. Joseph, *Cyprus: Ethnic Conflict and International Concern* (1985); C. Hitchens, *Cyprus* (1984); Opperman, *Cyprus, in* 12 EPIL 76–80 (1990). For legal analyses, *see* Evriviades, *The Legal Dimension of the Cyprus Conflict,* 10 Texas Int'l L.J., 227 (1975); Z. Necatigil, *The Cyprus Question and the Turkish Position in International Law* (1989); Symposium, *Cyprus: International Law and the Prospects for Settlement,* 78 Am. Soc. Int'l L. Proc. 107 (1984).

joint government, the Turkish Cypriots set up a Turkish Cypriot autonomous administration in December 1967. To manage their own affairs, the
Turkish Cypriots established a legislative body for prescribing laws for the
Turkish Cypriot population and an executive council which administered
the Turkish Cypriot enclaves throughout Cyprus. Prior to the 1974 invasion, nineteen "basic laws," on executive, judicial, and legislative matters
were promulgated.[97]

The Turkish invasion stopped at the "Attila line," which left the Turks
with control of the northern third of the island. As a result of measures
taken by both sides, about a third of the Cypriot population became refugees. More than two hundred thousand people were transferred across the
"Attila line," in both directions. This mass transfer resulted in the all-but-
complete separation of the two rival communities.

When hostilities subsided, the Turkish Cypriots first advocated a federal
solution to the Cypriot problem. The Turkish Cypriot autonomous body
reconstructed itself as the Turkish Cypriot Federated State (February 13,
1975), and afterwards was renamed the "Turkish Federated State of Cyprus." It held general elections in June 1975. After long years of stalemate
in negotiations for a political solution, the Turkish Cypriots abandoned
their proposal for a federated state, and instead opted for a looser confederation. In November 1983, a Turkish Republic of Northern Cyprus was
declared by a legislative assembly, invoking the right of the Turkish Cypriots to self-determination.[98] Its constitution was approved in a referendum in May 1985. Presidential and parliamentary elections held in Northern Cyprus in spring 1990 were interpreted as approving President Rauf
Denktash's unyielding position with respect to the peace talks with the
government of Cyprus.

While the Turkish Cypriot entity was still advocating a confederation
with the south, as of 1992, it was no more than a satellite of Turkey. It was
dependent on the military presence of a Turkish army, estimated to include
twenty thousand to thirty-six thousand troops. It was dependent on the
Turkish economy, and its economy was in fact united with that of Turkey,
as both used the same currency, the Turkish lira. The sociological ties with

[97] Even under the 1960 constitution of Cyprus, the two communities had separate local
administrations, separate educational systems, separate trade and labor unions, separate
presses and no national anthem. On the autonomous bodies, see Z. Nedjati, Administrative
Law 53–59 (1974); Necatigil, supra note 96, at 59–62.

[98] The change of name may signify a move away from the federative solution in favor of an
independent state for that part of the island. But the formal adherence to a federative solution
was reiterated in a letter that the representative of this entity to the United Nations sent to
the Secretary General, using the Turkish delegation as intermediaries. United Nations Yearbook 1983, at 253 (1987). See also Swan, Constitutional Majority Rule and the Cypriot Constitution: the 1983 Crisis in Critical Perspective, 5 Boston College Third World L.J. 1, at 32–33
(1984).

the mainland have been strengthened by the state-sponsored migration of Turks (an estimated sixty thousand people, comprising 50 percent of the indigenous Turkish Cypriot community) to Cyprus and their settlement in the Turkish-occupied part. To those immigrants, and to the Turkish Cypriots who were transferred from the south, the authorities have issued certificates of ownership to property left by the uprooted Greek Cypriots.[99]

THE INTERNATIONAL REACTION

Only Turkey has so far recognized this new entity. The UN General Assembly has adopted resolutions deploring the Turkish occupation and demanding its immediate withdrawal, and also deploring all unilateral actions that change the demographic structure of Cyprus or promote other faits accomplis.[100] The Security Council declared the 1983 declaration of independence of the Turkish Republic of Northern Cyprus legally invalid, and called upon all states not to recognize any Cypriot state other than the Republic of Cyprus.[101] In March 1990 the Security Council rejected Denktash's demand for the recognition of the existence of two peoples in Cyprus and their respective rights to self-determination, and called for a single bicommunal republic as the solution to the crisis.[102] The European Commission of Human Rights regarded Northern Cyprus as under the control of the Turkish army, and thus declared admissible the 1977 application of Cyprus against Turkey alleging violations of the European Convention on Human Rights in Northern Cyprus.[103]

APPRAISAL

What are the reasons for the negative reaction of the international community to the Turkish Republic of Northern Cyprus as opposed to the warm welcome extended to Bangladesh? Some basic conditions are similar

---

[99] *United Nations Yearbook, supra* note 98, at 244, 249.

[100] *See* General Assembly Resolution 3212(XXIX) of November 1, 1974; General Assembly Resolution 3395 (XXX) of November 20, 1975; General Assembly Resolution 33/15 of November 9, 1978; General Assembly Resolution 34/30 of November 20, 1979 (deploring "the fact that part of [the territory of the Republic of Cyprus] is still occupied by foreign forces"). In Resolution 37/253 of May 13, 1983, the General Assembly again deplored "the fact that part of the territory of the Republic of Cyprus is still occupied by foreign forces," and demanded "the immediate withdrawal of all occupation forces from the Republic of Cyprus."

[101] Security Council Resolution 541 of November 18, 1983. In a similar vein is Security Council Resolution 550 (1984).

[102] Security Council Resolution 649 of March 13, 1990.

[103] *Cyprus v. Turkey*, 21 Yearbook of the European Convention on Human Rights 100, 230–34, 62 ILR 5, 74–76 (European Commission of Human Rights, July 10, 1978).

in the two cases: both involved a political clash between two distinct communities, forced by the decolonization process into a single body-politic, in which one group managed to deprive the other of power.[104] But other crucial differences distinguish the two. The elements that seem to taint the Northern Cypriot claim for recognition are the continuing total dependency on Turkey, whose presence there was deemed the fruit of illegal aggression;[105] the vested interests of many Greek Cypriots in the northern part of the island, from which they fled or were forced to leave during the 1974 crisis; and maybe also the fact that before 1974 the Turkish Cypriots were not subjected to systematic abuses of human rights (as opposed to the deprivation of political rights). In contradistinction to the long distance that separates Bangladesh from Pakistan, the Turkish-imposed "Attila line" is only an arbitrary border, which cuts through a small island and which forced a massive relocation of peoples.

I would suggest that the mere presence of foreign Turkish troops on Cypriot soil may not be the reason for the nonrecognition of the Republic of Northern Cyprus, inasmuch as the Indian invasion of Bangladesh did not taint the latter's claim to sovereignty. Clearly the Turkish presence safeguards the interests of the Turkish Cypriot minority on the island. Had the international community recognized that minority's right to self-determination, Turkey's presence in the island would not have been condemned. Similarly, the case of Biafra tells us that it is safe to assume that the world would not have viewed favorably even a self-sustaining and independent Northern Cypriot entity. The criticism of the Turkish position is therefore rooted in the rejection of the Turkish Cypriot right to self-government. This attitude emphasizes the principle of territorial integrity, an emphasis that also loomed large in other failed secession attempts, such as the Katangan attempt to secede from the Republic of Kongo (1960–1963), and the Biafran attempt to secede from Nigeria (1967–1970). This attitude is based on apprehension concerning the possible ripple effects of a contrary decision, a fear of opening a Pandora's box of minority claims for self-government, without satisfactory criteria to draw a line between permitted secessions and illegal ones. The case of Bangladesh should therefore be viewed as a unique case of a successful secession. It seems that in the Bangladeshi case the accumulation of factors, and especially the geographic factor, were deemed so extraordinary, that there was no fear of embarking on

---

[104] Despite the distinctive features of the Turkish Cypriot community, it has not yet been recognized as a self-determination unit. It is suggested that this position stems from the concerns outlined below.

[105] The Turkish invasion was contrary to Article 2(4) of the UN Charter and the 1960 Treaty of Guarantee among Cyprus, Greece, Turkey, and the United Kingdom. *See* J. Dugard, *Recognition and the United Nations* 110 (1987).

a slippery slope that would lead to curtailment of the principle of territorial integrity.

Limited-Purpose Occupations: The Coalition Occupation of Southern and Northern Iraq and the Israeli Occupation of Southern Lebanon

Article 42 of the Hague Regulations stipulates that an invading army will be deemed an occupant only if it succeeds in placing the foreign territory under its authority. When is such "authority" established? Three recent occupations furnish an opportunity to explore the extent of this rule with respect to occupations that take effect during relatively short-term, limited-purpose invasions, in which the invading troops have no intention to remain in control over the area once the military goal of the invasion is achieved. The June 1982 Israeli invasion into southern Lebanon was an attack on Palestine Liberation Organization (PLO) bases inside that area. The IDF did not set up a military administration, nor did it proclaim the area to be under its authority or otherwise officially recognize the applicability of the law of occupation. The IDF plans called for a short-term operation that would not engage the Lebanese army. Israel probably assumed that any formal proclamation followed the 1967 example of establishing an occupation administration would be internationally regarded as yet another territorial expansion. Similarly, the spring 1991 coalition invasions into southern and later northern Iraq during the Persian Gulf War were not complemented with any formal act of this sort. Although some hundred thousand United States and other states' troops engaged during March and April 1991 in providing food, shelter, and medical care to tens of thousands of Iraqi refugees in southern Iraq, then under coalition occupation, no formal assertion regarding the status of these troops there was ever made. Although the occupation of part of northern Iraq from April through July of 1991 was an essential component in the scheme to resettle the scores of fleeing Kurdish refugees, a similar policy of blurring the legal status of the coalition forces there was used. The Bush administration coined the term "safe haven" as an informal term that would signify the humanitarian purpose of the occupation, and at the same time would not raise hopes, or fears, of a quasi-temporary situation.[106] It is not disputed that in all three cases, the invading armies were capable of exercising authority over a certain foreign area, and that the indigenous governments

---

[106] The *New York Times* quoted U.S. officials as saying that the designation of "informal safe havens" reflected "a compromise intended to sidestep problems of international law and regional sensitivities about the nature and future of the area." *Bush Sees Accord on "Safe Havens" for Kurds in Iraq*, N.Y. Times, April 12, 1991, at A1.

were unable to impose their rule in the same area without the formers' approval. Therefore, all three cases constituted occupations.

The judgment of the Israeli Supreme Court that determined that the Israeli presence in Lebanon was an occupation seems to be equally applicable to the southern and northern Iraq cases. The Court referred to Article 42 of the Hague Regulations and reasoned:

> A military force may invade or enter an area in order to pass through it to its intended goal, while leaving the area behind it *without* effective control. But if the military force gained effective and practical control over a certain area, it is immaterial that its presence in the territory is limited in time or that the intention is to maintain only temporary military control.[107]

Nevertheless, it is to be expected that few future occupants under similar circumstances will recognize the applicability of the law of occupation. By recognizing its applicability, the occupant would be obliged to assume duties toward the population, such as the duty to maintain public order and civil life. But the occupant who expects to leave the area as soon as the military objectives are met, and who concentrates all its efforts on specific military targets, has no incentive to recognize officially its status as an occupant. In fact, even the occupant who is able and willing to assume its duties toward the local population under the law of occupation has a very good reason to avoid the terminology of occupation. After more than two decades of criticism of Israeli policies in the territories it occupied in June 1967, the label "occupation" has acquired a pejorative connotation worldwide. The official assertion of "occupation" is therefore quite likely to be accepted as an intention to create at least a quasi-permanent situation, and as such to arouse indigenous sentiments against it.

The Law of Occupation That Emerges from Recent Occupations

Recent occupants did not view themselves as occupants and, for reasons discussed above, preferred to confer responsibility on local governments they established. As a result, occupants—except for Israel with regard to the territories occupied in 1967—did not have to struggle with the adaptation of the law of occupation to the contemporary challenges of administration. Thus, for example, aside from the interpretation of Article 43 of the Hague Regulations by Israeli institutions, no other state practice with regard to this basic article exists after World War II.

These attempts to avoid the status of occupant raise the very complicated

---

[107] *Tsemel et al. v. Minister of Defence et al.*, 37 (3) PD 365, 373 (1983).

question of the applicability of the law of occupation to various situations of foreign domination. When is the establishment of a new government to be accepted as lawful, and when would it be deemed illegal and invalid (and the law of occupation applicable)? Will all cases of annexation or secession of occupied territories be deemed unlawful and invalid, or will there be cases where such acts will be recognized as legal, for example, because of the occupied community's exercise of its right to self-determination? The first step toward a possible answer to these and similar questions is to acknowledge the fact that the question of the applicability of the law of occupation to a certain situation has come to be not a mere question of facts, but rather a question of law, and quite a sophisticated one. Whereas Article 42 of the Hague Regulations and Article 2 of the Fourth Geneva Convention put forward a simple factual test—the presence of foreign troops on an enemy's soil—the modern law complicates the issue by introducing normative criteria for analysis. Under certain conditions an occupant would be entitled to transform fundamentally the local political institutions (as in Grenada and Panama); in extreme cases an occupant could even effect a secession of an occupied area (as in Bangladesh). But on the other hand, political changes might be viewed as illegal (as in Afghanistan and until recently Kampuchea), and secessions or annexations also vehemently condemned (as in Cyprus, Kuwait, East Timor, and Western Sahara).

The key factor for formulating an inquiry into the legal criteria for recognizing a status of occupation seems to be the attitude of the occupied population toward the changing circumstances. A change of government definitely supported by the public would most certainly be internationally recognized; a change that did not enjoy public support would not. If an occupant controlled only a part of a state and that part was considered not to be a distinct unit entitled to self-determination, the occupant would not be entitled to effect the secession of the occupied area (as in Northern Cyprus). Similar considerations imply that the occupant would not be entitled to establish a new government in such a region even if its inhabitants supported such an act.

Another important lesson from the recent practice of occupants and the ensuing reactions is that the Hague and Geneva conception of an "ousted sovereign" does not exist any longer: since sovereignty inheres in the people that lives in the territory, the modern occupant needs to heed the political interests of this people, the sovereign, and not the historical claims of the ousted government. This impinges on the rules concerning the management of occupied territories, by diminishing the claim of an ousted government that does not truly represent the sovereign people to have its prescriptions retained.

The Law of Occupation in Contemporary International Instruments

Among the post–World War II documents dealing with issues related to the law of occupation, many reaffirm the traditional concepts. Other instruments, however, import new emphases that modify that traditional approach. The general drive of these latter instruments is to enhance indigenous rights, whether individual rights, through the emerging body of human rights prescriptions, or the collective right to self-determination. This section outlines these developments and their influence on the modern law of occupation.

Before exploring the new emphases that attempt to modify the law of occupation, it should be pointed out that its basic principles, namely, territorial integrity and inalienability of sovereignty through the use of force, have been reiterated in several UN documents. In some specific resolutions, taken with respect to specific events, the Security Council and the General Assembly have "[e]mphasiz[ed] the inadmissibility of the acquisition of territory by war."[108] The Declaration on Principles of International Law concerning Friendly Relations and Co-Operation among States in Accordance with the Charter of the United Nations (1970),[109] provided in Article 1, paragraph 11, a general reaffirmation of this principle:

> The territory of a State shall not be the object of acquisition by another State resulting from the threat or use of force. No territorial acquisition resulting from the threat or use of force shall be recognized as legal.

The Declaration on the Strengthening of International Security, adopted during the same session, repeats the same words.[110] The Helsinki Accord of 1975 also approved the principles of inviolability of frontiers and respect for the territorial integrity of the participating states.[111]

Struggle for Self-Determination in Occupied Territories

THE NATIONAL LIBERATION DOCTRINE

Parallel to the reaffirmation of territorial integrity, some instruments advanced the claim for the lawful struggle for self-determination of peoples

---

[108] This is a quote from the preamble of Security Council Resolution 242 of November 22, 1967 (concerning the Israeli occupation). For similar pronouncements with regard to other occupations, *see supra* note 10 (Western Sahara); text accompanying note 23 (East Timor); note 47 (Afghanistan); note 56 (Kampuchea); note 103 (Cyprus).

[109] General Assembly Resolution 2625 (XXV) of October 24, 1970.

[110] Article 5 of Resolution 2734 (XXV) of December 16, 1970.

[111] Articles 3 and 4 of the Final Act of the Conference on Security and Co-operation in Europe, 14 ILM 1292, 1294–95 (1975).

subject to alien domination. In some documents foreign occupation was likened to colonialism, and denounced along with the latter. The claim for self-determination depicted the situation of "alien occupation" as intrinsically illegal. In those instances where an existing government was labeled an illegal occupant, or colonial ruler, its opposition would supposedly be granted the right to struggle against the existing regime and, once in power, to introduce a new system of government in the "liberated" territory. Thus the claim of self-determination for a certain people, for "national liberation," could reverse the roles of occupant and occupied: as "national liberators," the invading forces would consider themselves the rightful sovereign, not subject to any limitations on its powers stemming from the law of occupation, whereas the ousted regime would be viewed as a defeated (illegal) occupant.

SPECIFIC FORMULATIONS

The claim of the lawful struggle for national liberation has been pronounced in a number of international instruments.[112] This claim was mentioned in the consensual Declaration of Principles of International Law concerning Friendly Relations. As we saw above, this declaration reaffirmed the principle of inalienability of territorial boundaries.[113] But it also recognized another element. After reiterating the principles of self-determination, freedom, and independence of peoples, the declaration went on to prescribe states' duties with regard to these principles:

> Every State has the duty to refrain from any forcible action which deprives peoples . . . of their right to self-determination and freedom and independence. In their actions against, and resistance to, such forcible action in pursuit of the exercise of their right to self-determination, such peoples are entitled to seek and to receive support in accordance with the purposes and principles of the Charter.[114]

[112] It is not relevant here to determine whether the international community recognized the right to use force in that struggle or not. This issue is hotly debated. *See, e.g.*, Reisman, *Coercion and Self-Determination: Construing Charter Article 2(4)*, 78 AJIL 642, 643 (1984) ("Each application of Article 2(4) must enhance opportunities for ongoing self-determination."). *See also* Reisman, *Criteria for the Lawful Use of Force in International Law*, 10 Yale Int'l L.J. 279 (1985). *Contra* Schacter, *The Legality of Pro-Democratic Invasion*, 78 AJIL 645, 648 (1984) ("[T]he rule against the unilateral recourse to force (except in self-defence) is a fundamental tenet of international law. In recent years, it has been widely characterized as *jus cogens*."); Y. Dinstein, *War, Aggression and Self-Defence* 88 (1988) ("[A] State using force in order to overthrow a despotic Government in another country would . . . run afoul of Article 2(4).").

[113] *Supra* text accompanying note 109.

[114] Resolution 2625, *supra* note 109, at 124.

In other words, the peoples deprived of their enumerated rights are entitled, according to the claim, to struggle to secure them with the aim of removing the existing institutions, while other states have the duty to aid such actions.[115] This, of course, impinges on occupation regimes that deprive peoples under their rule of the right of self-determination. Under this declaration, such regimes would be considered illegal, and the local populations would have the right to resist their rule. Other documents explicitly include occupations among the unlawful modalities of governance, similar to colonialism and apartheid.[116] The Charter of Economic Rights and Duties of States of December 12, 1974,[117] provides:

> 1. It is the right and duty of all States, individually and collectively, to eliminate colonialism, *apartheid*, racial discrimination, neo-colonialism and all forms of foreign aggression, occupation and domination, and the economic and social consequences thereof, as a prerequisite for development. States which practice such coercive policies are economically responsible to the countries, territories and peoples affected, for the restitution and full compensation for the exploitation and depletion of, and damages to, the natural and all other resources of those countries, territories and peoples. It is the duty of all States to extend assistance to them.
>
> 2. No State has the right to promote or encourage investments that may constitute an obstacle to the liberation of a territory occupied by force.

And General Assembly Resolution 3171 (XXVIII), Section 2, "[s]upports resolutely the efforts of the developing countries and of the peoples of the territories under colonial and racial domination and foreign occupation in their struggle to regain effective control over their natural resources."[118] Similar references to occupations as tantamount to colonialism and apartheid are found in Article 1(4) of the 1977 Additional Protocol I to the Geneva convention and in the 1979 International Convention against the Taking of Hostages.[119]

---

[115] The same message is conveyed in a later paragraph: "Nothing in the foregoing paragraphs shall be construed as authorizing or encouraging any action which would dismember or impair, totally or in part, the territorial integrity or political unity of sovereign and independent States *conducting themselves in compliance with the principle of equal rights and self-determination of peoples as described above and thus possessed of a government representing the whole people belonging to the territory without distinction as to race, creed or color.*" *Id.* (my emphasis).

[116] An important exception is the consensual Definition of Aggression (General Assembly Resolution 3314 (XXIX) of December 14, 1974). Article 7 refers to the right of peoples under "colonial and racist regimes or other forms of alien domination" to self-determination. There is no explicit mention of occupation.

[117] Article 16(1) of General Assembly Resolution 3281 (XXIX) of December 12, 1974.

[118] 28 UN GAOR, UN Doc. A/9400 (December 17, 1973).

[119] UN Doc. A/C.6/34/L.23, *reprinted in* 18 ILM 1456 (1979). Article 12 (12) provides that acts of hostage taking committed in the course of struggles against those regimes are not governed by that convention.

APPRAISAL

The claim of the lawful struggle for self-determination described above, coupled with the notion of illegal "foreign occupation" could seem to import major qualifications, indeed, a revolution, in the law of occupation. The accumulation of the abovementioned documents could be interpreted as asserting that if a state is constituted according to the principle of self-determination, its occupation, being an infringement, albeit a temporary one, of its people's right to freedom and independence, would seem to be illegal per se. Although the relevant documents lack explicit reference to the illegal occupant's powers in such a situation (except for the denial of its right to utilize the country's natural resources),[120] it would follow from the negative attitude toward it that the occupant's powers would be largely curtailed. Moreover, according to the same rationale, if a state is not constituted according to the principle of self-determination, its current government merits no respect, and the removal of such a government subsequent to invasion and the institution of a new government that conforms with the principle of self-determination are warranted. The creation of Bangladesh would seem a good example of this latter rule. Such a view would render the law of occupation as we have come to understand it irrelevant. It is suggested, however, that this was not the true meaning of those texts. The references to illegal "foreign occupation" should not be interpreted as advocating a virtual end to the temporary modality of government known as occupation. Rather, they should be viewed as politically motivated assertions, aimed at the Israeli occupation of the West Bank and Gaza, the only modern situation in which the occupant invoked the law of occupation. In order to bring these documents in line with the law of occupation, and in view of the context that prompted their adoption, I would suggest that they should be understood as referring only to occupations in which the occupant holds out in bad faith, and refuses to negotiate for its withdrawal in return for peace. Indeed, such an occupant abuses its powers and might taint its continuing presence in the occupied territory with illegality.

Human Rights in Occupied Territories

A strong claim for upholding human rights in occupied territories has been advanced in recent years, along with the general drive to promote human rights worldwide. Theoretically, there is an impressive body of documents elaborating on human rights that prima facie should impinge upon the powers and duties of the occupant. Concern for the humane treatment of

---

[120] See the Charter for Economic Rights and Duties of States, supra note 117.

the enemy's combatants and civilians has always been one of the scales that the law of war sought to balance.[121] This concern is reflected in the Hague Regulations and Fourth Geneva Convention, as well as in the Additional Protocol I of 1977. In fact, human rights considerations play a prominent role in both the Geneva Convention and the Additional Protocol I.[122] However, there is a debate about the formal applicability of the general body of laws on human rights to occupations. Some claim that when armed conflict erupts, most "peacetime" human rights are temporarily superseded by the humanitarian laws of war.[123] Others maintain the opposite, namely, that international human rights instruments are applicable to occupations.[124] The latter position has been espoused by the UN General Assembly,[125] and its Secretary General.[126] Yet another view expressed the need to adapt provisions from international human rights instruments to the law of occupation.[127]

---

[121] Dinstein, *Military Necessity, in* 3 EPIL 274 (1982) ("The laws of war are all based on a subtle balance between two opposing considerations: military necessity, on the one hand, and humanitarian sentiments, on the other."). For the growing convergence of humanitarian and human rights norms, *see* T. Meron, *Human Rights in Internal Strife: Their International Protection* (1987).

[122] The provisions of the protocol that refer to treatment of civilians under occupation are concerned exclusively with the humanitarian treatment of the population. *see* Articles 69–78).

[123] *See, e.g.*, Y. Dinstein, *Human Rights in Armed Conflict: International Humanitarian Law* in *Human Rights in International Law* 345, 350–52 (T. Meron, ed., 1985) (most human rights exist in peacetime but may disappear completely in wartime); J. Pictet, *Humanitarian Law and the Protection of War Victims* 15 (1975). During the drafting of the Fourth Geneva Convention, the majority rejected a Mexican proposal to include "a wording to the effect that the Occupying Power could only modify the legislation of an occupied territory if the legislation in question violated the principles of the 'Universal Declaration of the Rights of Man'." 2A *Final Record of the Diplomatic Conference of Geneva of 1949*, at 671.

[124] *See* Quigley, *The Relation between Human Rights Law and the Law of Belligerent Occupation: Does an Occupied Population Have a Right to Freedom of Assembly and Expression?* 12 Boston College Int'l and Comp. L. Rev. 1 (1989); Roberts, *What Is a Military Occupation?* 55 BYIL 249, 250, 287 (1985); *Id., Prolonged Military Occupation: The Israeli-Occupied Territories since 1967*, 84 AJIL 44, 72 (1990).

[125] *Basic Principles for the Protection of Civilian Population in Armed Conflicts*, General Assembly Resolution 2675 (XXV) December 9, 1970. The first "basic principle" for the protection of civilian population states: "Fundamental human rights, as accepted in international law and laid down in international instruments, continue to apply fully in situations of armed conflict." The vote was 109 to 0, with 8 abstentions.

Specific resolutions with respect to the Israeli occupation have also affirmed the applicability of human rights norms. *See, e.g.*, Resolution 2727 (XXV) of December 15, 1970, *reprinted in* United Nations Yearbook 1970, at 526–27, which called upon Israel to comply with the Universal Declaration of Human Rights.

[126] *Respect for Human Rights in Armed Conflict: Report of the Secretary General*, 24 UN GAOR, Supp. no. 61, at 12, UN Doc. A/7720 (November 20, 1969).

[127] Goodman, *The Need for Fundamental Change in the Law of Belligerent Occupation*, 37 Stan. L.Rev. 1539, 1600 (1985).

The question of the applicability of the human rights law to occupations is important to the extent that the former differs in important aspects from the Hague and Geneva laws, and the customary law that has developed around them. Human rights documents may complement the law of occupation in specific issues that are treated in more detail in the former.[128] But the real issue, where the human rights law seems to differ most dramatically from the law of occupation, lies in the area of civil and political rights. Civil and political rights receive extensive treatment in human rights instruments, yet are ignored by the Fourth Geneva Convention and the Additional Protocol I of 1977. Realistically, one cannot expect occupants to endanger the security of their forces for the purpose of allowing local residents to enjoy political rights that are usually granted in democracies in peacetime. If the political process is lawfully halted for the duration of the occupation, the suspension of political rights seems to be a sensible consequence. As I mentioned in Chapter 2, political rights are often among the first to be suspended by occupants, and this propensity has not been criticized as unlawful in principle.[129] In the interplay between the conflicting interests, the law of occupation concedes that certain civil and political rights will from time to time be subjected to other concerns. Ultimately, as in other cases, the occupant is required to balance its interests against those of the occupied community. Thus, as hostilities subside, and security interests can permit, the occupant could be expected to restore civil and political rights. Under such circumstances, the human rights documents may well serve as guidance for reestablishing civil and political rights in the occupied territory.[130]

Conclusion

The practice of recent occupants and recent international documents pose a serious challenge to the contemporary law of occupation. Using sophisticated claims, most—if not all—recent occupants avoided the acknowledgment that their presence on foreign soil was in fact an occupation. Emerging principles of self-determination and self-rule, as well as some international documents referring to "foreign occupation" as illegal per se, contributed to the growing complexity of the definition of occupation. Careful analysis reveals that in all of the recent cases of occupation, except for the Israeli control over the West Bank (not including East Jerusalem) and Gaza, the framework of the law of occupation was not followed even

---

[128] *See* Roberts, *Prolonged Military Occupation, supra* note 124, at 73.

[129] *See supra* Chapter 2, text accompanying note 38.

[130] *See* Benvenisti, *The Applicability of Human Rights Conventions to Israel and to the Occupied Territories*, 26 ISLR 24 (1992).

on a de facto basis. No occupant in the past two decades has established a temporary government that could effectively balance the conflicting interests of the occupant and occupied, nor did any occupant (except for Israel) invoke the Hague Regulations or Fourth Geneva Convention to justify its measures. This avoidance of recognition of occupation status served as a major stumbling block to international scrutiny of the conduct of most occupants. Moreover, the shunning of the Hague and Fourth Geneva rules by most occupants was reflected in contemporary legal discourse, which, by and large, failed to apply them to the recent practices. With the notable exception of Adam Roberts, the bulk of scholarly discussion regarding occupation was centered on Israeli practices.

One strategy for dealing with this pervasive phenomenon, namely, of occupants that avoid the recognition of the applicability of the law of occupation to their regimes, is to emphasize that the law of occupation applies without respect to the different claims regarding the relevant territory, and at the same time to concentrate on the elaboration of human rights. This strategy is taken up in the Additional Protocol I of 1977, whose preamble "[r]eaffirm[s] that the provisions of the Geneva Conventions of 12 August 1949 and of this protocol must be fully applied in all circumstances . . . without any adverse distinction based on the nature or origin of the armed conflict or on the causes espoused by or attributed to the Parties to the conflict." Instead of providing more refined formulas for defining occupations, this protocol reinforces and develops prescriptions regarding the human rights of people during armed conflicts. By emphasizing the plight of the individual and deemphasizing the issue of applicability of the law of occupation, it hoped to render the latter less crucial. The major problem with this route is that it does not give enough weight to the lesser rights of an occupant in an occupied territory or to the claim to sovereignty of the subjected population.

The other strategy to counter the practice of occupants is to explore existing enforcement mechanisms that could be used more rigorously to give authoritative determinations regarding the status of territories—whether occupied or not—and in case of an occupation, to delineate the responsibilities of the occupant toward the local population. The next chapter is dedicated to the assessment of this strategy.

7

Enforcement of the Law of Occupation on the Occupant: Existing Institutions

THE PREVIOUS chapters have exposed the two essential challenges that the law of occupation faces. First, from the observation of the practice of contemporary occupants, and the examination of their motives not to recognize their status as occupants,[1] one can extrapolate a pattern of denial that will probably be followed in future occupations. Second, even when an occupant recognizes, at most on a de facto basis, its duty to abide by the Hague Regulations and Fourth Geneva Convention, these laws can be interpreted by the occupant very broadly to confer upon it wide discretionary powers. Since the traditional conception views the occupant as entitled to keep the territory as a "pledge of his military success" until the other side yields to a peaceful settlement,[2] it is only natural to expect that the occupant would in the meantime use its internationally sanctioned rule to further its interests.

New definitions for occupation and stricter guidelines for the occupant do not seem to be the way to tackle these challenges. What is fundamentally flawed is the conception underlying the law of occupation, namely, that the occupant could serve as a loyal trustee to the occupied population. This conception has been refuted too many times in this century, and can no longer serve as the basic assumption upon which the law of occupation is founded. Instead, the basic assumption should be the very opposite: an occupant who is left without external supervision would tend to advance its own interests, even at the expense of the interests of the occupied population. The key to a satisfactory response to the abovementioned challenges is the employment of external institutions that will enforce the law of occupation upon the occupant by giving authoritative judgments regarding the status of the forces stationed on foreign soil and the lawfulness of measures taken by the power in control of that country. This chapter examines existing institutions that might take up such a role.

[1] *See supra* Chapter 6.
[2] This is Oppenheim's remark. *See Supra* Chapter 5, text accompanying note 181.

Enforcement through Adjudication

Judicial review of occupation measures could be an important vehicle for the enforcement of the law of occupation on the occupant. To explore the promise of judicial review it is necessary to distinguish between the various judicial institutions that are possible candidates for this task.

Courts in Occupied Territory

Courts under occupation face a dilemma. They have to apply the local laws, and sometimes the temporarily ousted national authorities might expect them also to apply the ousted government's new prescriptions. At the same time, the occupant requires them to respect its own measures. Their refusal to fulfill the occupant's demand might cost them their jurisdiction. Generally, courts tend to acquiesce to this demand rather than find themselves stripped of their powers, and their people left without recourse to an indigenous court system. Only under extreme conditions will courts under occupation resist the occupant's demands. Therefore, aside from very few exceptions, the tendency of judges in occupied territories has been to refrain from making any assertions questioning the validity of the occupant's measures under the law of occupation. A brief survey of the positions taken by local courts under occupation will support this observation.

In 1916, the Belgian Court of Cassation's first reported judicial reference to a German occupation measure[3] asserted:

> [T]he difficulties with regard to the alleged non-compliance [of the occupant] with [Article 43 of the Hague Regulations] merely concerns international relations, and their solution can only lead to the application of the sanction as set out by Article 3 of the [1907 Hague] Convention;[4] . . . if they attempted to solve these difficulties, the judicial authorities of the occupied territory would encroach upon the prerogative of the competent national power, [and therefore] they must . . . abstain from doing so under pain of acting *ultra vires*.[5]

Thus the court denied the Belgian citizen's right to challenge occupation measures under Article 43 of the Hague Regulations in local courts. This denial, of course, gave the status of unchallengeable law to every occupa-

---

[3] The order established special courts to adjudicate landlord-tenant controversies. *See supra* Chapter 3, text accompanying note 43.

[4] Article 3 of that convention provides in relevant part: "A belligerent party which violates the provisions of the [Hague] Regulations shall, if the case demands, be liable to pay compensation."

[5] Judgment of May 18, 1916, 1 ILN 136 (1916).

tion enactment.[6] This procedural stumbling block, however, was not enough. To fully respect the occupant's orders, the court had to reject as inapplicable any conflicting decrees issued by the Belgian king from his exile. The Court of Cassation did not want to rely for that purpose on the German decree of January 4, 1915,[7] which had denied any effect to the king's decrees after the commencement of the occupation.[8] Instead, the court developed the following theory: by incorporating the Hague Regulations into Belgian law in 1910, the Belgian legislature had conceded that whoever would occupy Belgium would enjoy full legislative powers. In other words, the court reasoned, Belgian law delegated to the occupant the power to enact laws. Thus, any law enacted pursuant to this grant should enjoy the same status as any other local laws.[9] This theory did not eliminate a possible conflict between occupation orders and the king's decrees, since any new Belgian decree could subordinate occupation orders or even abrogate them entirely. However, due to the fact that the king's decrees could not be published in the official bulletin as the law required, the applicability of these decrees was subject to an examination by the court as to whether they had been made sufficiently known to the general public within occupied Belgium. For that reason, the Court of Cassation created a rebuttable presumption against the applicability of any new Belgian decree.[10] I have not found a case where such a decree was held sufficiently known and therefore applicable.[11] The Belgian courts continued to operate in this mo-

[6] The Court of Appeal of Liège, however, was ready to examine the occupant's orders under Article 43. In a decision of February 13, 1917, 2 ILN 111 (1917), it held the same order valid under international law.

[7] *Supra* Chapter 3, note 6.

[8] The court did not follow a prior decision of the Tribunal Civil de Tournai, *La Belgique Industrielle c. Masure*, judgment of March 9, 1916, 2 ILN 169 (1917), which did rely on that order to reject a conflicting Belgian law.

[9] This was the rationale of the decision of May 18, 1916, *supra* note 5, which said, in part: "Whereas the Belgian laws of 25th May and 8th August 1910, while recording the assent given to the [1907 Hague] treaty by the Houses of Parliament, contain formal directions that the Convention is to receive full and complete effect in Belgium . . . [consequently] the measures contained in Article 43 must . . . be observed, not because the occupant exercises the legislative powers of the occupied territory by reason of his strength, nor because these measures are the orders of a foreign military authority, or that they possess the virtue of having, in themselves, any legal effect although not assented to by the legal authority, but solely because it is ordered by a Belgian law."

[10] Decision of November 13, 1916, 2 ILN 79 (1917). The trial judge was still required to inquire whether the law had become adequately known despite that fact, and if so, the law would have effect. 2 ILN 169–70 (1917).

[11] Despite the general enforceability of occupation orders in Belgian courts, the Court of Cassation could still decline jurisdiction to entertain certain thorny issues. Thus it refused to entertain petitions against the Belgian fiscal administration, which was enforcing the tenfold "absence tax" (on this tax, *see supra* Chapter 3, text accompanying note 31). The ground for the ruling was that the court's jurisdiction to review decisions in matters of direct taxation

dus vivendi with the occupant until early 1918, when the Court of Cassation found it impossible to cope with the German attempt to divide Belgium. After the occupant deported some of this court's judges and relieved the rest from their posts, the court decided to suspend its sessions until further notice.[12]

The jurisprudence of the Belgian courts after the war was diametrically opposed to their prior position during the war. After liberation, almost no occupation order was upheld by them. Second, all Belgian decrees promulgated during the occupation were held retroactively applicable.[13] The courts developed what was later termed the Belgian school, a theory according to which the occupant's orders do not have any legal value whatsoever, being merely de facto commands enforced through the occupant's coercive power.[14] The Court of Appeal of Liège, which during the war had conceded wide lawmaking powers to the occupant,[15] subsequently denied any legal effect of *any* occupation order, regardless of its contents.[16] The Court of Appeal of Brussels reached a similar decision.[17] The same rationale was applied to determine the legal effect of the Belgian decrees promulgated by the exiled government during the war. Several such decrees received recognition after the war, including the same decree that was rejected in 1916[18] by the Court of Cassation,[19] and even laws that imposed criminal sanctions for giving aid to the occupant were enforced.[20] These courts' jurisprudence again reversed itself during the German occupation in World War II, when the Court of Cassation consistently refused to pass

---

had been confined to taxation imposed by the national government only. *Francq v. l'Administration des finances de Belgique*, 2 ILN 170 (1917).

[12] *See supra* Chapter 3, text accompanying note 64.

[13] This position conformed with the Belgian decree-law of April 8, 1917, which asserted that only the king's prescriptions had the force of law in Belgium. *See supra* Chapter 3, text accompanying note 66.

[14] For the doctrine, *see* the influential article of de Visscher, *L'occupation de guerre d'apres la jurisprudence de la Cour de cassation de Belgique*, 34 LQR 72–81 (1918).

[15] *Supra* note 6. In that case the court upheld the special court for landlord-tenant disputes.

[16] *Mathot v. Longue*, [1919–1922] AD Case no. 329 (Court of Appeal of Liège, February 19, 1921). This case was the second in a row dealing with a German order that had declared void all purchases of vegetables not yet gathered. It reversed the same court's prior ruling, *Borchart v. Committee of Supplies of Corneux*, [1919–22] AD Case no. 327 (February 28, 1920), which had upheld the validity of the order.

[17] *De Brabant and Gossselin v. T. and A. Florent*, [1919–1922] AD Case no. 328 (July 22, 1920).

[18] *See supra* note 5.

[19] *See* the decision of the Court of Cassation of December 9, 1920, 1 Pasicrisie Belge 177 (1921). *Accord De Nimal v. De Nimal*, [1919–1922] AD Case no. 311 (Court of Appeal of Brussels, April 23, 1919).

[20] *Auditeur Militaire v. Van Dieren*, [1919–1922] AD Case no. 310 (Council of War of Brabant, January 31, 1919); *see also* the Editor's Note, *id.*

judgment on the measures dictated by the occupant through the Belgian secretaries-general.[21]

As the following brief survey shows, courts in other occupied jurisdictions, during World War II and afterwards, acted in much the same way as the Belgian courts did. The Dutch courts declined jurisdiction to review legislative acts of the Germans, based on the guidance of their Supreme Court.[22] That Court held that the occupation measures had the status of Dutch legislation and were therefore nonreviewable, and that the framers of the Hague Regulations had no intention of confering on the local courts such a function of judicial review.[23] The French Tribunal Civil de la Seine refused to hear a claim contesting the validity of a decree restricting the right of Jews to draw freely from their bank accounts, saying that "[t]he decrees of the occupying authorities bind all within the occupied territories."[24] The Conseil d'État also hinted that it did not regard itself as competent to determine the legality of measures taken by local authorities if such a determination involved "the interpretation of acts of an international nature" or "touch[ed] upon the rights of the occupying power."[25] In a later case,[26] the Conseil d'État made it clear that it would not entertain petitions that involved a claim against the legality of occupation measures.[27] The attitude of both the Greek Court of Cassation and the Greek Conseil d'État during World War II was to regard as Greek laws the legislative measures taken by the occupant or by the so-called government established by the latter, thus denying any possibility of judicial review under

[21] *In re Anthoine*, [1919–1942] AD Case no. 151 (October 24, 1940); and other cases mentioned in the Editor's Note to that case.

[22] *In re Jurisdiction of the Dutch Supreme Court for Economic Matters*, [1919–1942] AD (Supp.) Case no. 161 (Supreme Court of Holland, January 12, 1942). In this case the court dismissed a claim against the institution of a new tribunal by the Germans ("for the Trial of Criminal Cases concerning Economic Life").

[23] Admittedly, the Dutch Supreme Court was headed by a Nazi appointee during the occupation, and the Dutch government in exile condemned the court's general attitude, but on this issue, the outcome reached by the court conformed to similar outcomes in other jurisdictions.

The Note of the editor of the Annual Digest, which precedes the reported Dutch Supreme Court decision, *id.*, admonishes that "judicial decisions rendered in Holland during the occupation are not to be regarded as being of any considerable value in the interpretation of the law of nations in the field of belligerent occupation." *Id.* at 290. The Dutch authorities, upon their return, suspended the members of the Supreme Court, and prosecuted the Court's president (appointed after the ousting of the former, Jewish president) in the Special War Crimes Court for having assisted the enemy by his activity in the Court.

[24] *In re C.*, [1919–1942] AD (Supp.) Case no. 157 (May 31, 1941).

[25] *In re Lecoq and Others*, [1943–1945] AD Case no. 161 (January 7, 1944).

[26] *In re Hiriat*, judgment of November 22, 1944, *cited in* the Editor's Note to the *Lecoq* case, *id.*

[27] In considering the position taken by the Conseil d'État, we should remember that its jurisdiction is confined by French law to acts of French authorities acting under French law.

international law.[28] During the post–World War II occupation period, the Austrian Administrative Court[29] and Constitutional[30] Court, as well as the Italian Court of Cassation,[31] also declined jurisdiction to review occupation measures. As in the case of postwar Belgian jurisprudence, upon the termination of World War II, some courts reversed their earlier position, and assumed, ex post facto, powers of judicial review over occupation orders.[32]

Norway experienced a unique situation. In reacting to a German decree that was to facilitate the Nazification of the Norwegian courts, the Norwegian Supreme Court sent a letter to the authorities giving its opinion regarding the illegality of that measure. The decree was not repealed, and the Court was advised to abstain from "political questions," whereupon all the members of the Court resigned, explaining that under the circumstances they could not fulfill their duty to review occupation measures. The occupation authorities appointed new members to the Court, which subsequently declared itself incompetent to review the formers' measures.[33] Despite these developments, there is one reported case of a district court decision in which a certain enactment was quashed as illegal under Article 43.[34]

In the Israeli-occupied West Bank, a similar declaration of judicial incompetence was rendered by the highest court in that region, the Court of Appeals sitting in Ram'alla.[35] This court reversed a decision of the Hebron

---

[28] *In re Law 900 of 1943*, [1943–1945] AD Case no. 152 and Editor's Note, at 441 (Court of Cassation, Judgment no. 68 of 1944).

[29] *See, e.g., Booty (Qualification by the Occupant) Case*, [1949] AD Case no. 187 (February 1, 1949).

[30] *See, e.g., Requisition of Private Property (Austria) Case*, [1949] AD Case no. 188 (June 23, 1949); *Billeting of Troops Case*, [1950] AD Case no. 135 (March 22, 1950); *Booty (Requisitioned Car) Case*, [1951] AD Case no. 219 (May 16, 1951).

[31] *See, e.g., Tanfani v. Carlletti*, [1949] AD Case no. 185 (February 10, 1949); *Magri v. Di Marco*, [1951] AD Case no. 212 (February 8, 1951).

[32] The Dutch Special Court of Cassation (which had replaced the suspended Supreme Court) asserted such powers in *In re Contractors Knols*, [1946] AD Case no. 144 (December 2, 1946). Other courts acted similarly. *In re G.*, [1943–1945] AD Case no. 151 (Greek Criminal Court of Heraklion [Crete], 1945); *Randsfjordsbruket and Jevnaker Kommune v. Viul Tresliperi*, [1951] AD Case no. 199 (Norwegian Supreme Court, November 30, 1951).

[33] Upon the liberation of Norway, that court was dismissed, and its Nazi judges were indicted for treason. On these developments, *see* the Editor's Note to *Public Prosecutor v. X*, [1919–1942] AD Case no. 160 (1940), and the Editor's Note to *Overland's Case*, [1943–1945] AD Case no. 156 (District Court of Aker, August 25, 1943).

[34] *Overland's Case, supra* note 33. The court held that "the courts will in all circumstances be obliged to refuse to base their decisions on legislation which is obviously in contradiction to Article 43 of the Hague Regulations." According to the court's view, its opinion was compatible with the position of the "Nazi" Supreme Court, as the latter supposedly recognized the possibility of reviewing decrees as "being obviously beyond one's powers."

[35] *Al-Ja'bari v. Al-Awiwi*, 42 ILR 484, 486 (1971) ("[T]his Court holds that the courts in

Magistrate's Court, which had declared invalid a certain occupation order,[36] and sided with a decision of the Bethlehem Magistrate's Court on
the same point.[37]

The nearly consistent attitude of courts under occupation reflects the
local judges' concern that the occupant will retaliate against unfavorable
court decisions by restricting the courts' jurisdiction or by replacing the
judges, thus depriving the local population of an indigenous judiciary sym-
pathetic to their interests. The aftermath of the two incidents where courts
did clash with the occupant, in Belgium during World War I and in Norway during World War II, demonstrates that the decision to decline judicial review is a clear choice for the preservation of the preoccupation
judicial institution. Therefore, the courts of the occupied territory cannot
be relied upon as a potential watchdog for reviewing the legality of the
occupant's conduct.[38]

Judicial Review and the Occupant's Courts

During the occupation, the courts of the occupying power, those within
its borders and those established in the occupied area, may find themselves
facing claims against the validity of occupation measures. There are many
situations, before various courts, where such claims might arise. Military
or other tribunals established by the occupant often adjudicate claims
against locals or members of the occupation army, or against other nationals of the occupant; some occupants would be subject to their country's

---

the occupied area are not competent to consider whether or not an imperative need exists
tha: requires additional or amending legislation.").

[36] The order in question, which gave Israeli lawyers the right to represent clients in the
West Bank courts, was held by the Hebron Court as invalid, being inconsistent with international law, which limited, according to the decision, the occupant's legislative powers to
the protection of the occupation forces. The decision is mentioned in Blum, *The Missing
Reversioner: Reflections on the Status of Judea and Samaria*, 3 ISLR 279, 279–80 (1968).

[37] *See* Blum, *id.* at 280–81. *But cf. El-Alami v. Income Tax Authorities in Gaza* (unpublished
decision of the Gazan District Court, March 7, 1970), cited in M. Drori, *The Legislation in
the Area of Judea and Samaria* 65 n.45 (1975), where the court held itself competent to review
occupation measures.

[38] Courts that are situated in the unoccupied part of an occupied country usually have little
influence on life in the occupied part. The practice of many occupants has been to sever the
legal ties between courts in the occupied and unoccupied parts of a country. When the higher
court was situated in the unoccupied part, as in Cyrenaica (Libya), Venezia Giulia (Italy),
and the West Bank, the occupants would suspend the right to appeal to it from cases decided
by courts in the occupied part. An exception to this common practice was during the Armistice Occupation of Germany after 1918, when the access to appeals procedures in the unoccupied part of Germany was not barred. For an assessment of the influence of the German
Reichsgericht, *see supra* Chapter 3, text accompanying notes 101–15).

administrative court, which could be asked to review the occupant's measures; finally, the courts of the occupant's home country might confront such claims.

Military tribunals set up by many occupants either refused to review the occupant's measures on the gound that these acts were outside their jurisdiction, or reviewed such measures only to uphold them as legal.[39] Administrative or judicial institutions of the occupant's home country would also hesitate before imposing limits on their forces who are in charge of administering the occupied territory. The British Act-of-State doctrine, which denies British courts the jurisdiction to review acts of the Executive with respect to other states or their residents,[40] also applies to the reviewability of occupation measures. The French Conseil d'État decided during the occupation of Germany after World War II that the French commander-in-chief was, when acting in occupied Germany, not an organ of the French state and thus not amenable to the court's jurisdiction.[41] In 1913, the U.S. Supreme Court did reject an order of the U.S. occupant of Puerto Rico as being an infringement of the Fifth Amendment of the Constitution.[42] On the other hand, a 1990 decision ruled that U.S. forces operating abroad, including armed forces, were not subject to the requirement of the Constitution's Fourth Amendment.[43] Claims of foreigners against the U.S. government for the recovery of damages alledgedly caused by U.S. military forces operating abroad are routinely dismissed by lower federal courts.[44] Thus, as of 1992 the Israeli Supreme Court remains the only national court that is ready to review occupation measures of its national institutions under both Israeli administrative law and international law.[45] Given this

[39] The Allied military tribunals in post–World War II Germany rejected the applicability of the Hague Regulations, on the basis of their claim that the Allies were exercising sovereign rights. *See, e.g., Grahame v. Director of Prosecutions*, [1947] AD Case no. 103 (Germany, British Zone of Control, Control Commission Court of Criminal Appeal); *Dalldorf et al. v. Director of Prosecutions*, [1949] AD Case no. 159 (same court, December 31, 1949). Some of the Israeli military tribunals have agreed to review occupation measures, but there is no reported case of striking down a measure as illegal. *See supra* Chapter 5, note 43.

[40] On the British Act of State doctrine, *see, e.g.*, Morgenstern, *Judicial Practice and the Supremacy of International Law*, 27 BYIL 42, 72–80 (1950).

[41] *In re Société Bonduelle et Cie*, [1951] AD Case no. 177 (June 29, 1951).

[42] *Ochoa v. Hernandez y Morales*, 230 U.S. 139 (1913).

[43] *United States v. Verdugo-Urquidez*, 110 S. Ct. 1056, 29 ILM 441 (1990). This case involved the question of whether or not searches and seizures conducted on non-Americans abroad are protected by the Fourth Amendment of the U.S. Constitution. Five Justices held that such actions were not protected.

[44] *Committee of U.S. Citizens Living in Nicaragua et al. v. Ronald Reagan*, 859 F.2d 929 (D.C. Cir. 1988) (U.S. operations in Nicaragua); *Saltany et al. v. Ronald Reagan*, 886 F.2d 438 (D.C. Cir. 1989) (air raid on Libya); *Industria Panificadora, S.A., et al. v. United States*, 763 F. Supp. 1154 (D.D.C. 1991) (occupation of Panama).

[45] On the jurisprudence of the Israeli Supreme Court, which is not entirely satisfactory, *see supra* Chapter 5, text accompanying notes 55–84.

general tendency of national courts to refrain from enforcing the law of occupation upon their governments, it seems that the courts of the occupant cannot be considered to have the potential of imposing meaningful constraints on the occupant's measures.

Judicial Review by Courts in Third Countries

Review by courts in third countries is important to this study as long as decisions taken by these courts may have some influence on the occupant's measures. Theoretically, courts in third countries could have an important impact on occupation measures, especially by refusing to recognize titles to property conferred upon the claimant through occupation measures that those courts would declare incompatible with international law and therefore invalid. The impact could be significant if that property were immovable property, or minerals and other commodities that were taken and shipped from occupied territories in defiance of the law of occupation. Courts in third countries could use the law of occupation, particularly the Hague Regulations dealing with the occupant's powers and duties regarding the use of private and public property as the test for the legality of the title. Many international lawyers have pointed out this opportunity.[46]

My observation is, however, that judges in third countries often avoid an even-handed scrutiny of occupation measures. They opt for this hesitant approach because of their concern for the negative ramifications a bolder position could have for the interests of their countries. A decision of a national court, for example, that the entitlement for an oil shipment is vested in the original owner (illegally deprived of its title by the occupant) could lead to adverse economic results in the forum state: the occupant (or the person upon whom the title was conferred) would seek other jurisdictions where such an outcome could be avoided, and ship the resources only to those destinations. Since the judge cannot be assured that his or her decision would be followed in those other jurisdictions, he or she might very well be inclined to give precedence to the occupant's effective power. Another factor that looms large in these circumstances, and stands in the

---

[46] This, for example, is the opinion of Morgenstern: "It has . . . been affirmed by writers of authority that the legitimate acts of the occupant will—and ought to be—recognized by the courts of neutral states. . . . With regard to [illegitimate acts of the former] there is some authority to the effect that third states must deny recognition and enforcement to acts of the occupant which are contrary to international law." *Validity of Acts of the Belligerent Occupant*, 28 BYIL 291, 316–17 (1951). Quincy Wright held a similar view: "Doubtless there are definite rules of international law limiting the authority of a military occupant during the course of war. Acts of such a *de facto* authority which ignore these limitations, even though functioning locally, should be regarded as *ultra vires* and void by a foreign Court." *British Courts and Ethiopian Recognition*, 31 AJIL 683, 687 n2 (1937).

way of the satisfactory application of the law of occupation by third-country courts, is the courts' inclination to defer to their governments in matters they consider pertinent to the realm of foreign policy.

Two decisions of Dutch courts during World War I may illustrate both the promise and the difficulties of third-country adjudication. The two courts of first instance, the district courts of Breda[47] and of Rotterdam[48] reviewed an order issued by the German Governor General in occupied Belgium in light of Article 43 of the Hague Regulations. The order, which provided for the abrogation of a moratorium that had been enacted by the Belgian king at the beginning of the War, was upheld by both courts.[49] While those two decisions appear to be truly objective applications of the law of occupation, their background is not without relevance. As a result of the British blockade of Germany during that war, the Netherlands had become Germany's most important outlet for foreign trade.[50] A hostile attitude of the Dutch courts might have jeopardized this arrangement. In any case, this earlier trend to apply the Hague Regulations has been subsequently overcome in all Benelux countries, in which the more modern trend of the courts has been to defer to the occupant of the relevant territory (the cases involved the Soviet occupation of the Baltic republics and the German occupation of Poland).[51]

In Anglo-American courts, issues relating to foreign occupations were dealt with through the question of recognition of foreign entities illegally established by the occupant. The courts tended to defer this question to the Executive, and refrained from expressing their independent judgment.[52] Thus, during the appeasement policy of Britain on the eve of World War II, which prompted its recognition of Italy's sovereignty over Ethiopia, the British Chancery Division validated an act of the Italian occupant on the basis of that recognition.[53] A Soviet measure in Estonia was

---

[47] Judgment of May 22, 1917, 2 *ILN* 127 (1917).

[48] *Cillekens v. De Haas*, [1919–1922] AD Case no. 336 (May 14, 1919).

[49] The Rotterdam court reasoned that the limitation imposed in Article 43 "has clearly in view the laws which were in force before the war and not legal measures of a special character (such as moratorium) taken during the war and in connection with it." *Id*. Moreover, "it would in any case be in the interest of public order and safety to restrict the moratorium to the shortest possible term." Id.

[50] *See* L. von Köhler, *The Administration of the Occupied Territories* 149–50 (W. Dittmar trans., 1942) (1927); *see generally supra* Chapter 3.

[51] J. Verhoeven, *Relations internationales de droit privé en l'absence de reconnaissance d'un état, d'un gouvernement ou d'une situation*, 192 (III) Recueil des cours 9, at 122–23 (1985).

[52] Although this tendency, in this and in other matters that pertain to international law, is characteristic of Anglo-American courts, this trend also prevailed in the early jurisprudence of the French, Italian, and Belgian courts. Verhoeven, *id*. at 115–16, 118–19, 121.

[53] *Bank of Ethiopia v. National Bank of Egypt and Liguori*, [1937] Ch. 513 (validating an act by the Italian occupant, based on assumed de facto sovereignty of Italy).

validated on the same grounds.[54] In the United States, the New York State courts refused to recognize the power of the German administrator of Dutch companies (under occupation) on the basis of the refusal of the U.S. government to recognize what the court called the "German military control of Holland."[55] For similar reasons, the same courts refused to recognize measures of the Soviet occupant in the Baltic republics.[56] The Supreme Court of Victoria, Australia, approached similarly the question of the German annexation of parts of Czechoslovakia.[57] None of these rulings mentioned the relevance of the law of occupation.[58]

In a recent British case concerning the Turkish occupation of Northern Cyprus (not recognized de facto or de jure by the British Foreign Office), the House of Lords avoided a scrutiny of Turkish measures under international law by declaring its lack of jurisdiction to decide issues linked to immovables situated in foreign territories.[59]

I have found only three decisions that offered a credible application of the law of occupation by courts of third states. Significantly, in all of these cases, the litigation took place long after the occupant had been defeated and the territory liberated,[60] when adverse economic and political reper-

---

[54] *A/S Talinna Laevauhisus v. Estonian State Steamship Line*, [1946] AD Case no. 6 (de facto recognition of Soviet annexation validated the latter's measures within the occupied territory).

[55] *Koninklijke Lederfabriek "Oisterwijk" N.V. v. Chase National Bank of the City of New York*, 30 N.Y.S.2d 518, [1941–1942] AD Case no. 172 (1941); *Amstelbank, N.V. v. Guaranty Trust Co. of New York*, 31 N.Y.S.2d. 194, [1941–1942] AD Case no. 171 (1941).

[56] *See, e.g., Latvian State Cargo and Passenger S.S. Line v. McGrath, Attorney-General*, [1951] AD Case no. 27 (D.D.C. 1951). In other incidents, the law of the annexing state was declared valid, again on grounds of recognition policies. *Eck v. N.V. Netherlandsch Amerikaansche Stoomvaart Maatschappij*, 52 N.Y.S. 2d 367, [1946] AD Case no. 13 (1944) (German law applicable to Austrian territory).

[57] *Anglo-Czechoslovak and Prague Credit Bank v. Janssen*, [1943] A.L.R. 427, [1943–1945] AD Case no. 11 (August 1943). Since in this case the government's statement was not conclusive, the Court accepted judicial notice of the fact of the de facto German control over Czechoslovakia.

[58] Morgenstern, *Validity of Acts, supra* note 46, at 318 n.1, points out that "[a]ltogether the question of recognition of annexation has served to distract courts from the real problem before them of the legal effect of acts of a belligerent occupant."

[59] *Hesperides Hotels Ltd. v. Muftizade*, [1979] A.C. 508, [1978] 2 All E.R. 1168, [1978] 3 W.L.R. 378 (H.L. 1978).

[60] Two of the cases were decided by U.S. courts. *Aboitz and Co. v. Price*, 99 F. Supp. 602 (D. Utah, 1951) ("[T]he Japanese fiat currency was valid [under international law], but the prohibition of traffic between the internees and their friends was not."); *State of the Netherlands v. Federal Reserve Bank of New York*, 201 Fed. Rep. 2d 455, 18 ILR no. 174 (2d. Cir. 1953) ("The legitimate sovereign should be entitled to legislate over occupied territory insofar as such enactments do not conflict with the legitimate rule of the occupying power."). The third case, decided by the court of appeals of Paris, did not explicitly invoke the Hague Regulations: *Administration des domaines c. Dame Sorkin*, judgment of July 21, 1953, [1954] Revue Crit. 539, note Loussouarn. The court declared that a testament made by a Jew in

cussions from such a judicial position could no longer be feared. Of course, after the occupation period, the importance of judicial scrutiny by third-country courts is very much reduced.

As international cooperation increases, and activity in world markets becomes more and more coordinated, the transaction costs involved in reaching a communitywide rejection of entitlements gained through violations of international law diminish substantially. A decision common to many states to resist illegal occupation measures can be expected to find followers. Such a coordinated policy may well reduce the "risk" taken by national courts in rejecting illegal occupation measures. Therefore, despite past experience, there is today a potential for meaningful contribution of national courts to the enforcement of the law of occupation. The basic condition of such an contribution, a joint effort of governments, is attainable. It is to be hoped that increased awareness of this promise will prompt such joint effort.

Supranational Tribunals

International and regional tribunals are free from the constraints under which third-country courts operate. They can be expected to apply the law of occupation free of national biases in adjudicating claims regarding occupation measures. Even here, however, one should distinguish among the different international tribunals. Quite surprisingly, the permanent international tribunals have demonstrated hesitations similar to those of national courts. The advisory opinion of the International Court of Justice (ICJ) regarding South African rule in Namibia held that the South African presence there was illegal occupation.[61] Although the court declared the South African administration illegal under international law, it stopped short of extending this illegality to private transactions based on the laws of the illegal regime.[62] Earlier, the Permanent Court of International Justice (PCIJ) had also refrained from translating breaches of international

---

Auschwitz in 1942 according to the Polish law was valid despite its invalidity under the then-effective German law. As the court said, neither annexation nor forceful occupation could render the Polish law nonexistent. Id. at 540.

[61] *Advisory Opinion on Legal Consequences for States of the Continued Presence of South Africa in Namibia (South West Africa) Notwithstanding Security Council Resolution 276 (1970)* [1971] ICJ Rep. 16.

[62] *Id.* at paragraph 125, stating that "while official acts performed by [South Africa with respect to Namibia] are illegal and invalid, this invalidity cannot be extended to those acts, such as, for instance, the registration of births, deaths and marriages, the effects of which can be ignored only to the detriment of the inhabitants of the Territory."

obligations to the sphere of private law.[63] Its opinion in *Interpretation of the Statute of the Memel Territory*,[64] despite having declared the action under scrutiny incongruent with treaty obligations, stopped short of referring to the implications of such a holding for municipal law, and explicitly refrained from declaring the unlawful act void. This tendency of the international courts has been explained by Felice Morgenstern as a result of "the imperfections of international organization."[65] Those courts were clearly aware of the limits of their powers, and did not want to emphasize these limits by giving decisions that would not be followed. In comparison to the ICJ and the PCIJ approach, the international ad hoc arbitral tribunals, established after both world wars, produced a more resolute jurisprudence.[66] These tribunals considered the issues before them free from any institutional concerns, and did not hesitate to declare invalid certain occupation measures.

The main problem of supranational tribunals is, of course, the lack of consent of states to have these issues adjudicated. A lesser, though still difficult, problem is that some modern occupants tend not to recognize their responsibility for measures in territories they occupy. A case in point is the 1978 application of Cyprus against Turkey to the European Commission of Human Rights, related to acts allegedly committed by Turkey in the northern part of Cyprus. Turkey responded by saying that it was not responsible for acts of the Turkish Federated State of Cyprus, which was not subject to the commission's jurisdiction. The commission rejected the Turkish argument and declared the application admissible, after satisfying itself that northern Cyprus was within Turkish jurisdiction in the sense of Article 1 of the European Convention on Human Rights.[67] The commis-

---

[63] Compare Morgenstern's observation, in *Validity of Acts, supra* note 46, at 301: "[I]nternational courts are, as a rule, reluctant to regard as void municipal acts which are contrary to international law, even when international law appears to limit the competence of the municipal organ concerned."

[64] *Publications of the P.C.I.J.*, Series A/B, nos. 49, 294, at 336 (decision of August 11, 1932).

[65] Morgenstern, *Judicial Practice, supra* note 40, at 44.

[66] *See Affaire relative a l'or de la banque nationale d'Albanie*, 12 RIAA 19 (1953) (restitution of gold taken by the German occupant in Rome); *Affaire de forêts du Rhodope central (fond)*, 3 RIAA 1405 (1933) (Greece v. Bulgaria) (invalidity of Bulgarian measure transferring entitlements over Greek forces); *Kemeny v. Yugoslavia*, 8 Rec. Dec. Trib. Arb. Mixtes 588, [1927–1928] AD Case no. 374 (Hung.-Yugo., 1928) (Yugoslav decree regulating mining concessions in territory occupied during Armistice Occupation held valid); *Ville d'Anvers v. État Allemand*, 5 Rec. Dec. Trib. Arb. Mixtes 712 (Ger.-Belg., 1925) (German order imposing liability on boroughs for violations of public order incompatible with Article 43); *Herwyn v. Muller*, 2 Rec. Dec. Trib. Arb. Mixtes 368 (Ger.-Belg., 1923) (Belgian decree of exiled government prohibiting trade with Germans declared of no effect during occupation).

[67] Application 8007/77, *Cyprus v. Turkey*, 21 Yearbook of the European Convention on Human Rights 100, 230–34, 62 ILR 5, 74–76 (1978).

sion's approach, of looking to the actual presence of Turkish soldiers on the island and disregarding legalistic claims regarding their formal status, is highly commendable. It is the only possible response to such formalistic claims, which are unfortunately not uncommon in modern occupations.

Enforcement through Protecting Powers

Since occupations involve the use of force in declared or undeclared international armed conflicts, protecting powers, respectable institutions in customary and treaty law, may be regarded as potential international agencies, capable of ensuring compliance with the law of occupation.

Protecting Powers under the 1949 Fourth Geneva Convention

Article 9 of the Fourth Geneva Convention (common Article 8 of the first three Geneva conventions) delineates the arrangements with regard to protecting powers. The goal of the institution is stated in the opening sentence: "The present Convention shall be applied with the co-operation and under the scrutiny of the Protecting Powers whose duty is to safeguard the interests of the Parties to the conflict." The Geneva conventions do not prescribe the procedure for appointing and recognizing protecting powers. In these crucial matters they rely on customary law.

A protecting power is a state that has agreed to look after the interests of another state (in our case, the occupied state) in a territory controlled by a third state (in our case, the occupant), after the latter has expressed its consent. Especially with respect to occupation, this arrangement is theoretically very promising. Not only is the protecting power put in the position of a mediator, even an umpire, enabling a flow of communications between the parties to the conflict, pointing at common objectives, but, in addition, the protecting power has direct access to the occupied population, which is entitled under Article 30 to apply directly to it. However, despite its promise, this arrangement is deficient, especially in a situation of occupation. What was left out of Article 9, namely, the appointing and recognizing procedure, is the major drawback to its implementation. As mentioned throughout the preceding chapter, the majority of occupants attempted to set up new entities, annex existing ones, or recognize new governments. The formal position of such an occupant would be that the government that appointed the protecting power has no legal standing and therefore the appointment is invalid.[68] On the other hand, governments

---

[68] This happened often during World War II. *See* J. Pictet, ed., *Commentary: The Fourth Geneva Convention*, 83–84 (1958).

that did not recognize the occupant (as in the case of the Arab states in conflict with Israel) would not appoint such a protecting power as this would amount to recognizing the occupant as a state. Finally, although the Geneva conventions provide for mandatory supervision by a protecting power, they did not create a procedure for its appointment. Therefore, even if there were no problems of mutual recognition, one belligerent could stall its acceptance of the state appointed as a protecting power by the other side. There is no duty to accept any state, and there is no mechanism for selecting one in case of such a default.

Article 11 of the Fourth Geneva Convention tries to mitigate the results of the non-appointment of protecting powers by imposing a duty on the occupant (the "Detaining Power") to "request a neutral State, or such an organization, to undertake the functions performed . . . by a protecting power." And if this is not possible, the occupant "shall request, or shall accept, . . . the offer of the services of a humanitarian organization, such as the International Committee of the Red Cross, to assume the humanitarian functions performed by protecting power." This solution will not impress an occupant that does not concede its function to be that of a "Detaining Power," such as an occupant that claims to be merely "assisting" a new entity or government, which it had set up. Moreover, the opportunity this article gives the occupant unilaterally to appoint a protecting power gives the occupant too much power vis-à-vis the ousted government.[69] The last option, the assumption of humanitarian functions by a humanitarian organization, is limited in scope. "Humanitarian functions" include only "those activities which bring directly and immediately to the persons protected by this Conventions the care which their condition demands." They do not include the power to supervise the management of the affairs of the occupied territory.[70]

The deficiencies of Articles 9 and 11 of the Fourth Geneva Convention resulted in their disregard by occupants in subsequent conflicts. The system of protecting powers has been used only twice, in the Suez conflict in 1956 and in Goa in 1961. In the war that led to the creation of Bangladesh, India did not accept the nomination of Switzerland as a protecting power.[71] The ICRC has never formally assumed a role of a substitute for a

---

[69] Indeed, ten countries made reservations to the effect that such unilateral appointments would be illegal unless approved by the ousted government. Id. at 104. Pictet maintains that such a problem does not exist, since as long as the ousted government is represented by any protecting power, then the occupant may not use its appointing power under Article 11. Id. at 107. If this is the case, then we are left with the incomplete arrangement of Article 9.

[70] Id. at 109; see also id. at 102.

[71] I. de Lupis, The Law of War 323 (1987). On the failure of this system, see also E. Rosenblad, International Humanitarian Law of Armed Conflict 15–17 (1979).

protecting party.[72] Instead, it has acted to alleviate personal suffering through its general grant, embodied in Article 10 of the Fourth Convention, to undertake "humanitarian activities . . . for the protection of civilian persons and their relief."[73]

Protecting Powers under Additional Protocol I of 1977

Additional Protocol I of 1977 set forth a new arrangement for protecting powers, one that was designed to overcome the critical lacunae in Articles 9 and 11 of the Fourth Geneva Convention. It establishes a complete system for appointing protecting powers, and at the same time tries to suppress the effects of problems of nonrecognition between belligerents.

Article 5 of the 1977 protocol provides for a process for appointing protecting powers. Upon the beginning of a conflict, each belligerent is under a duty to designate a protecting power, and to permit the activities of the protecting power designated by the other party (paragraph 2). The belligerents are reassured that this designation and acceptance shall not affect the legal status of the parties or of any territory, including occupied territory (paragraph 5). In case difficulties occur, the ICRC is to offer its good offices and suggest protecting powers (paragraph 3). Even if there is still disagreement, the ICRC, or any other organization that offers impartiality and efficacy, may offer to act as a substitute (paragraph 4). Are the parties obligated to accept this offer? One reading of the paragraph is affirmative: the parties are required to respect the designation.[74] Another view emphasizes the second sentence of this paragraph, which states that "[t]he functioning of such a substitute is subject to the consent of the Parties to the conflict."[75] At any rate, this is a theoretical question. It is improbable that a substitute will assume authority unless this was sanctioned by both parties to the conflict. The ICRC, for example, has declared that it would offer to act as a substitute only if it had the consent of both parties.[76] Thus, as a

[72] *See* Y. Sandoz, C. Swinarski, and B. Zimmerman, eds., *Commentary on the Additional Protocols* 85, paragraph 213 (1987). It should be noted that the ten countries that made reservations to Article 11 also made explicit their concern with respect to international or humanitarian organizations acting on behalf of parties who have no standing under Article 11 to approve such a mission. *See* Pictet, supra note 68, at 104 n.1.

[73] This is, for example, the basis for the ICRC activities in the Arab-Israeli conflict. ICRC, *The Middle East Activities of the ICRC,* 10 Int'l. Rev. Red Cross 425, 429 (1970).

[74] *See* Sandoz et al., *supra* note 72, at 86.

[75] *See* M. Bothe, K. Partsch, and W. Solf, *New Rules for Victims of Armed Conflicts* 78 (1982). The issue of a fallback institution was the hottest topic of discussion concerning Article 5, and the result reflects this. For a concise description of the drafting history of this article, *see id.* at 66–71.

[76] *Id.* at 78; *see also* Sandoz et al., *supra* note 72, at 86.

matter of fact, the protocol does not improve on the Geneva system. There is still no mechanism for imposing a protecting power on an unwilling occupant. This could explain why the protocol mechanism has not been used by parties to subsequent conflicts. Until the existing shortcomings of this system are addressed, it is not likely that protecting powers will be referred to in situations of occupation.

Enforcement through Other International Processes

Since the previous two systems do not seem at present to be capable of meeting the challenges facing the law of occupation, attention should be given to the regular processes of the international community: the reactions of governments, regional and international organizations, Non-Governmental Organizations (NGOs), and international financial institutions.

Among these processes, it is the collective power behind international global and regional organizations that offers the most promising concerted and hence powerful reaction to unlawful occupation measures. These organizations, however, sometimes are plagued with internal cleavages that stultify their joint response. In the past, these organizations did not exhaust their full potential to deal with cases of recalcitrant occupants. Until recently, the United Nations proved ineffective in enforcing international law on post–World War II occupants. Similarly, the Organization of African Unity (in the Western Sahara case), the Organization of American States (in the Grenada and Panama cases), and the Non-Aligned Movement (in the case of East Timor) have also proved largely ineffective in calling their members to order.

Recently, however, the potential contribution of such organizations to the management of occupations was more apparent. In 1989–1990 The United Nations assumed a crucial role in the transition of Namibia from South African occupation to independence. Encouraged by the achievements in Namibia, the Secretary General set even more ambitious roles for the United Nations in monitoring the referendum in Western Sahara, and in supervising the transition to peace in Kampuchea, according to a plan for UN administration of the country for at least a year, until the holding of general elections.[77] The decisive role played by the Security Council in ending of the Iraqi occupation of Kuwait and subsequently establishing a peacekeeping force to protect the Kurds in northern Iraq, are so far the strongest evidence of the profound potential of this organization. It is to be hoped that the momentum gathered in the recent past will pave the way for a more responsible UN role with respect to other occupied territories.

---

[77] *U.N. Seeks Expanded Cambodia Role*, N.Y. Times, January 11, 1990, at A3.

This new role might be best accomplished through the creation of permanent procedures under UN auspices that would require any of future occupant to provide full information on a regular basis regarding its activities, and to cooperate with the international community in administering the occupied territory. These procedures could lead to authoritative assertions regarding the validity of various occupation measures and thereby reduce much of the controversy concerning various aspects of the law of occupation.

In addition to intergovernmental organizations, the contribution of several NGOs to the welfare of populations under occupation is of extreme importance. In addition to their direct aid to peoples under occupation, their continuous monitoring and disseminating of data on the situation in occupied territories promises an informal restraint on the occupant's powers, through the enlightenment of world public opinion. The mass media is another important source of information on occupation measures. Since such a monitoring function, of both the NGOs and the mass media, could be influential as an informal check upon the occupant, it is necessary to recognize the occupant's duty under the law of occupation to enable them free access to and within the occupied area, in order to facilitate their unhindered gathering of information in pursuit of the inhabitants' well-being, subject to the occupant's security considerations.

8

Conclusion: The Contemporary Law of Occupation

THE PREVIOUS chapters described different codifications of the law of occupation, state practice, and other developments in international law that bear upon this law. On the basis of this account I shall conclude with an attempt to cull and assess the contemporary law of occupation. In this concluding chapter I suggest my own reading of this law, in an effort to accommodate it to contemporary challenges.

Major Developments That Have Influenced the Law of Occupation

The law of occupation has been influenced by the recognition of the increasing role of the central government in the life of its nation, and the growing emphasis in the international community on personal and communal rights. Also of importance has been the tendency of many occupants, especially in most recent history, not to acknowledge their rule as occupation.

The Emergence of the Welfare State

The idea of the welfare state was totally incompatible with the laissez-faire approach of the 1899 and 1907 Hague Regulations. The laissez-faire theory, which was shared by all nineteenth-century powers, implied minimal intervention by the government in economic and social life. This approach, which was coupled with a minimalistic conception of war and the war effort, made possible the conception of a laissez-faire type of government even in wartime. The assumption was that the separation of governments from citizens, and of public from private interests, would also hold true in times of war. It was this assumption that underlay Article 43: the peaceful cohabitation of the local population with the enemy's army, with the minimal necessary friction between them. That separation of interests provided room for a simple balancing principle of disengagement.

But the principles underlying the law of occupation had already been on the decline even by the time of the first Hague Peace Conference of 1899.

Toward the end of the nineteenth century, the national governments of some European countries began to expand their functions by greater involvement in their countries' economic and social lives. The later rise of communism brought with it an unbridgeable gap between competing national ideologies concerning the proper functions of the national government. The increasing involvement of central governments in economic activities multiplied and intensified the occupant's interest in the various resources that the occupied territory had to offer. As a result of these factors, the balancing mechanism of Article 43 was put under tremendous strain. These factors did not erase the fundamental difference between occupant and sovereign, but the theoretical peaceful coexistence between the occupant and the local population, and the international consensus over the legitimate functions of the occupation administration could not be realistically expected any longer. More and more issues gradually became the objects of unbridgeable conflicts of interests, as occupants sought to intervene in the affairs of the territories under their control. In many cases, such acts had the potential of causing profound effects in both the public and the private sectors. With the recognition of the necessity of some regulation of social and economic activities, came the realization that policies and goals had to be decided upon and implemented by the controlling institutions. Thus the mandate to "restore and ensure public order and civil life" became at best an incomplete instruction to the occupant. Even the simplest conservative function of restoring public order, at a minimal level of intervention, became a profound policy decision, with extensive potential effects.

At the heart of almost every modern occupation lies a conflict of interests among the occupant, the local population, and the ousted government, a conflict over policies and goals. The modern occupant is no longer the impartial trustee of indigenous private interests, as was envisaged in the Hague Regulations. Rather, it is usually an interested party, with short- and long-term objectives, and with the effective capability to implement those objectives.

The Emerging International Recognition of Individual and Communal Rights

While the nineteenth-century law of occupation concentrated primarily on the interests of ruling elites, the twentieth-century law shifted its attention to the concerns of the indigenous population subjected to foreign rule. The shift is apparent in two related processes. The first is the prescription of norms aimed at the protection of individuals; the second is the international community's increasing approval of claims of indigenous communities at the expense of the interests of the ousted governments.

The first process was first discernible in the 1949 Fourth Geneva Convention. This convention delineated a bill of rights for the occupied population. Moreover, the very decision to dedicate this convention to persons and not to governments was an early sign of the growing awareness in international law of the idea that peoples were not merely the resources of states, but worthy of being the subject of international norms. This general awareness was bound to find its way into the area of the law of occupation, and diminish the claim of ousted governments to return to areas that they had controlled before the occupation but in which they were not supported by the indigenous population. This was a striking departure from the 1899 and 1907 Hague Regulations, which had called for preservation of the ousted governments' bases of power within the occupied territories, as well as preservation of their property.

International prescription after World War II further bolstered the rights of peoples vis-à-vis their ousted governments. Two trends are apparent in this respect: the further delineation of personal rights (human, civil, political, economic, social, and cultural rights), and the recognition of the communal rights of self-determination and self-rule. The first trend represents an attempt to influence the discretion of the occupant in prescribing policies for the administration of the occupied territory, so that occupation policies will conform with the international law of human rights. The second trend looms large in the process of ascertaining the legitimate sovereign of an occupied territory. This second trend was mature enough to lead the international community to sanction the secession of East Pakistan as independent Bangladesh (through the Indian occupation) and, on the other hand, to resolve that Morocco's annexation of Western Sahara was an occupation despite the acquiescence of Spain, the former colonialist, to the Moroccan takeover.

The Changing Circumstances of Occupations

Chapter 6 outlined the practice of recent occupants. They tended not to recognize the applicability of the law of occupation to their actions in foreign countries under their control. This common practice is not accidental. Rather, there are crucial reasons that prevent states from acknowledging the status of occupant. In many cases, an attempt to justify the resort to force, such as the claim of coming to the aid of the purported or real indigenous government, would determine the invader's explanation of its subsequent status in the foreign territory. In other cases, an interest in permanent and exclusive control over foreign lands would prompt occupants not to acknowledge the applicability of the law of occupation. When the title to a territory is disputed, the likelihood of an occupant's acknowledging an occupation is minimal even if the occupant is not necessarily interested in everlasting control. Finally, "occupation" has over the last two decades acquired a pejorative connotation, and as a result, occupants would tend to prefer euphemistic titles to portray their position. It is therefore my expectation that few future occupants will voluntarily recognize the applicability of the law of occupation. Occupants who deny its applicability are likely not to consider themselves bound by its commands, even on a de facto basis. Thus, the tendency to ignore the basic commands of the law of occupation seems to pose the most potentially destructive challenge to its survival.

The Response to Contemporary Challenges

The Duty to Establish a Direct System of Administration in Occupied Territories

The duty of the occupant to establish a system of direct administration in the occupied territory was self-evident to the framers of the Hague Regulations. Nowadays, faced with occupants' reluctance to abide by this rule, this point requires emphasis. The establishment of such an administration is a decisive indication of the occupant's intentions regarding the treatment of the population under its rule and the final disposition of the territory. The failure to abide by this requirement signifies a potential reluctance to abide by other limitations that the law of occupation imposes on the occupant.

Aside from reemphasizing this point, the law of occupation can and should reinforce it through the idea that any measures whatsoever introduced by the occupant or its illegal surrogates would merit no respect in international law. The illegality of the occupation regime would taint all its measures, and render them null and void. The occupant who fails to establish the required regime does not seek international protection for its policies in the occupied area, and, indeed, is not entitled to expect any deference for these policies. As such an occupant fails to share power with the lawful government under the auspices of international law, the latter is not precluded from taking whatever countermeasures it can in order to protect its interests during and after the occupation. Thus, under such circumstances, the ousted government, from its exile or upon its return, is under no obligation to respect those measures that would have been lawful had the occupant respected the basic norm of the law of occupation. Moreover, states are under a duty not to recognize such an illegal regime or its prescriptions. This rule sends a straightforward message to the prospective occupant: there is but one way you can secure recognition of your measures, and that is by administering the territory as an occupant, acknowledging all the constraints the law of occupation imposes.

The Management of Occupied Territories: Balancing Conflicting Interests

The basic principle that must guide the occupant is the requirement to balance the competing relevant concerns involved in an occupation, namely, the occupant's security against indigenous interests. There may be certain auxiliary considerations that can aid in determining the proper balance in specific issues, such as the right to carry arms, freedom of movement, and political freedoms, but even these will be subject to the ultimate test: the ad hoc weighing of the conflicting values that are relevant to any specific case.

Who is endowed with the power to balance the conflicting interests: the occupation administration or the occupant's national government? The fact that the administration of the occupied territories is bureaucratically distinct and theoretically independent of its national government led some to maintain that the power and duty to balance the interest lie only in the occupation administration. This position, which overlooks the fact that the bureaucracy of the occupation administration would usually be heavily influenced by—if not entirely dependent on—its own national government, could open the way for national governments to claim that they are not subject to the duty to balance those interests in formulating policies that could affect the occupied territories. A clear example of such a claim is the Israeli decision to impose a VAT in the West Bank and Gaza. In considering whether or not such a measure was legal, the Israeli Supreme Court[1] relied on the bureaucratic distinction between the national government and the occupation administration, arguing that the discretion of the latter was restricted by prior acts of the Israeli government (acts that, according to this rationale, were not subject to scrutiny under international law). It is therefore necessary to emphasize that the duty to blance the conflicting interests applies not only to the occupation administration but also to the national institutions of the occupant: legislature, Executive, and courts. Whenever their acts impinge upon the interests of the people subject to their occupation, they must abide by the commands of the law of occupation.

[1] See *Abu-Aita et al. v. Commander of Judea and Samaria et al.*, 37 (2) PD 197 (1983), 7 Selected Judgments of the Supreme Court of Israel 1 (1983–1987). For a discussion of this case, *see supra* Chapter 5, text accompanying notes 179–81.

What are the relevant considerations that must be included in the process of weighing alternatives in prescribing policies? From the occupant's viewpoint, we find the interest in the protection of its troops and administration personnel inside the occupied area. Note that these interests do not include the national interests of the occupant state itself, which are deemed irrelevant. On the occupied side, the occupant must take into consideration the needs of the occupied community and the interests of the ousted legitimate government. In case of conflict between the two, it would seem that the occupant would have discretion as to which one to prefer. During the period of occupation, especially if the occupation becomes protracted, the occupant would face quite a few problems connected with many aspects of the economic and social life of the occupied community. While these issues may have little influence on its security concerns, the occupant is nevertheless required, as part of the duty to "ensure public order and civil life," to take up those issues and find a proper answer to them. In forming the policies regarding these issues, the occupant has to encourage the participation of the indigenous community and of the ousted government, subject to the occupant's safety concerns. It should always be kept in mind that occupants might be prejudiced in favor of their own larger interests at the expense of the indigenous community. Therefore it is pertinent to emphasize their duty to give ample weight to indigenous views regarding the relevant issues. These views could be learned from the solutions offered by the ousted government in the unoccupied part of the country, or from the views taken by locally elected officials, such as mayors and other representatives.

Supplementing the basic principle of ad hoc balancing of interests is a set of standards that the occupation regime must observe, as specified in the Fourth Geneva Convention. These standards represent the entrenched rights of the local population. They include a few basic human rights, such as respect for the the occupied population's persons, their honor, family rights, religious convictions, and manners and customs, all of which are nonderogable, even by an occupant. Article 27, which enumerates these basic rights, adds the general duty to treat the population "with the same consideration . . . without any adverse distinction, based, in particular, on race, religion and political opinion." These basic standards must be observed by the occupants "at all times."

The Power and the Duty to Terminate the Occupation Administration

The traditional law of occupation recognized only one way to end an occupation regime: a peace treaty between the occupant and the ousted government. The 1899 and 1907 Hague Regulations do not mention any duty on the occupant's part to promote such a peaceful solution. It would seem that the occupant could stay put until the ousted government offered good enough terms in return for the occupant's withdrawal.

This concept has undergone changes in two important aspects. First, international law seems to acquiesce under certain circumstances in transfer of authority from the occupant to indigenous elements, bypassing the ousted government. Second, it would seem that an occupant that in bad faith stalls efforts for a peaceful ending to its rule would be considered an aggressor and its rule be tainted with illegality.

The Power to Terminate the Occupation Regime Unilaterally

The survey of contemporary occupations, and of recent international instruments, has shown that the modern occupant is considered to be relieved of its duties as occupant once its forces have transferred control over an occupied territory that is considered a self-determination unit to an indigenous government that enjoys the support of the majority of the population, the claims of the ousted government notwithstanding. Thus, some modern occupants were not infringing the law when they affected secession, as in Bangladesh, or when they formed new governments, as in Kampuchea, Grenada, and Panama. This proposition emanates from the principles of self-determination and self-rule, which embody the idea that sovereignty lies in a people rather than its government, and is backed by state practice. For the same reason, no agreement between the occupant and an ousted regime that is not the country's legitimate sovereign could affect the occupant's status. Therefore Morocco cannot rely on the Madrid Agreement in explaining its presence in Western Sahara, and Indonesia cannot benefit from a possible Portuguese recognition of its purported annexation of East Timor.

The Duty to Terminate an Occupation

In the nineteenth century, occupations were quickly resolved by peace agreements. Nowadays, occupations usually tend to be quite protracted. In the nineteenth century, occupations were perceived as a possible burden on the occupant, and there was even a concern that some occupants would not be interested in assuming control over local affairs. Nowadays, many occupants find the occupation rather useful. Many of them would not view occupation as a burden, but rather as a bounty. In view of these tendencies, it is necessary to rethink the allocation of the burdens of a political stalemate under the law of occupation. If the occupant is entitled to adopt a policy of "wait and see," and hold on to the occupied territory until it is fully satisfied by the ousted government's terms for settlement, then the burden of stalemate in the settlement process rests solely with the ousted government. Such an allocation of the burden of stalemate is not conducive to political solutions; rather, it encourages the ousted government to seek military responses. This situation ought to be altered. The law of occupation ought not to condone an occupant who holds out in bad faith, using its control of the occupied territory as leverage. Indeed, such a position is no different from outright annexation. Instead, a more appropriate system of incentives would denounce such acts as illegal, would view the continued rule of the recalcitrant occupant as an aggression, and would treat measures aimed at the occupant's own interests as illegal and void. I concede that there is a fine line between reasonable bargaining and obstinate holdout, a line that is very difficult to draw and one upon which there would sometimes be more disagreement than consent. In many instances, however, it would not be too difficult to conclude that there is, beyond reasonable doubt, bad faith on the part of the occupant that could taint its status in the territory under its control.

Monitoring the Occupants and Enforcing the Law

In discussing the contemporary principles of the law of occupation, I did not try to formulate a code of conduct for the scrupulous occupant, or any other set of strict definitions and minutely drafted rules. Codes and strict definitions would fail to accommodate the contingencies that occupants face during their rule, as much as they would fail to instruct any other government. Moreover, it is unlikely to expect that minutely defined powers would stand in the way of an occupant who wanted to deviate from them. Instead, I opted for more open-ended principles, such as the balancing of interests, and other tests that rely on ample evidence, such as the support of the local population. Open-ended principles, like stricter ones, are liable to be abused either by occupants or by their opponents. In applying these principles to specific cases, it is therefore imperative to rely on full, fresh, and objective information. It is therefore necessary to recognize the occupant's duty to supply this information, and not to obstruct independent efforts to gather relevant information; indeed, such a duty is required to ensure public order and civil life.

It is to be hoped that in the future the realizations of these and other shortcomings of the law of occupation will pave the way for the creation of international institutions that will be entrusted with the task of monitoring activities in occupied territories, give authoritative opinions regarding their legality, and assist in the enforcement of those decisions upon recalcitrant occupants.

Bibliography

Agoncillo, T., *Filipino Nationalism 1872–1970* (1974).

Allen, H., *The Rhineland Occupation* (1923).

Ando, N., *Surrender, Occupation, and Private Property in International Law* (1991).

Arnold, A., *Afghanistan: The Soviet Invasion in Perspective* (rev. ed. 1985).

Association for Civil Rights in Israel, *Reflections on the Civil Rights in the Administered Territories: The Judicial and Administrative System* (1985).

Aubin, D., *Enemy Legislation and Judgments in Jersey* (n.d.).

Bagge, *The Legal Position of the Allied Powers in Germany*, 1 Jus Gentium 23 (1949).

Bar-Yaacov, *The Applicability of the Laws of War to Judea and Samaria (the West Bank) and the Gaza Strip*, 24 ISLR 485 (1990).

Batiffol, H., and P. Lagarde, *Droit international privé* (7th ed. 1983).

Baxter, *The Duty of Obedience to the Belligerent Occupant*, 27 BYIL 235 (1950).

Becker, E., *When the War Was Over* (1986).

Bell, G., *Review of the Civil Administration in Mesopotamia* (Cmd 1061, 1920).

Ben-Israel, *On Social Rights for Workers of the Administered Areas*, 12 IYHR 141 (1982).

Benvenisti, E., *The Applicability of Human Rights Conventions to Israel and to the Occupied Territories*, 26 ISLR 24 (1992).

Bilder, Gordon, Rovine, and Wallace, *Report of the American Bar Association Committee on Grenada* (1984).

Blum, *The Missing Reversioner: Reflections on the Status of Judea and Samaria*, 3 ISLR 279 (1968).

Bothe, M., *Belligerent Occupation, in* 4 EPIL 65 (1982).

Bothe, M., K. Partsch, and W. Solf, *New Rules for Victims of Armed Conflicts* (1982).

Bracha, *Service of Documents to the Administered Territories*, 4 Mishpatim [Hebrew U. L. Rev.] 119 (1972–1973) (in Hebrew).

Bradsher, H., *Afghanistan and the Soviet Union* (1983).

Brownlie, I., *International Law and the Use of Force by States* (1963).

Budardjo, C., and L. Soei Liong, *The War against East Timor* (1984).

Buss, C., *War and Diplomacy in Eastern Asia* (1941).

Caponera and Althéritiere, *Principles for International Groundwater Law*, 18 Natural Resources J. 589 (1978).

Carroll, *The Israeli Demolition of Palestinian Houses in the Occupied Territories: An Analysis of Its Legality in International Law*, 11 Mich. J. Int'l L. 1195 (1990).

Castrén E., *The Present Law of War and Neutrality* (1954).

Civil War in East Pakistan, 4 N.Y.U. J. Int'l L. and Pol. 524 (1971).

Clark, *The "Decolonization" of East Timor and the United Nations Norms on Self-Determination and Aggression*, 7 Yale J. World Public Order 2 (1980).

Cohen, E., *Human Rights in the Israeli-Occupied Territories 1967–1982* (1985).

Coles, H., and A. Weinberg, *Civil Affairs: Soldiers Become Governors* (1964).

Crawford, J., *The Creation of States in International Law* (1979).

Crawford, J., *The Creation of the State of Palestine: Too Much Too Soon?* 1/2 European J. Int'l L. 307 (1990).

Cruickshank, C., *The German Occupation of the Channel Islands* (1975).

Dallin, A. *German Rule in Russia* (1957).

D'Amato, *The Invasion of Panama Was a Lawful Response to Tyranny*, 84 AJIL 516 (1990).

Das, S., *Japanese Occupation and Ex Post Facto Legislation in Malaya* (1960).

Day, A., ed., *Keesing's Border and Territorial Disputes* (2d ed. 1987).

Debbasch, O., *L'occupation militaire* (1962).

de Jaer, B., *L'armée Belge d'occupation et son droit de jurisdiction* (1928).

Delaume, *Enemy Legislation and Judgments in France*, 30 JCLIL 32 (1948).

de Lupis, I., *The Law of War* (1987).

de Visscher, *L'occupation de guerre d'après la jurisprudence de la Cour de cassation de Belgique*, 34 LQR 72 (1918).

Dinstein, Y., *Zion Shall Be Redeemed in International Law*, 27 Hapraklit 5 (1971) (in Hebrew).

———, *Legislative Power in Occupied Territory*, 2 Tel Aviv U. L. Rev. 505 (1972) (in Hebrew).

———, *The International Law of Belligerent Occupation and Human Rights*, 8 IYHR 104 (1978).

———, *Deportations from Administered Territories*, 13 Tel Aviv U. L. Rev. 403 (1988) (in Hebrew).

———, *The Israeli Supreme Court and the Law of Belligerent Occupation: Reunification of Families*, 18 IYHR 173 (1988).

———, *Military Necessity*, 3 EPIL 274 (1982).

———, *War, Aggression and Self-Defence* (1988).

Donnison, F., *British Military Administration in the Far East 1943–46* (1956).

Drori, M., *The Legislation in the Area of Judea and Samaria* (1975).

———, *The Legal System in Judea and Samaria: A Review of the Previous Decade with a Glance at the Future*, 8 IYHR 144 (1978).

Dugard, J., *Recognition and the United Nations* (1987).

Dunn, J., *Timor: A People Betrayed* (1983).

El-Hindi, *The West Bank Aquifer and Conventions Regarding the Laws of Belligerent Occupation*, 11 Mich. J. Int'l L. 1400 (1990).

Elliott, *The East Timor Dispute*, 27 ICLQ 238 (1978).

Evriviades, *The Legal Dimension of the Cyprus Conflict*, 10 Texas Int'l L.J. 227 (1975).

Farer, *Panama: Beyond the Charter Paradigm*, 84 AJIL 503 (1990).

Feilchenfeld, E., *The International Economic Law of Belligerent Occupation* (1942).

Fraenkel, E., *Military Occupation and the Rule of Law* (1944).

Franck, *The Stealing of the Sahara*, 70 AJIL 694 (1976).

Franck and Hoffman, *The Right of Self-Determination in Very Small Places*, 8 N.Y.U. J. Int'l L. and Pol. 331 (1976).

Franck and Rodley, *The Law, The United Nations and Bangladesh*, 2 IYHR 142 (1972).

Fraser, *Grenada: Sovereignty of a People*, 7 West Indian L.J. 205 (1983).

Freeman, *War Crimes by Enemy Nationals: Administering Justice in Occupied Territory*, 41 AJIL 579 (1947).

Fried, *Transfer of Civilian Manpower from Occupied Territories*, 40 AJIL 303 (1946).

Garber, L., *Elections in Grenada: Return to Parliamentary Democracy* (1985).

Garner, J., *International Law and the World Order* (1920).

Gerson, A., *Israel, the West Bank and International Law* (1977).

Gilmore, W., *The Grenada Intervention* (1984).

Goldstein, *International Jurisdiction Based on Service on the Defendant*, 10 Mishpatim [Hebrew U. L. Rev.] 409 (1980) (in Hebrew).

Goodman, *The Need for Fundamental Change in the Law of Belligerent Occupation*, 37 Stan. L. Rev. 1539 (1985).

Graber, D., *The Development of the Law of Belligerent Occupation 1863–1914* (1949).

Greenspan, M., *The Modern Law of Land Warfare* (1959).

Hannum, *International Law and the Cambodian Genocide: The Sounds of Silence*, 11 Human Rights Q. 82 (1989).

Hardt, *Grenada Reconsidered*, 11 Fletcher Forum 277 (1987).

Harris, C., *Allied Military Administration of Italy 1943–1945* (1957).

Hartendorf, A., *The Japanese Occupation of the Philippines* (1967).

Harvard Research in International Law, *Draft Convention on the Rights and Duties of States in Case of Aggression*, 33 AJIL (Supp.) 827 (1939).

Hiorth, F., *Timor: Past and Present* (South East Asian Monograph no. 17, 1985).

Hitchens, C., *Cyprus* (1984).

Hull, W., *The Two Hague Conferences and Their Contributions to International Law* (1908).

Hyde, C., *International Law* (2d ed. 1945).

Hyman, A., *Afghanistan under Soviet Domination 1964–83* (1984).

(British) Imperial War Museum, *The Occupation of the Rhineland 1918–1929* (facsimile ed. 1987) (1944).

Indonesia, Republic of, Department of Foreign Affairs, *Decolonization in East Timor* (n.d.).

International Commission of Jurists, *East Pakistan Staff Study*, 8 ICJ Rev. 23 (1972).

International Committee of the Red Cross, *The Middle East Activities of the ICRC*, 10 Int'l Rev. Red Cross 425 (1970).

Ireton, *The Rhineland Commission at Work*, 17 AJIL 460 (1923).

Israeli Section of the International Commission of Jurists, *The Rule of Law in the Areas Administered by Israel* (1981).

Jacob, P., *Les lois de l'occupation en France* (1942).

Jennings, *Government in Commission*, 23 BYIL 135 (1946).

Jolliffe, J., *East Timor: Nationalism and Colonialism* (1978).

Joseph, J., *Cyprus: Ethnic Conflict and International Concern* (1985).

Joyner, *Reflections on the Lawfulness of Invasion*, 78 AJIL 131 (1984).

Kahan, D., *Agriculture and Water Resources in the West Bank and Gaza (1967–1987)* (1987).

Kawakami, K., *Manchoukuo—Child of Conflict* (1933).

Kegel, G., *Internationales Privatrecht* (6th ed. 1987).

Kelsen, *The Legal Status of Germany According to the Declaration of Berlin*, 39 AJIL 518 (1945).

Khadduri, M., *Modern Libya—A Study in Political Development* (1963).

Kulski, *Some Soviet Comments on International Law*, 45 AJIL 347 (1951).

Langr, R., *Seizure of Territory* (1947).

Lapidoth, *International Law within the Israeli Legal System*, 24 ISLR 451 (1990)

Laserson, M., *International Conciliation-Documents for the Year 1943* (1993).

Lauterpacht, H., *Oppenheim's International Law* (7th ed. 1948).

———, *The Limits of the Operation of the Law of War*, 30 BYIL 206 (1953).

Laval, *German Law in the Occupied Territories of Belgium*, [1916] ILN 20.

Lawrence, *East Timor*, 12 EPIL 94 (1990).

Lebra, J., ed., *Japan's Greater East Asia Co-Prosperity Sphere in World War II* (1975).

Lemkin, R., *Axis Rule in Occupied Europe* (1944).

Leurquin, *The German Occupation of Belgium and Article 43 of the Hague Regulation of the 18th October, 1907*, [1916] ILN 55.

Lyons, *The Courts of Singapore under the Japanese Occupation*, 30 BYIL 507 (1953).

Malanczuk, *Israel: Status, Territory and Occupied Territories*, in 12 EPIL 149 (1990).

Mann, F., *The Legal Aspect of Money* (2d ed. 1953).

Massart, J., *Belgians under the German Eagle* (1916).

McDougal, M., and F. Feliciano, *Law and Minimum World Public Order* (1961).

McNair, A., Lord, and A. Watts, *The Legal Effects of War* (4th ed. 1966).

Mérignhac A., *Traité de droit public international* (1912).

Meron, T., *Applicability of Multilateral Conventions to Occupied Territories*, 72 AJIL 542 (1978).

———, ed., *Human Rights in International Law* (1985).

———, *Human Rights in Internal Strife: Their International Protection* (1987).

Moore, *Law and the Grenada Mission* (1984).

Mordacq, *L'évacuation anticipée de la Rhénanie*, 51 Revue des deux mondes 761 (1929).

Morgenstern, *Judicial Practice and the Supremacy of International Law*, 27 BYIL 42 (1950).

———, *Validity of Acts of the Belligerent Occupant*, 28 BYIL 291 (1951).

Mossner, *The Hague Peace Conferences of 1899 and 1907*, 3 EPIL 204 (1982).

———, *Military Government*, 3 EPIL 269 (1982).

Nanda, *The Tragic Tale of Two Cities—Islamabad (West Pakistan) and Dacca (East Pakistan)*, 66 AJIL 321 (1972).

———, *The Validity of United States Intervention in Panama under International Law*, 84 AJIL 494 (1990).

Nathan, *Israel Civil Jurisdiction in the Administered Territories*, 13 IYHR 90 (1983).

Nawaz, *Bangladesh and International Law*, 11 Indian J. Int'l L. 459 (1971).

Necatigil, Z., *The Cyprus Question and the Turkish Position in International Law* (1989).

Nedjati, Z., *Administrative Law* (1974).

Negbi, M., *Justice under Occupation* (1981) (in Hebrew).

Niboyet, *L'occupation du Palatinat durant l'armistice*, 16 Revue droit int'l privé et de droit pénal int'l 46 (1920).

———, *Question de droit international privé en Alsace-Lorraine durant l'armistice*, 16 Revue droit int'l privé et droit pénal int'l 78 (1920).

Nicol, B., *Timor: The Stillborn Nation* (1978).

Noorani, *Afghanistan and the Rule of Law*, 24 ICJ Rev. 37 (1980).

North, P., and J. Fawcett, *Cheshire and North's Private International Law* (11th ed. 1987).

Nussbaum, A., *Money in the Law* (1950).

O'Connell, D., *State Succession in Municipal Law and International Law* (1967)

Oppenheim, L., *International Law* (2d ed. 1912; 3d ed. 1921).

Opperman, *Cyprus, in* 12 EPIL 76–80 (1990).

O'Shaughnessy, H., *Grenada: Revolution, Invasion and Aftermath* (1984).

Pao-Min, C., *Kampuchea between China and Vietnam* (1985).

Picone, P., and B. Conforti, *La Giurisprudenza italiana di dirito internationale publico* (1988).

Pictet, J., *Humanitarian Law and the Protection of War Victims* (1975).

———, ed., *Commentary: The Fourth Geneva Convention* (1958).

Pillet, A., *Les lois actuelles de la guerre* (2d ed. 1901).

Pirenne, J., and M. Vauthier, *La legislation et l'administration Allemandes en Belgique* (1925).

Quigley, *The Relation between Human Rights Law and the Law of Belligerent Occupation: Does an Occupied Population Have a Right to Freedom of Assembly and Expression?* 12 Boston College Int'l and Comp. L. Rev. 1 (1989).

Reisman, *Coercion and Self-Determination: Construing Charter Article 2(4)*, 78 AJIL 642 (1984).

———, *Criteria for the Lawful Use of Force in International Law*, 10 Yale Int'l L.J. 279 (1985).

———, *Sovereignty and Human Rights in Contemporary International Law*, 84 AJIL 866 (1990).

Reisman and Silk, *Which Law Applies to the Afghan Conflict?* 82 AJIL 459 (1988).

Lord Rennel of Rodd, *British Military Administration of Occupied Territories in Africa* (1948).

Riggs, *Grenada: A Legal Analysis* 109 Military L. Rev. 1 (1985).

Roberts, *What Is a Military Occupation?* 55 BYIL 249 (1985)

———, *Prolonged Military Occupation: The Israeli-Occupied Territories since 1967*, 84 AJIL 44 (1990).

Rolin, A., *Le droit moderne de la guerre* (1920).

Romig, *The Legal Basis for United States Military Action in Grenada*, Army Lawyer, April 1985, at 1.

Ross, *Denmark's Legal Status during the Occupation*, 1 Jus Gentium 1 (1949).

Rostow, *Palestinian Self-Determination: Possible Futures for the Unallocated Territories of the Palestine Mandate*, 5 Yale Studies in World Public Order 147 (1979).

———, Letter to the Editor, 84 AJIL 717 (1990).

Rubinstein, *The Changing Status of the "Territories" (West Bank and Gaza): From Escrow to Legal Mongrel*, 8 Tel-Aviv U. Studies in Law 59 (1988).

Sandoz, Y., C. Swinarski, and B. Zimmerman, eds., *Commentary on the Additional Protocols* (1987).

Scelle, M., *Le conflit italo-éthiopien devant le droit international* (1938).

Schacter, *The Legality of Pro-Democratic Invasion*, 78 AJIL 645 (1984).

Schindler, D., and J. Toman, eds., *The Laws of Armed Conflicts* (2d ed. 1981).

Schwarzenberger, G., *The Law of Belligerent Occupation: Basic Issues*, 30 Nordisk Tidsskrift for Int'l Ret 18 (1960).

——, *International Law—The Law of Armed Conflict* (1968).

Schweisfurth, T., *Germany, Occupation after World War II*, 3 EPIL 196 (1982).

Schwenk, *Legislative Power of the Military Occupant under Article 43, Hague Regulations*, 54 Yale L.J. 393 (1945.

Sen Gupta, B., *Afghanistan: Politics, Economics and Society* (1986).

Shamgar, M., *The Observance of International Law in the Administered Territories*, 1 IYHR 262 (1971).

——, ed., *Military Government in the Territories Administered by Israel 1967–1980—The Legal Aspects* (1982).

Shamir, *"Landmark Cases" and the Reproduction of Legitimacy: The Case of Israel's High Court of Justice*, 24 Law and Society Rev. 781 (1990).

——, *Legal Discourse, Media Discourse, and Speech Rights: The Shift from Content to Identity—The Case of Israel*, 19 Int'l J. of the Sociology of Law 45 (1991).

Skubiszewski, K., *Pieniadz na Terytorium Okupowanym* [Money in Occupied Territories] (1960).

Solansky, A., *German Administration in Belgium* (1928).

Sommer, *Eppur si applica—The Geneva Convention (IV) and the Israeli Law*, 11 Tel Aviv U. L. Rev. 263 (1986) (in Hebrew).

Spaight, J., *War Rights on Land* (1911).

Stabel, *Enemy Legislation and Judgments in Norway*, 31 JCLIL 3 (1949).

Stein, *Application of the Law of the Absent Sovereign in Territories under Belligerent Occupation: The Schio Massacre*, 46 Mich. L. Rev. 341 (1948).

Stone, J., *Legal Controls of International Conflicts* (1954).

Strupp, K., *Das Internationale Landkriegsrecht* (1914).

Swan, *Constitutional Majority Rule and the Cypriot Constitution: The 1983 Crisis in Critical Perspective*, 5 Boston College Third World L.J. 1 (1984).

Symposium, *Cyprus: International Law and the Prospects for Settlement*, 78 Am. Soc. Int'l L. Proc. 107 (1984).

Teson, F., *Humanitarian Intervention* (1988).

United Kingdom, *see* Imperial War Museum; War Office.

U.S. Army, *American Military Government of Occupied Germany 1918–1920* (1943).

——, *Military Government and Civil Affairs* (U.S. Army Field Manual, FM 27-5, 1943).

——, *Japanese Administration of Occupied Areas—Philippine Islands* (1944).

——, *The Law of Land Warfare* (U.S. Army Field Manual, FM 27-10, 1956).

——, *The Rules of Land Warfare* (U.S. Army Field Manual, FM 27-5, 1940).

United States Departments of State and Defense, *Grenada, A Preliminary Report* (1983).

United States Judge Advocate General's School, *Legal Aspects of Civil Affairs* (1960).

Vagts, *International Law under Time Pressure: Grading the Grenada Take-Home Examination*, 78 AJIL 169 (1984).

Vanard, *La Jurisdiction civile des tribunaux Allemands en territoire occupé*, 19 Revue de droit int'l privé 205 (1923–1924).

Vance, *Recognition as an Affirmative Step in the Decolonization Process: The Case of Western Sahara*, 7 Yale J. World Public Order 45 (1980–1981).

van de Craen, *Palestine, in* 12 EPIL 275 (1990).

Verzijl, J., *International Law in Historical Perspective* (1978).

Vickery, M., *Cambodia 1975–82* (1984).

von Glahn, G., *The Occupation of Enemy Territory* (1957).

———, *Law among Nations* (5th ed. 1986).

von Köhler, L., *The Administration of the Occupied Territories* (W. Dittmar trans., 1942) (1927).

von Laun, *The Legal Status of Germany*, 45 AJIL 267 (1951).

Warbrick, *Kampuchea: Representation and Recognition*, 30 ICLQ 234 (1981).

(British) War Office, *British Military Administration of Occupied Territories in Africa during the Years 1941–43* (Cmd 6589, 1945).

———, *The Law of War on Land, Being Part III of the Manual of Military Law* (1958).

Watts, *The British Military Occupation of Cyrenaica, 1942–1949*, 37 TGS 69 (1951).

Weatherbee, D., *The Situation in East Timor* (Occasional Paper, University of South Carolina, Institute of International Studies, 1980).

Weiler, J., *Armed Intervention in a Dichotomized World: The Case of Grenada*, in A. Cassese (ed.), *The Current Legal Regulation of the Use of Force*, 240 (1986).

Wilson, *The Laws of War in Occupied Territory*, 18 TGS 17 (1933).

Wolff, *Municipal Courts in Enemy Occupied Territory*, 29 TGS 99 (1944).

Woodward, L., *British Foreign Policy in the Second World War* (1971).

Wright, Q., *Courts and Ethiopian Recognition*, 31 AJIL 683 (1937).

———, *The Existing Legal Situation as It Relates to the Conflict in the Far East* (1939).

———, *The Outlawry of War and the Law of War*, 47 AJIL 365 (1953).

Zamir, *The Rule of Law and Control of Terrorism*, 8 Tel-Aviv U. Studies in Law 81 (1988).

Zepos, *Enemy Legislation and Judgments in Liberated Greece*, 30 JCLIL 27 (1948).

Table of Cases

Belgium

In re Anthoine, [1919–1942] AD Case no. 151 (1940), 195n.

Auditeur Militaire v. Van Dieren, [1919–1922] AD Case no. 310 (1919), 194n.

Borchart v. Committee of Supplies of Corneux, [1919–1922] AD Case no. 327 (1920), 194n.

Bourseaux v. Kranz, [1948] AD Case no. 171, 25n.

De Brabant and Gosselin v. T. and A. Florent, [1919–1922] AD Case no. 328 (1920), 194n.

De Nimal v. De Nimal, [1919–1922] AD Case no. 311 (1919), 194n.

Francq v. l'Administration des finances de Belgique, 2 ILN 170 (1917), 194n.

In re Hoogeveen, [1943–1945] AD Case no. 148 (1944), 24n.

Kauhelen Case, [1919–1922] AD Case no. 323 (1920), 44n.

Krott v. Merkens, [1947] 3 Pasicrisie Belge 10, [1946] AD Case no. 148 (1946), 25n.

La Belgique Industrielle c. Masure, 2 ILN 169 (1917), 193n.

Mathot v. Longue, [1919–1922] AD Case no. 329 (1921), 194n.

Judgment of May 18, 1916, Court of Cassation, 1 ILN 136 (1916), 192, 193.

Judgment of February 13, 1917, Liège Court of Appeals, 2 ILN 111 (1917), 193n.

Judgment of December 9, 1920, Court of Cassation, [1921] 1 Pasicrisie Belge 177, 194n.

Egypt

Judgment of November 26, 1950, [1950] ILR Case no. 98 (Port Said, 1950), 70n.

France

Administration des domaines c. Dame Sorkin, judgment of July 21, 1953, 1954 Revue crit. 539, note Loussouarn, 201n.

In re Bauerle, [1949] AD 292 Case no. 93, 93n.

In re C., [1919–1942] AD Case no. 157 (1941), 195n.

In re Friess and Ronnenberger, [1947] AD Case no. 80, 21n.

In re Hiriat, [1943–1945] AD Case no. 161, Editor's note (1944), 195n.

In re Lecoq and Others, [1943–1945] AD Case no. 161 (1944), 195n.

In re Société Bonduelle et Cie, [1951] AD Case no. 177, 198n.

In re Weber, [1919–1922] AD Case no. 313 (1919), 50n.

In re Ziwi, [1931–1932] AD Case no. 231 (1932), 50n.

Germany

Loss of Requisitioned Motor Car (Germany) Case, [1952] ILR 621, 93n.

Rhineland (German Decrees) Case, [1919–1922] AD Case no. 315 (1921), 54n, 55n.

Judgment of October 25, 1920, 1 FJG Case no. 205, 54n.

Judgment of May 10, 1921, 1 FJG Case no. 225, 55n.

Judgment of June 7, 1921, 1 FJG Case no. 228, 55n.

Judgment of November 11, 1921, 1 FJG Case no. 245, 55n.

Judgment of February 22, 1922, 1 FJG Case no. 251, 56n.

Judgment of March 7, 1922, 1 FJG Case no. 253, 54n, 55n.

Judgment of April 22, 1922, 1 FJG Case no. 259, 55n.

Judgment of May 12, 1922, 1 FJG Case no. 262, 55n.

Judgment of May 2, 1923, 1 FJG Case no. 287, 55n, 56n.

Judgment of November 5, 1924, 1 FJG Case no. 332, 55n.

Judgment of November 20, 1924, 1 FJG Case no. 335, 55n.

Judgment of November 10, 1926, 1 FJG Case no. 375, 55n, 56n.

Judgment of March 9, 1929, 1 FJG Case no. 407, 55n.

Greece

In re G., [1943–1945] AD Case no. 151 (1945), 196n.

L. v. N. (Bulgarian Occupation of Greece), [1947] AD Case no. 110, 25n.

In re Law 900 of 1943, [1943–1945] AD Case no. 152 (1944), 196n.

Occupation of Cavalla Case, [1929–1930] AD Case no. 292 (1930), 24n.

In re P. (Komotini Case), [1948] AD Case no. 187, 25n, 66n.

Thrace (Notarial Services) Case, [1949] AD Case no. 167, 25n.

In re X.Y., [1943–1945] AD Case no. 147 (1945), 24n.

Israel

Abu-Aita et al. v. Commander of Judea and Samaria et al., 37 (2) PD 197 (1983), 7 Selected Judgments of the Supreme Court of Israel 1 (1983–1987), 9n, 10n, 16n, 17n, 124n, 125n, 141n, 142–43.

Abu-Atiya v. Arabtisi, 39 (1) PD 365 (1985), 133n.

Abu-Gosh v. Military Commander of the Corridor to Jerusalem, 7 PD 941 (1953), 120n.

Abu-Ita v. Ya'akobi, C.A. 425/81, unpublished decision (1981), 133n, 134n.

Abu-Tir v. Israeli Police, Case 7-4/1985 (1989), 135.

In re Jurisdiction of the Dutch Supreme Court for Economic Matters, [1919–1942] AD Case no. 161 (1992), 195n.

Mr. P. (Batavia) v. Mrs. S. (Bandoeng), [1947] AD Case no. 118 (Netherlands East Indies), 26n, 62n.

Procurator v. X (Incest Case), [1943–1945] AD Case no. 154 (1944), 196n.

In re Rauter, [1949] AD Case no. 193, 67n.

Rotterdam Bank Ltd. (Robaver) v. Nederlandsch Beheers-instituut, [1949] AD Case no. 154, 24n.

Judgment of District Court of Breda, May 22, 1917, 2 ILN 127 (1917), 200n.

Norway

Overland's Case, [1943–1945] AD Case no. 156 (1943), 196n.

Public Prosecutor v. Lian, [1943–1945] AD Case no. 155 (1945), 24n.

Public Prosecutor v. Reidar Haaland, [1943–1945] AD Case no. 154 (1945), 24n.

Public Prosecutor v. X, [1919–1942] AD Case no. 160 (1990), 196n.

Randsfjordsbruket and Jevnaker Kommune v. Viul Tresliperi, [1951] AD Case no. 199, 196n.

Philippines

Gibbs et al. v. Rodriguez et al., [1951] AD Case no. 204, 25n.

Haw Pia v. China Banking Corp., [1951] AD Case no. 203, 25n.

Poland

B. v. T., [1957] ILR 962, 26n.

In re Greiser, [1946] AD Case no. 166, 70n.

In re Will of Josef K., [1951] ILR 966, 26n.

Switzerland

Ammon v. Royal Dutch Co., 21 ILR 25 (1954), 19n.

United Kingdom

A/S Talinna Laevauhisus v. Estonian State Steamship Line, [1946] AD Case no. 6, 201n.

Bank of Ethiopia v. National Bank of Egypt and Liguori, [1937] Ch. 513, 200n.

Chaplin v. Boys, [1969] 2 All E.R. 1085, 139n.

Index